THE COLORED PATRIOTS OF THE AMERICAN REVOLUTION,
WITH SKETCHES OF SEVERAL DISTINGUISHED COLORED PERSONS:
TO WHICH IS ADDED A BRIEF SURVEY OF THE CONDITION AND PROSPECTS OF COLORED AMERICANS.

WM. C. NELL.

WITH AN INTRODUCTION BY HARRIET BEECHER STOWE.

TABLE OF CONTENT

INTRODUCTION.

THE colored race have been generally considered by their enemies, and sometimes even by their friends, as deficient in energy and courage. Their virtues have been supposed to be principally negative ones. This little collection of interesting incidents, made by a colored man, will redeem the character of the race from this misconception, and show how much injustice there may often be in a generally admitted idea.

In considering the services of the Colored Patriots of the Revolution, we are to reflect upon them as far more magnanimous, because rendered to a nation which did not acknowledge them as citizens and equals, and in whose interests and prosperity they had less at stake. It was not for their own land they fought, not even for a land which had adopted them, but for a land which had enslaved them, and whose laws, even in freedom, oftener oppressed than protected. Bravery, under such circumstances, has a peculiar beauty and merit.

It is to be hoped that the reading of these sketches will give new self-respect and confidence to the race here represented. Let them emulate the noble deeds and sentiments of their ancestors, and feel that the dark skin can never be a badge of disgrace, while it has been ennobled by such examples.

And their white brothers in reading may remember, that generosity, disinterested courage and bravery, are of not particular race and complexion, and that the image of the Heavenly Father may be reflected alike by all. Each record of worth in this oppressed and despised should be pondered, for it is by many such that the cruel and unjust public sentiment, which has so long proscribed them, may be reversed, and full opportunities given them to take rank among the nations of the earth.

H. B. STOWE.

ANDOVER, October, 1855.

INTRODUCTION TO PAMPHLET EDITION.

The following pages are an effort to stem the tide of prejudice against the colored race. The white man despises the colored man, and has come to think him fit only for the menial drudgery to which the majority of the race has been so long doomed. "This prejudice was never reasoned up and will never be reasoned down." It must be lived down. In a land where wealth is the basis of reputation, the colored man must prove his sagacity and enterprise by successful trade or speculation. To show his capacity for mental culture, he must BE, not merely claim the right to be, a scholar. Professional eminence is peculiarly the result of practice and long experience. The colored people, therefore, owe it to each other and to their race to extend liberal encouragement to colored lawyers, physicians, and teachers — as well as to mechanics and artisans of all kinds. Let no individual despair. Not to name the living, let me hold up the example of one whose career deserves to be often spoken of, as complete proof that a colored man can rise to social respect and the highest employment and usefulness, in spite not only of the prejudice that crushes his race, but of the heaviest personal burthens. Dr. DAVID RUGGLES, poor, blind, and an invalid, founded a well-known Water-Cure Establishment in the town where I write, erected expensive buildings, won honorable distinction as a most successful and skillful practitioner, secured the warm regard and esteem of this community, and left a name embalmed in the hearts of many who feel that they owe life to his eminent skill and careful practice. Black though he was, his aid was sought sometimes by those numbered among the Pro-Slavery class. To be sure, his is but a single instance, and I know it required preeminent ability to make a way up to light through the overwhelming mass of prejudice and contempt. But it is these rare cases of strong will and eminent endowment, — always sure to make the world feel them whether it will or no, — that will finally wring from a contemptuous community the reluctant confession of the colored man's equality.

I ask, therefore, the reader's patronage of the following sheets on several grounds; first, as an encouragement to the author, Mr. NELL, to pursue a subject which well deserves illustration on other points beside those on which he has labored; secondly, to scatter broadly as possible the facts here collected, as instances of the colored man's success — a record of the genius he has shown, and the services he has rendered society in the higher departments of exertion; thirdly to encourage such men as RUGGLES to perseverance, by showing a generous appreciation of their labors, and a cordial sympathy in their trials.

Some things set down here go to prove colored men patriotic though denied a country: — and all show a wish, on their part, prove themselves men, in a land whose laws refuse to recognise their manhood. If the reader shall, sometimes, blush to find that, in the days of our country's weakness, we remembered their power to help or harm us, and availed ourselves gladly of their gone services, while we have, since, used our strength only to crush them the more completely, let him resolve henceforth to do them justice himself and claim it for them of others. If any shall be convinced by these facts, that they need only a free path to show the same capacity and reap the same rewards as other races, open every door to their efforts, and hasten the day when to be black shall not, almost necessarily, doom a man to poverty and the most menial drudgery. There is touching eloquence, as well as something of Spartan brevity, in the appeal of a well-known colored man, Rev. PETER WILLIAMS, of New York: — "We are NATIVES Of this country: we ask only to be treated as well as FOREIGNERS. Not a few of our fathers suffered and bled to purchase its independence; we ask only to be treated as well as those who fought against it. We have toiled to cultivate it, and to raise it to its present prosperous condition; we ask only to share equal privileges with those who come from distant lands to enjoy the fruits of our labor."

WENDELL PHILLIPS.

NORTHAMPTON, Oct. 25, 1852.

AUTHOR'S PREFACE.

IN the month of July, 1847, the eloquent Bard of Freedom, JOHN G. WHITTIER, contributed to the National Era a statement of facts relative to the Military Services of Colored Americans in the Revolution of 1776, and the War of 1812. Being a member of the Society of Friends, he disclaimed any eulogy upon the shedding of blood, even in the cause of acknowledged justice, but, says he, "when we see a whole nation doing honor to the memories of one class of its defenders, to the total neglect of another class, who had the misfortune to be of darker complexion, we cannot forego the satisfaction of inviting notice to certain historical facts, which, for the last half century, have been quietly elbowed aside, as no more deserving of a place in patriotic recollection, than the descendants of the men, to whom the facts in question relate, have to a place in a Fourth of July procession, [in the nation's estimation.] Of the services and sufferings of the Colored Soldiers of the Revolution, no attempt has, to our knowledge, been made to preserve a record. They have had no historian. With here and there an exception, they have all passed away, and only some faint traditions linger among their descendants. Yet enough is known to show that the free colored men of the United States bore their full proportion of the sacrifices and trials of the Revolutionary War."

In my attempt, then, to rescue from oblivion the name and fame of those who, though "tinged with the hated stain," yet had warm hearts and active hands in the "times that tried men's souls," I will first gratefully tender him my thanks for the service his compilation has afforded me, and my acknowledgments also to other individuals who have kindly contributed facts for this work. Imperfect as these pages may prove, to prepare even these, journeys have been made to confer with the living, and even pilgrimages to grave-yards, to save all that may still be gleaned from their fast disappearing records.

There is now an institution of learning in the State of New York, (Central College,) where the chair of Professorship in Belles Lettres has been filled by three colored young men, CHARLES L. REASON, WILLIAM G. ALLEN, and GEORGE B. VASHON, each of whom has worn the

Professor's mantle gracefully, giving proof of good scholarship and manly character.

These men, as teachers, especially in Colleges open to all, irrespective of accidental differences, are doing a mighty work in uprooting prejudice. The influences thus generated are already felt. Many a young white man or woman who, in early life, has imbibed wrong notions of the colored man's inferiority, is taught a new lesson by the colored Professors at McGrawville; and they leave its honored walls with thanksgiving in their hearts for their conversion from pro-slavery heathenism to the Gospel of Christian Freedom, and are thus prepared to go forth as pioneers in the cause of Human Brotherhood.

But the Orator's voice and Author's pen have both been eloquent in detailing the merits of Colored American, in these various ramifications of society, while a combination of circumstances has veiled from the public eye a narration of those military services which are generally conceded as passports to the honorable and lasting notice of Americans.

I was born on Beacon Hill, and from early childhood, have loved to visit the Eastern wing of the State House, and read the four stones taken from the monument that once towered from its summit. One contains the following inscription: —

"Americans, while from this eminence scenes of luxuriant fertility, of flourishing commerce, and the abodes of social happiness, meet your view, forget not those who by their exertions have secured to you these blessings."

These words became indelibly impressed upon my mind, and have contributed their share in the production of this book, which, like the labors of "Old Mortality," rendered immortal by the genius of Scott, I humbly trust will deepen in the heart and conscience of this nation the sense of justice, that will ere long manifest itself in deeds worthy a people who, "free themselves," should be "foremost to make free."

WILLIAM C. NELL.

BOSTON, October, 1855.

OMISSION.

The following brief account of the organization of a colored military company in Boston, accidentally omitted from the body of this work, is inserted here, (though somewhat out of place,) as a matter too important to be overlooked in a book of this character: —

The "Massasoit Guards," a military company originating among some of the colored citizens of Boston, having been refused a loan of State arms, have equipped themselves in preparation for volunteer service. They do not wish to be considered a castecompany, and hence invite to their ranks any citizens of good moral character who may wish to enrol their names.

Many query, "Why call themselves 'Massasoit Guards?' why not 'Attucks' Guards,' after one of their own race, and the first martyr of American Independence, on the 5th of March, 1770?

Perhaps, as the name of Attucks has been already appropriated by colored military companies in New York and Cincinnati, they accepted Massasoit as their patron saint. He was one of those Indian chiefs, who, in early colonial times, proved himself signally friendly to the interests of the Old Bay State. Their pride of loyalty may have prompted the choice, though we believe a better selection could have been made. Still, if they are satisfied, the preferences of others are superfluous.

We earnestly hope they will revive the efforts for erasing the word white from the military clause in the statute-book, for, until that is accomplished, their manhood and citizenship are under proscription.

CHAPTER I: MASSACHUSETTS.

ON the 5th of March, 1851, the following petition was presented to the Massachusetts Legislature, asking an appropriation of $1,500, for the erection of a monument to the memory of CRISPUS ATTUCKS, the first martyr in the Boston Massacre of March 5th, 1770: —

To the Honorable the Senate and House of Representatives of the State of Massachusetts, in General Court assembled:

The undersigned, citizens of Boston, respectfully ask that an appropriation of fifteen hundred dollars may be made by your Honorable Body, for a monument to be erected to the memory of CRISPUS ATTUCKS, the first martyr of the American Revolution.

WILLIAM C. NELL,
CHARLES LENOX REMOND,
HENRY WEEDEN,
LEWIS HAYDEN,
FREDERICK G. BARBADOES,
JOSHUA B. SMITH,
LEMUEL BURR.
BOSTON, Feb. 22d, 1851.

This petition was referred to the Committee on Military Affairs, who granted a bearing to the petitioners, in whose behalf appeared Wendell Phillips, Esq., and William C. Nell, but finally submitted an adverse report, on the ground that a boy, Christopher Snyder, was previously killed. Admitting this fact, (which was the result of a very different scene from that in which Attucks fell,) it does not offset the claims of Attucks, and those who made the 5th of March famous in our annals the day which history selects as the dawn of the American Revolution.

Botta's History, and Hewes's Reminiscences (the tea party survivor), establish the fact that the colored man, ATTUCKS, was of and with the people, and was never regarded otherwise.

Botta, in speaking of the scenes of the 5th of March, says: — "The people were greatly exasperated. The multitude ran towards King street, crying, 'Let us drive out these ribalds; they have no business here!' The rioters rushed furiously towards the Custom House; they approached the sentinel, crying, 'Kill him, kill him!' They assaulted him with snowballs, pieces of ice, and whatever they could lay their hands upon. The guard were then called, and, in marching to the Custom House, they encountered," continues Botta, "a band of the populace, led by a mulatto named ATTUCKS, who brandished their clubs, and pelted them with snowballs. The maledictions, the imprecations, the execrations of the multitude, were horrible. In the midst of a torrent of invective from every quarter, the military were challenged to fire. The populace advanced to the points of their bayonets. The soldiers appeared like statues; the cries, the howlings, the menaces, the violent din of bells still sounding the alarm, increased the confusion and the horrors of these moments; at length, the mulatto and twelve of his companions, pressing forward, environed the soldiers, and striking their muskets with their clubs, cried to the multitude: 'Be not afraid; they dare not fire: why do you hesitate, why do you not kill them, why not crush them at once?' The mulatto lifted his arm against Capt. Preston, and having turned one of the muskets, he seized the bayonet with his left hand, as if he intended to execute his threat. At this moment, confused cries were heard: 'The wretches dare not fire!' Firing succeeds. ATTUCKS is slain. The other discharges follow. Three were killed, five severely wounded, and several others slightly."

ATTUCKS had formed the patriots in Dock Square, from whence they marched up King street, passing through the street up to the main guard, in order to make the attack.

ATTUCKS was killed by Montgomery, one of Capt. Preston's soldiers. He had been foremost in resisting, and was first slain. As proof of a front engagement, he received two balls, one in each breast.

John Adams, counsel for the soldiers, admitted that Attucks appeared to have undertaken to be the hero of the night, and to lead the people. He and Caldwell, not being residents of Boston, were both buried from Faneuil Hall. The citizens generally participated in the solemnities.

The Boston Transcript of March 7, 1851, published an anonymous communication, disparaging the whole affair; denouncing CRISPUS ATTUCKS as a very firebrand of disorder and sedition, the most conspicuous, inflammatory, and uproarious of the misguided populace, and who, if he had not fallen a martyr, would richly have deserved hanging as an incendiary. If the leader, ATTUCKS, deserved the epithets above applied, is it not a legitimate inference, that the citizens who followed on are included, and hence should swing in his company on the gallows? If the leader and his patriot band were misguided, the distinguished orators who, in after days, commemorated the 5th of March, must, indeed, have been misguided, and with them, the masses who were inspired by their eloquence; for John Hancock, in 1774, invokes the injured shades of Maverick, Gray, Caldwell, ATTUCKS, Carr; and Judge Dawes, in 1775, thus alludes to the band of "misguided incendiaries": — "The provocation of that night must be numbered among the master-springs which gave the first motion to a vast machinery, — a noble and comprehensive system of national independence."

Ramsay's History of the American Revolution, Vol. I., p. 22, says — "The anniversary of the 5th of March was observed with great solemnity; eloquent orators were successively employed to preserve the remembrance of it fresh in the mind. On these occasions, the blessings of liberty, the horrors of slavery, and the danger of a standing army, were presented to the public view. These annual orations administered fuel to the fire of liberty, and kept it burning with an irresistible flame."

The 5th of March continued to be celebrated for the above reasons, until the Anniversary of the Declaration of American Independence was substituted in its place; and its orators were expected to honor the feelings and principles of the former as having given birth to the latter.

On the 5th of March, 1776, Washington repaired to the intrenchments. "Remember," said he, "it is the 5th of March, and avenge the death of your brethren!"

In judging, then, of the merits of those who launched the American Revolution, we should not take counsel from the Tories of that or the present day, but rather heed the approving eulogy of Lovell, Hancock, and Warren.

Welcome, then, be every taunt that such correspondents may fling at ATTUCKS and his company, as the best evidence of their merits and their strong claim upon our gratitude! Envy and the foe do not labor to traduce any but prominent champions of a cause.

The rejection of the petition was to be expected, if we accept the axiom that a colored man never gets justice done him in the United States, except by mistake. The petitioners only asked for justice, and that the name of CRISPUS ATTUCKS might be honored as a grateful country honors other gallant Americans.

And yet, let it be recorded, the same session of the Legislature which had refused the ATTUCKS monument, granted one to ISAAC DAVIS, of

Concord. Both were promoters of the American Revolution, but one was white, the other was black; and this is the only solution to the problem why justice was not fairly meted out.

In April, 1851, Thomas Sims, a fugitive slave from Georgia, was returned to bondage from the city of Boston, and on Friday, June 2d, 1854, Anthony Burns, a fugitive from Virginia, was dragged back to slavery, — both marching over the very ground that ATTUCKS trod. Among the allusions to the man, and the associations clustering around King street of the past and State street of the present, the following are selected. The first is from a speech of the Hon. ANSON BURLINGAME, in Faneuil Hall, Oct. 13, 1852, on the rendition of Thomas Sims: —

"The conquering of our New England prejudices in favor of liberty 'does not pay.' It 'does not pay,' I submit, to plat our fellow-citizens under practical martial law; to beat the drum in our streets; to clothe our temples of justice in chains, and to creep along, by the light of the morning star, over the ground wet with the blood of CRISPUS ATTUCKS, the noble colored man, who fell in King street before the muskets of tyranny, away in the dawn of our Revolution; creep by Faneuil Hall, silent and dark; by the Green Dragon, where that noble mechanic, Paul Revere, once mustered the sons of liberty; within sight of Bunker Hill, where was first unfurled the glorious banner of our country; creep along, with funeral pace, bearing a brother, a man made in the image of God, not to the grave, — O, that were merciful, for in the grave there is no work and no device, and the voice of a master never comes, — but back to the degradation of a slavery which kills out of a living body an immortal soul. O, where is the man now, who took part in that mournful transaction, who would wish, looking back upon it, to avow it!"

"Thousands of agitated people came out to see the preacher [Burns] led off to slavery, over the spot where Hancock stood and ATTUCKS fell.

"And at high 'change, over the spot where, on the 5th of March, 1770, fell the first victim in the Boston Massacre, — where the negro blood of CHRISTOPHER ATTUCKS stained the ground, — over that spot, Boston authorities carried a citizen of Massachusetts to Alexandria as a slave."

"A short distance from that sacred edifice, [Faneuil Hall,] and between it and the Court House, where the disgusting rites of sacrificing a human being to slavery were lately performed, was the spot which was first moistened with American blood in resisting slavery, and among the first victims was a colored person."

"Nearly all those who had watched the trial of poor Burns, who heard his doom, saw the slave-guard march from the Court House, that had been closed so long, through State street, swept as if by a pestilence, down to the vessel that, under our flag, bore him out of the Bay the Pilgrims entered, into captivity, would rather have looked on a funeral procession, rather have heard the rattling of British guns again . . . . . Sad, shocking, was the sight of the harmless, innocent victim of all that mighty machinery, as he passed down Queen's street and King's street, all hung in mourning. Better to have seen the halter and the coffin for a criminal again paraded through our streets, than the cutlasses and the cannon for him. As he went down to the dock into which the tea was thrown, the spirits that lingered about the spots he passed vanished and fled, whilst dire and frightful images arose in their place."

HENRY HILL, a colored man, and a Revolutionary Soldier, died in Chilicothe, on the 12th of August, 1833, aged eighty years. He was buried with the honors of war, — a singular tribute of respect to the memory of a colored man, but no doubt richly merited in this case. Henry, I should infer from an obituary notice in the Chilicothe Advertiser, was at the battle of Lexington, Brandywine, Monmouth, Princeton, and Yorktown.

Swett, in his "Sketches of Bunker Hill Battle," alludes to the presence of a colored man in that fight. He says: — "Major Pitcairn caused the first effusion of blood at Lexington. In that battle, his horse was shot under him, while he was separated from his troops. With presence of mind, he feigned himself slain; his pistols were taken from his holsters, and he was left for dead, when he seized the opportunity, and escaped. He appeared at Bunker Hill, and, says the historian, 'Among those who mounted the works was the gallant Major Pitcairn, who exultingly cried out, "The day is ours!" when a black soldier named SALEM shot him through, and he fell. His agonized son received him in his arms, and tenderly bore him to the boats.' A contribution was made in the army for the colored soldier, and he was presented to Washington as having performed this feat."

Besides SALEM, there were quite a number of colored soldiers at Bunker Hill. Among them, TITUS COBURN, ALEXANDER AMES, and BARZILAI LEW, all of Andover; and also CATO HOWE, of Plymouth, — each of whom received a pension. Lew was a fifer. His daughter, Mrs. Dalton, now lives within a few rods of the battle field.

SEYMOUR BURR was a slave in Connecticut, to a brother of Col. Aaron Burr, from whom he derived his name. Though treated with much favor by his master, his heart yearned for liberty, and he seized an occasion to induce several of his fellow slaves to escape in a boat, intending to join the British, that they might become freemen; but being pursued by their owners, armed with the implements of death, they were compelled to surrender.

Burr's master, contrary to his expectation, did not inflict corporeal punishment, but reminded him of the kindness with which he had been treated, and asked what inducement he could have for leaving him. Burr replied, that he wanted his liberty. His owner finally proposed, that if he would give him the bounty money, he might join the American army, and at the end of the war be his own man. Burr, willing to make any sacrifice for his liberty, consented, and served faithfully during the campaign, attached to the Seventh Regiment, commanded by Colonel, afterwards Governor Brooks, of Medford. He was present at the siege of Fort Catskill, and endured much suffering from starvation and cold. After some skirmishing, the army was relieved by the arrival of Gen. Washington, who, as witnessed by him, shed tears of joy on finding them unexpectedly safe.

Burr married one of the Punkapog tribe of Indians, and settled in Canton, Mass. He received a pension from Government. His widow died in 1852, aged over one hundred years.

JEREMY JONAH served in the same Regiment, (Col. Brooks's,) at the same time with Seymour Burr. The two veterans used to make merry together in recounting their military adventures, especially the drill on one occasion, when Jonah stumbled over a stone heap; for which he was severely caned by the Colonel. He drew a pension.

LEMUEL BURR, (grandson of Seymour,) a resident of Boston, often speaks of their reminiscences of DEBORAH GANNETT. In confirmation of this part of their history, I give the following extract from the Resolves of the General court of Massachusetts during the session of 1791: —

XXIII. — Resolve on the petition of DEBORAH GANNETT, granting her £34 for services in the Continental Army. January 20,1792.

On the petition of DEBORAH GANNETT, praying for compensation for services performed in the late army of the United States:

Whereas, it appears to this Court that the said DEBORAH GANNETT enlisted, under the name of Robert Shurtliff, in Capt. Webb's company, in the 4th Massachusetts Regiment, on May 20th, 1782, and did actually perform the duty of a soldier, in the late army of the United States, to the

23d day of October, 1783, for which she has received no compensation; and, whereas, it further appears that the said Deborah exhibited an extraordinary instance of female heroism, by discharging the duties of a faithful gallant soldier, and at the same time preserving the virtue and chastity of her sex unsuspected and unblemished, and was discharged from the service with a fair and honorable character; therefore,

Resolved, That the Treasurer of this Commonwealth be, and he hereby is, directed to issue his note to the said Deborah for the sum of thirty four pounds, bearing interest from Oct. 23, 1783.

Joshua B. Smith has stated to me that he was present at a company of distinguished Massachusetts men, when the conversation turned upon the exploits of Revolutionary times; and that the late Judge Story related an incident of a colored Artillerist who, while having charge of a cannon with a white fellow soldier, was wounded in one arm. He immediately turned to his comrade, and proposed changing his position, exclaiming that he had yet one arm left with which he could render some service to his country. The change proved fatal to the heroic soldier, for another shot from the enemy killed him upon the spot. Judge Story furnished other incidents of the bravery of colored soldiers, adding, that he had often thought them and their descendants too much neglected, considering the part they had sustained in the wars; and he regretted that he did not, in early life, gather the facts into a shape for general information.

The late Governor Eustis, of Massachusetts, the pride and boast of the Democracy of the East, himself an active participant in the war, and therefore a most competent witness, states that the free colored soldiers entered the ranks with the whites. The time of those who were slaves was purchased of their masters, and they were induced to enter the service in consequence of a law of Congress, by which, on condition of their serving in the ranks during the war, they were made freemen. This hope of liberty inspired them with fresh courage to oppose their breasts to the Hessian bayonet at Red Bank, and enabled them to endure with fortitude the cold and famine of Valley Forge.

At the close of the Revolutionary War, John Hancock presented the colored company, called "the Bucks of America," with an appropriate banner, bearing his initials, as a tribute to their courage and devotion throughout the struggle. The "Bucks," under the command of Colonel Middleton, were invited to a collation in a neighboring town, and, en route, were requested to halt in front of the Hancock Mansion, in Beacon street, where the Governor and his son united in the above presentation.

LYDIA MARIA CHILD gives the following sketch of Col. MIDDLETON, commander of the "Bucks": —

"Col. Middleton was not a very good specimen of the colored man. He was an old horse-breaker, who owned a house that he inhabited at the head of Belknap street. He was greatly respected by his own people, and his house was thronged with company. His morals were questioned, — he was passionate, intemperate, and profane. We lived opposite to him for five years; during all this time, my father treated this old negro with uniform kindness. He had a natural compassion for the ignorant and the oppressed, and I never knew him fail to lift his hat to this old neighbor, and audibly say, with much suavity, 'How do you do, Col. Middleton?' or 'Good morning, colonel.' My father would listen to the dissonant sounds that came from an old violin that the colonel played on every summer's evening, and was greatly amused at his power in subduing mettlesome colts. He would walk over and compliment the colonel on his skill in his hazardous employment, and the colonel would, when thus praised, urge the untamed animal to some fearful caper, to show off his own bold daring. Our negroes, for many years, were allowed peaceably to celebrate the abolition of the slave trade; but it became a frolic with the white boys to deride them on this day, and finally, they determined to drive them, on these occasions, from the Common. The colored people became greatly incensed by this mockery of their festival, and this infringement of their liberty, and a rumor reached us, on one of these anniversaries, that they were determined to resist the whites, and were going armed, with this intention. About three o'clock in the afternoon, a shout of a beginning fray reached us. Soon, terrified children and women ran down Belknap street, pursued by white boys, who enjoyed their fright. The sounds of battle approached; clubs and brickbats were flying in all directions. At this crisis, Col. Middleton opened his door, armed with a loaded musket, and, in a loud voice, shrieked death to the first white who should approach. Hundreds of human beings, white and black, were pouring down the street, the blacks making but a feeble resistance, the odds in numbers and spirit being against them. Col. Middleton's voice could be heard above every other, urging his party to turn and resist to the last. His appearance was terrific, his musket was levelled, ready to sacrifice the first white man that came within its range. The colored party, shamed by his reproaches, and fired by his example, rallied, and made a short show of resistance. Capt. Winslow Lewis and my father determined to try and quell this tumult. Capt. Lewis valiantly grappled with the ringleaders of the whites, and my father coolly surveyed the scene from his own door, and instantly determined what to do. He calmly approached Col. Middleton, who called to him to stop, or he was a dead man! I can see my father at this distance of time, and never can forget the feelings his family expressed, as they saw him still approach this armed man. He put aside his musket, and, with his countenance all serenity, said a few soothing words to the colonel, who burst into tears, put up his musket, and, with great emotion, exclaimed, loud enough for us to hear across the street, 'I will do it for you, for you have always been kind to me,' and retired into his own house, and shut his door upon the scene."

When a boy, living in West Boston, I was familiar with the person of "Big Dick," and have heard the following account of him (which is taken from the Boston Patriot) confirmed. It is not wholly out of place in this collection. "RICHARD SEAVERS," said that journal, a few days after his decease, "was a man of mighty mould." A short time previous to his death, be measured six feet five inches in height, and attracted much attention when seen in the street. He was born in Salem, or vicinity, and when about sixteen years old, went to England, where he entered the British navy. When the war of 1812 broke out, be would not fight against his country, gave himself up as an American citizen, and was made a prisoner of war.

"A surgeon on board an American privateer, who experienced the tender mercies of the British Government in Dartmoor prison, during the War of 1812, makes honorable mention of "King Dick," as he was there called: —

"'There are about four hundred and fifty negroes in prison No. 4, and this assemblage of blacks affords many curious anecdotes, and much matter for speculation. These blacks have a ruler among them, whom they call King Dick. He is by far the largest, and, I suspect, the strongest man in the prison. He is six feet five inches in height, and proportionably large. This black Hercules commands respect, and his subjects tremble in his presence. He goes the rounds every day, and visits every berth to see if they are all kept clean. When he goes the rounds, he puts on a large bearskin cap, and carries in his hand a huge club. If any of his men are dirty, drunken, or grossly negligent, he threatens them with a beating; and if they are saucy, they are sure to receive one. They have several times conspired against him, and attempted to dethrone him, but he has always conquered the rebels. One night, several attacked him, while asleep in his hammock; he sprang up and seized the smallest of them by his feet, and thumped another with him. The poor negro who had thus been made a beetle of was carried next day to the hospital, sadly bruised, and provokingly laughed at. This ruler of the blacks, this King Richard IV.; is a man of good understanding, and he exercises it to a good purpose. If any one of his color cheats, defrauds, or steals from his comrades, he is sure to be punished for it.'"

CHARLES BOWLES, (says his biographer, Rev. John W. Lewis,) "was born in Boston, 1761. His father was an African; his mother was a daughter of the celebrated Col. Morgan, who was distinguished as an officer in the Rifle Corps of the American army, during the revolutionary struggle for independence. At the early age of twelve, he was placed in the family of a Tory; but his young heart did not fancy his new situation, for at the tender age of fourteen, we find him serving in the colonial army, in the capacity of waiter to an officer. He remained in this situation for two years, and then enlisted, — a mere boy, — in the American army, to risk his life in defence of the holy cause of liberty. He served during the entire war, after which he went to New Hampshire, and engaged in agricultural pursuits. He succeeded in drawing a pension, became a Baptist preacher, and died March 16, 1843, aged 82."

PRIMUS HALL, a native Bostonian, was the son of Prince Hall, founder of the Masonic Lodge of that name in Boston. Primus Hall was long known to the citizens as a soap-boiler. Besides his revolutionary services, be was among those who, in the war of 1812, repaired to Castle Island, in Boston Harbor, to assist in building fortifications.

The following anecdote of Primus is extracted from Godey's Lady's Book for June, 1849, to which it was communicated by Rev. HENRY F. HARRINGTON: —

"Throughout the Revolutionary War, PRIMUS HALL was the body servant of Col. PICKERING, of Massachusetts. He was free and communicative, and, delighted to sit down with an interested listener and pour out those stores of absorbing and exciting anecdotes with which his memory was stored.

"It is well known that there was no officer in the whole American army whose memory was dearer to WASHINGTON, and whose counsel was more esteemed by him, than that of the honest and patriotic Col. PICKERING. He was on intimate terms with him, and unbosomed himself to him with as little reserve as, perhaps, to any confidant in the army.

Whenever he was stationed within such a distance as to admit of it, he passed many hours with the Colonel, consulting him upon anticipated measures, and delighting in his reciprocated friendship.

"WASHINGTON was, therefore, often brought into contact with the servant of Col. PICKERING, the departed PRIMUS. An opportunity was afforded to the negro to note him, under circumstances very different from those in which he is usually brought before the public, and which possess, therefore, a striking charm. I remember two of these anecdotes from the mouth of PRIMUS. One of them is very slight, indeed, yet so peculiar as to be replete with interest. The authenticity of both may be fully relied upon.

"WASHINGTON once came to Col. PICKERING'S quarters, and found him absent.

"'It is no matter,' said he to PRIMUS 'I am greatly in need of exercise. You must help me to get some before your master returns.'

Under WASHINGTON'S directions, the negro busied himself in some simple preparations. A stake was driven into the ground about breast high, a rope tied to it, and then PRIMUS was desired to stand at some distance and hold it horizontally extended. The boys, the country over, are familiar with this plan of getting sport. With true boyish zest, WASHINGTON ran forwards and backwards for some time, jumping over the rope as he came and went, until he expressed himself satisfied with the 'exercise.'

"Repeatedly afterwards, when a favorable opportunity offered, he would say — 'Come, PRIMUS, I am in need of exercise;' whereat the negro would drive down the stake, and WASHINGTON would jump over the rope until he had exerted himself to his content.

"On the second occasion, the great General was engaged in earnest consultation with Col. PICKERING in his tent until after the night had fairly set in. Head-quarters were at a considerable distance, and WASHINGTON signified his preference to staying with the Colonel over night, provided he had a spare blanket and straw.

"O, yes,' said PRIMUS, who was appealed to; 'plenty of straw and blankets — plenty.'

"Upon this assurance, WASHINGTON continued his conference with, the Colonel until it was time to retire to rest. Two humble beds were spread, side by side, in the tent, and the officers laid themselves down, while PRIMUS seemed to be busy with duties that required his attention before he himself could sleep. He worked, or appeared to work, until the breathing of the prostrate gentlemen satisfied him that they were sleeping;

and then, seating himself upon a box or stool, he leaned his head on his hands to obtain such repose as so inconvenient a position would allow. In the middle of the night, WASHINGTON awoke. He looked about, and descried the negro as he sat. He gazed at him awhile, and then spoke.

"'PRIMUS!' said he, calling; 'PRIMUS!'

"PRIMUS started up and rubbed his eyes. 'What, General?' said he.

"WASHINGTON rose up in his bed, 'PRIMUS,' said he, 'what did you mean by saying that you had blankets and straw enough? Here you have given up your blanket and straw to me, that I may sleep comfortably, while you are obliged to sit through the night.'

"'It's nothing, General,' said PRIMUS. 'It's nothing. I'm well enough. Don't trouble yourself about me, General, but go to sleep again. No matter about me. I sleep very good.'

"'But it is matter — it is matter,' said WASHINGTON, earnestly. 'I cannot do it, PRIMUS. If either is to sit up, I will. But I think there is no need of either sitting up. The blanket is wide enough for two. Come and lie down here with me.'

"'O, no, General!' said PRIMUS, starting, and protesting against the proposition. 'No; let me sit here. I'll do very well on the stool.'

"'I say, come and lie down here!' said WASHINGTON, authoritatively. 'There is room for both, and I insist upon it!'

He threw open the blanket as be spoke, and moved to one side of the straw. PRIMUS professes to have been exceedingly shocked at the idea of lying under the same covering with the commander-in-chief, but his tone was so resolute and determined that he could not hesitate. He prepared himself, therefore, and laid himself down by WASHINGTON, and on the same straw, and under the same blanket, the General and the negro servant slept until morning."

JAMES EASTON, of Bridgewater, was one who participated in the erection of the fortifications on Dorchester Heights, under command of Washington, which the next morning so greatly surprised the British soldiers then encamped in Boston.

Mr. Easton was a manufacturing blacksmith, and his forge and nail factory, where were also made edge tools and anchors, was extensively known, for its superiority of workmanship. Much of the iron work for the Tremont Theatre and Boston Marine Railway was executed under his supervision. Mr. Easton was self-educated. When a young man, stipulating for work, he always provided for chances of evening study. He was welcome to the business circles of Boston as a man of strict integrity, and the many who resorted to him for advice in complicated matters styled him "the Black Lawyer." His sons, Caleb, Joshua, Sylvanus, and Hosea, inherited his mechanical genius and mental ability.

The family were victims, however, to the spirit of color-phobia, then rampant in New England, and were persecuted even to the dragging out of some of the family from the Orthodox Church, in which, on its enlargement, a porch had been erected, exclusively for colored people. After this disgraceful occurrence, the Easton's left the church. They afterwards purchased a pew in the Baptist church at Stoughton Corner, which excited a great deal of indignation. Not succeeding in their attempt to have the bargain cancelled, the people tarred the pew. The next Sunday, the family carried seats in the waggon. The pew was then pulled down; but the family sat in the aisle. These indignities were continued until the separation of the family.

HOSEA EASTON published a Treatise on the Intellectual Condition of the Colored People, in which was shown the heart of a philanthropist and the head of a philosopher. His work did great execution among those who proclaim the innate inferiority of colored men. Here is a chapter from his experience: —

"I, as an individual, have had a sufficient opportunity to know something about prejudice and its destructive effects. At an early period of my life, I was extensively engaged in mechanism, associated with a number of other colored men, of master spirits and great minds. The enterprise was followed for about twenty years perseveringly, in direct opposition to public sentiment and the tide of popular prejudice. So intent were the parties in carrying out the principles of intelligent, active freemen, that they sacrificed every thought of comfort and ease to the object. The most rigid economy was adhered to, at home and abroad. A regular school was established for the youth, connected with the factory; the rules of morality were supported with surprising assiduity, and ardent spirits found no place in the establishment. After the expenditure of this vast amount of labor and time, together with many thousands of dollars, the enterprise ended in a total failure. By reason of the repeated surges of the tide of prejudice, the establishment, like a ship in a boisterous hurricane at sea, went beneath the waves, — richly laden, well manned and well managed, sank to rise no more. It fell, and with it fell the hearts of several of its projectors in despair, and their bodies into their graves."

QUACK MATRICK, of Stoughton Corner, was a regular Revolutionary soldier, and drew a pension.

JOB LEWIS, of Lancaster, (formerly a slave,) enlisted for two terms of three years each; and a third time for the remainder of the war. He died in November, 1797. His Son, JOEL W. LEWIS, when a boy, was very persevering in study, and as he depended mainly upon himself, when away from a brief country school term, busied himself for seven weeks in solving one complicated lesson in arithmetic. Mr. Lewis is now proprietor of an extensive blacksmithing establishment in Boston, where he gives employment to several white and colored mechanics.

PRINCE RICHARDS, of East Bridgewater, was a pensioned Revolutionary soldier. While a slave, he learned to write with a charred stick; thus evincing a burning desire to improve, even against the command of his self-styled owner.

PHILIP ANDREWS, a colored man, was drowned in Ludlow, on the 30th of May, 1842. He was over eighty years of age. He was the servant of a captain of the British army, in the Revolution, and, at the age of sixteen, deserted to the American army, and has remained in this country ever since.

JACK GROVE, of Portland, while steward of a brig, sailing from the West Indies to Portland, in 1812, was taken by a French vessel, whose commander placed a guard on board. Jack urged his commander to make an effort to retake the vessel, but the captain saw no hope. Says Jack, "Captain McLellan, I can take her, if you will let me go ahead." The captain checked him, warning him not to lisp such a word, — there was danger in it; but Jack, disappointed though not daunted, rallied the men on his own hook. Captain McLellan and the rest, inspired by his example, finally joined them, and the attempt resulted in victory. They weighed anchor, and took the vessel into Portland. The owners of the brig offered Jack fifty hogsheads of molasses for his valor and patriotism, but Jack demanded one half of the brig, which being denied him, he commenced a suit, engaging two Boston lawyers in his behalf. I have not been able to learn how the case was decided, if, indeed, a decision has yet been made.

BOSSON WRIGHT resided in Massachusetts upwards of eighty years, and could well remember when the British burned the town of Portland. He assisted in building two of the Forts, and parted with two of his companions on their way to join the American army. He was a tax-payer for more than fifty years.

Bosson said that one Mayberry, a slave from Gorham, saw a British sailor in the act of setting fire to the old Parish church, (now the First Parish in Portland,) when he (Mayberry) seized him, and carried him before the leading men, who, being Tories, ordered the sailor's discharge.

Being one afternoon on a sailing excursion down Portland harbor, Bosson directed attention to the Fort as not being properly located, indicating the spot which he would have selected. Some years after, when President Munroe visited the Eastern States, the same observation was made by him, and the same spot pointed out as had been by Bosson Wright.

One of his acquaintances, a colored soldier at the Battle of Saratoga, walked up, quite elated, to Cornwallis, after his surrender, saying: — "You used to be named Cornwallis, but it is Corn-wallis no longer; it must now be Cob-wallis, for General Washington has shelled off all the corn."

COLONIAL REMINISCENCES.

Extract from the Speech of Hon. CHARLES SUMNER, of Massachusetts, in reply to Senator Butler, of South Carolina, in the Senate of the United States, June, 28, 1854.

"Sir, slavery never flourished in Massachusetts; nor did it ever prevail there at any time, even in early colonial days, to such a degree as to be a distinctive feature in her powerful civilization. Her few slaves were merely for a term of years, or for life. If, in point of fact, their issue was, sometimes held in bondage, it was never by sanction, of any statute law of Colony or Commonwealth. (Lanesboro' vs. Westfield, 16 Mass., 73.) In all her annals, no person was ever born a slave on the soil of Massachusetts. This of itself is a response to, the imputation of the Senator.

"A benign and brilliant act of her Legislature, as, far back as 1646, shows her sensibility on this subject. A Boston ship had brought home two negroes, seized on the coast of Guinea. Thus spoke Massachusetts: —

"'The General Court, conceiving themselves bound by the first opportunity to bear witness against the heinous and crying sin of man-stealing, also, to prescribe such timely redress for what is past, and such a law for the future as may sufficiently deter all those belonging to us to have to do in such vile and most odious conduct, justly abhorred of all good and just men, do order that the negro interpreter, with others unlawfully taken, be, by the first opportunity, at the charge of the country, for the present, sent to his native country of Guinea, and a letter with him of the indignation of the Court thereabout and justice thereof.'"

"The Colony that could issue this noble decree was inconsistent with itself, when it allowed its rocky face to be pressed by the footsteps of a single slave. But a righteous public opinion earnestly and constantly set its face against slavery. As early as 1701, a vote was entered upon the records of Boston to the following effect: — 'The Representatives are desired to promote the encouraging the bringing of white servants, and to put a period to negroes being slaves.' Perhaps, in all history, this is the earliest testimony from any official body against negro slavery, and I thank God that it came from Boston, my native town. In 1705, a heavy duty was imposed upon every negro imported into the province; in 1712, the importation of Indians as servants or slaves was strictly forbidden, but the general subject of slavery attracted little attention till the beginning of the controversy which ended in the Revolution, when the rights of the blacks were blended by all true patriots with those of the whites. Sparing all unnecessary details, suffice it to say, that, as early as 1769, one of the courts of Massachusetts, anticipating, by several years, the renowned judgment in Somersett's case, established within its jurisdiction the principle of emancipation; and under its touch of magic power, changed a slave into a freeman. Similar decisions followed in other places."

An author, who signs himself "Old Style Freeman," says that "the contest commenced in 1761, in the town of Boston, in the old court-house, in the masterly speech of James Otis against the writs of assistance. He boldly asserted the rights, not only of the white, but of the black man . . . . Our colonial charters make no difference between black and white colonists.

"Massachusetts passed resolutions, in 1764, in which the rights of all the colonists were declared, without respect to mark or color, and James Otis, under the sanction of the House of Representatives, published his work on the Rights of the British Colonies, in which it was 'declared that all the colonists are, by the law of nature, 'freeborn, as, indeed, all men are, white or black; nor can any logical inference in aid of slavery,' said Otis, 'be drawn from a flat nose or a long or short face.'"

June 23d, 1773, the following petition was presented to the General Court, which was read, and referred to the next session: —

PETITION OF SLAVES IN BOSTON.
PROVINCE OF MASSACHUSETTS BAY.

To His Excellency, Thomas Hutchinson, Esq., Governor: —

To the Honorable, His Majesty's Council, and to the Honorable House of Representatives, in general court assembled at Boston, the 6th day of January, 1773: — The humble petition of many slaves living in the town of Boston, and other towns in the province, is this, namely: —

That Your Excellency and Honors, and the Honorable the Representatives, would be pleased to take their unhappy state and condition under your wise and just consideration.

We desire to bless God, who loves mankind, who sent his Son to die for their salvation, and who is no respecter of persons, that he hath lately put it into the hearts of multitudes, on both sides of the water, to bear our burthens, some of whom are men of great note and influence, who have pleaded our cause with arguments, which we hope will have their weight with this Honorable Court.

We presume not to dictate to Your Excellency and Honors, being willing to rest our cause on your humanity and justice, yet would beg leave to say a word or two on the subject.

Although some of the negroes are vicious, (who, doubtless, may be punished and restrained by the same laws which are in force against others of the King's subjects,) there are many others of a quite different character, and who, if made free, would soon be able, as well as willing, to bear a part in the public charges. Many of them, of good natural parts, are discreet, sober, honest and industrious; and may it not be said of many, that they are virtuous and religious, although their condition is in itself so unfriendly to religion, and every moral virtue, except patience? How many of that number have there been, and now are, in this province, who had every day of their lives embittered with this most intolerable reflection, that, let their behavior be what it will, neither they nor their children, to all generations, shall ever be able to do or to possess and enjoy any thing — no, not even life itself — but in a manner as the beasts that perish!

We have no property! we have no wives! we have no children! we have no city! no country! But we have a Father in heaven, and we are determined, as far as his grace shall enable us, and as far as our degraded condition and contemptuous life will admit, to keep all his commandments; especially will we be obedient to our masters, so long as God, in his sovereign providence, shall suffer us to be holden in bondage.

It would be impudent, if not presumptuous, in us to suggest to Your Excellency and Honors, any law or laws proper to be made in relation to our unhappy state, which, although our greatest unhappiness, is not our fault; and this gives us great encouragement to pray and hope for such relief as is consistent with your wisdom, justice and goodness.

We think ourselves very happy, that we may thus address the great and general court of this province, which great and good court is to us the best judge, under God, of what is wise, just and good.

We humbly beg leave to add but this one thing more: we pray for such relief only, which by no possibility can ever be productive of the least wrong or injury to our masters, but to us will be as life from the dead.

In January, 1774, a bill was brought in, which passed all the forms in the two Houses, and was laid before Governor Hutchinson for his approval, March 8th. The negroes had deputed a committee respectfully to solicit the Governor's consent; but he told them that his instructions forbade. His successor, General Gage, gave them the same answer, when they waited on him.

The blacks had better success in the judicial court. A pamphlet containing the case of a negro who had accompanied his master from the West Indies to England, and had there sued for and obtained his freedom, was reprinted here, and this encouraged several others to sue their masters for their freedom, and recompense for their services.

The first trial of this kind was in 1770. James, a servant of Richard Lechmere, of Cambridge, brought an action against his master for detaining him in bondage. The negroes collected money among themselves to carry on the suit and the verdict was in favor of the plaintiff. Other suits were instituted between that time and the Revolution, and the juries invariably gave their verdicts in favor of liberty.

During the Revolutionary War, public opinion was so strongly in favor of the abolition of slavery, that, in some of the country towns, votes were passed in town meetings that they would have no slaves among them; and that they would not exact of the masters any bonds for the maintenance of liberated blacks, should they become incapable of supporting themselves. A liberty-loving antiquarian copied the following from the Suffolk Probate Record, and published it in the Boston Liberator, February, 1847: —

"Know all men by these presents, that I, Jonathan Tackson, of Newburyport, in the county of Essex, gentleman, in consideration of the impropriety I feel, and have long felt, in beholding any person in constant bondage, — more especially at a time when my country is so warmly contending for the liberty every man ought to enjoy, — and having sometime since promised my negro man Pomp, that I would give him his freedom, and in further consideration of five shillings, paid me by said Pomp, I do hereby liberate, manumit, and set him free; and I do hereby remise and release unto said Pomp, all demands of whatever nature I have against said Pomp.

"In witness whereof, I have hereunto set my hand and seal, this nineteenth June, 1776.

"JONATHAN JACKSON. [Seal.]

"Witness — MARY COBURN,

WILLIAM NOYES."

It only remains to say a word respecting the two parties to the foregoing instrument.

JONATHAN JACKSON, Of Newburyport, we well remember to have heard spoken of, in our younger days, by honored lips, as a most upright and thorough gentleman of the old school, possessing talents and character of the first standing. He was the first Collector of the Port of Boston, under Washington's administration, and was Treasurer of the Commonwealth of Massachusetts for many years, and died in 1810. A tribute to his memory and his worth, said to be from the pen of the late John Lowell, appeared in the Columbian Centinel, March 10, 1810. His immediate descendants have long resided in this city, are extensively known, and as widely and justly honored.

POMP took the name of his late master, upon his emancipation, and soon after enlisted in the army, as POMP JACKSON, served through the whole war of the Revolution, and obtained an honorable discharge at its termination. He afterwards settled in Andover, near a pond still known as "Pomp's Pond," where some of his descendants yet live. In this case of emancipation, it appears, instead of "cutting his master's throat," he only slashed the throats of his country's enemies.

Rev. Charles Lowell, in a letter to the Boston Courier, May 17, 1847, says: — "I well remember, myself, when I was a boy at Andover Academy, being often told by an intelligent old black man, who sold buns, that my father was the friend of the blacks, and the cause of their being freed, or something to that effect, and that I often had a bun or two extra on that account. I may further state, that in October, 1773, an action was brought against Richard Greenleaf, of Newburyport, by Cæsar (Hendrick), a colored man, whom he claimed as his slave, for holding him in bondage. He laid the damages at fifty pounds. The counsel for the plaintiff, in whose favor the jury brought in their verdict, and awarded him eighteen pounds, damages and costs, was John Lowell, Esq., afterwards Judge Lowell."

From the archives in the State House, I have gleaned many petitions and resolves of Revolutionary times, on questions concerning the rights of Massachusetts colored citizens, some of which I have deemed of sufficient historical value to be recorded in this volume.

LEGISLATIVE ACTION TO REDEEM TWO SLAVES.

I find the following Resolution on the records of the House of Representatives, Sept. 13, 1776. The Council concurred, Sept. 16, 1776: —

Whereas, this House is credibly informed that two negro men, lately brought into this State as prisoners taken on the high seas, are advertised to be sold at Salem, the 17th inst., by public auction, —

Resolved, That the selling and enslaving the human species is a direct violation of the natural rights alike vested in all men by their Creator, and utterly inconsistent with the avowed principles on which this and the other United States have carried their struggles on for liberty, even to the last appeal; and therefore, that all persons concerned with the said negroes be, and they hereby are, forbidden to sell them, or in any manner to treat them otherway than is already ordered for the treatment of prisoners of war taken in the same vessel, or others in the like employ, and if any sale of the said negroes shall be made, it hereby is declared null and void.

AN ACT FOR PREVENTING THE PRACTICE OF HOLDING PERSONS AS SLAVES — A. D. 1777.

Whereas, the practice of holding Africans and the children born of them, or any other persons, in slavery, is unjustifiable in a civil government, at a time when they are asserting their natural freedom; wherefore, for preventing such a practice for the future, and establishing to every person residing within the State the invaluable blessing of liberty, —

Be it enacted, by the Council and House of Representatives, in General Court assembled, and by the authority of the same, — That all persons, whether black or other complexion, above 21 years of age, now held in slavery, shall, from and after the — day of — next, be free from any subjection to any master or mistress, who have claimed their servitude by right of purchase, heirship, free gift or otherwise, and they are hereby entitled to all the freedom, rights, privileges and immunities that do, or ought to of right, belong to any of the subjects of this State, any usage or custom to the contrary notwithstanding.

And be it enacted, by the authority aforesaid, that all written deeds, bargains, sales or conveyances, or contracts, without writing, whatsover, for conveying or transferring any property in any person, or to the service and labor of any person whatsoever, of more than twenty-one years of age, to a third person, except by order, of some court of record for some crime that has been, or hereafter shall be, made, or by their own voluntary contract for a term not exceeding seven years, shall be and hereby are declared null and void.

And, whereas, divers persons now have in their service negroes, mulattoes, or others who have been deemed their slaves or property, and who are now incapable of earning their living by reason of age or infirmities, and may be desirous of continuing in the service of their masters or mistresses, — be it therefore enacted, by the authority aforesaid, that whatever negro or mulatto, who shall be desirous of continuing in the service of his master or mistress, and shall voluntarily declare the same before two justices of the county in which said master or mistress resides, shall have a right to continue in the service, and to a maintenance from their master or mistress, and if they are incapable of earning their living, shall be supported by the said master or mistress, or their heirs, during the lives of said servants, any thing in this act to the contrary notwithstanding.

Provided, nevertheless, that nothing in this act shall be understood to prevent any master of a vessel or other person from bringing into this State any persons, not Africans, from any other part of the world, except the United States of America, and selling their service for a term of time not exceeding five years, if 21 years of age, or, if under 21, not exceeding the time when he or she so brought into the State shall be 26 years of age, to pay for and in consideration of the transportation and other charges said master of vessel or other person may have been at, agreeable to contracts made with the persons so transported, or their parents or guardians in their behalf, before they are brought from their own country.

Ordered to lie until second session of the General Court.

SECOND PETITION OF MASSACHUSETTS SLAVES.

The petition of a great number of negroes, who are detained in a state of slavery in the very bowels of a free and Christian country, humbly showing, —

That your petitioners apprehend that they have, in common with all other men, a natural and inalienable right to that freedom, which the great Parent of the universe hath bestowed equally on an mankind, and which they have never forfeited by any compact or agreement whatever. But they were unjustly dragged by the cruel hand of power from their dearest friends, and some of them even torn from the embraces of their tender parents, — from a populous, pleasant and plentiful country, and in violation of the laws of nature and of nations, and in defiance of all the tender feelings of humanity, brought hither to be sold like beasts of burthen, and, like them, condemned to slavery for life — among a people possessing the mild religion of Jesus — a people not insensible of the sweets of national freedom, nor without a spirit to resent the unjust endeavors of others to reduce them to a state of bondage and subjection.

Your Honors need not to be informed that a life of slavery like that of your petitioners, deprived of every social privilege, of every thing requisite to render life even tolerable, is far -worse than nonexistence.

In imitation of the laudable example of the good people of these States, your petitioners have long and patiently waited the event of petition after petition, by them presented to the legislative body of this State, and cannot but with grief reflect that their success has been but too similar.

They cannot but express their astonishment that it has never been considered, that every principle from which America has acted, in the course of her unhappy difficulties with Great Britain, bears stronger than a thousand arguments in favor of your humble petitioners. They therefore humbly beseech Your Honors to give their petition its due weight and consideration, and cause an act of the legislature to be passed, whereby they may be restored to the enjoyment of that freedom, which is the natural right of all men, and their children (who were born in this land of liberty) may not be held as slaves after they arrive at the age of twenty-one years. So may the inhabitants of this State (no longer chargeable with the inconsistency of acting themselves the part which they condemn and oppose in others) be prospered in their glorious struggles for liberty, and have those blessings secured to them by Heaven, of which benevolent minds cannot wish to deprive their fellow-men.

And your petitioners, as in duty bound, shall ever pray: —
LANCASTER HILL,
PETER BESS,
BRISTER SLENFEN,

PRINCE HALL,

JACK PIERPONT, [his X mark.]

NERO FUNELO, [his X mark.]

NEWPORT SUMNER, [his X mark.]

In 1778, Lieut. THOMAS KENCH presented a petition to the Legislature, asking for the appointment of a colored regiment. The Legislature responded thus: —

STATE OF MASSACHUSETTS BAY:

The Committee of both Houses upon the letter of THOMAS KENCH, with other papers accompanying it, have attended to that service, and report —

That there be one regiment of volunteers raised, as soon as possible, to serve during the war, to consist of the same number of officers and privates as those of a continental regiment; — That one sergeant in each company, and every higher officer in said regiment, shall be white men, and that all the other sergeants, inferior officers and privates shall be negroes, mulattoes, or Indians.

At a later date, Lieut. KENCH addressed the following letter to the Council: —

To the Honorable Council:

The letter I wrote before I heard of the disturbance with Col. Seaver, Mr. Spear, and a number of other gentlemen, concerning the freedom of negroes, in Congress, street. It is, a pity that riots should be committed on the occasion, as it is, justified that negroes should have their freedom, and none among, us be held as slaves, as freedom and liberty is the grand controversy that we are contending for, and I trust, under the smiles of Divine Providence, we shall obtain it, if all our minds can be united; and putting the negroes into the service will prevent much uneasiness, and give more satisfaction to those that are offended at the thoughts of their servants being free.

I will not enlarge, for fear I should give offence, but subscribe myself,

Your faithful servant,

THOMAS KENCH.

CASTLE ISLAND, April 7, 1778.

FORMATION OF A COLORED REGIMENT IN RHODE ISLAND.

STATE OF RHODE ISLAND AND PROVIDENCE PLANTATIONS, IN GENERAL ASSEMBLY.

February Session, 1778.

Whereas, for the preservation of the rights and liberties of the United States, it is necessary that the whole power of Government should be exerted in recruiting the Continental battalions; and, whereas, His Excellency, General Washington, hath inclosed to this State a proposal made to him by Brigadier General Varnum, to enlist into the two battalions raising by this State such slaves as should be willing to enter into the service; and, whereas, history affords us frequent precedents of the wisest, the freest and bravest nations having liberated their slaves and enlisted them as soldiers to fight in defence of their country; and also, whereas, the enemy have, with great force, taken possession of the capital and of a great part of this State, and this State is obliged to raise a very considerable number of troops for its own immediate defence, whereby it is in a manner rendered impossible for this State to furnish recruits for the said two battalions without adopting the said measures so recommended, —

It is Voted and Resolved, That every able-bodied negro, mulatto, or Indian man-slave in this State may enlist into either of the said two battalions, to serve daring the continuance of the present war with Great Britain; — That every slave so enlisting shall be entitled to and receive all the bounties, wages and encouragements allowed by the Continental Congress to any soldiers enlisting into this service.

It is further Voted and Resolved, That every slave so enlisting shall, upon his passing muster by Col. Christopher Greene, be immediately discharged from the service of his master or mistress, and be absolutely free, as though he had never been incumbered with any kind of servitude or slavery. And in case such slave shall, by sickness or otherwise, be rendered unable to maintain himself, he shall not be chargeable to his master or mistress, but shall be supported at the expense of the State.

And, whereas, slaves have been by the laws deemed the property of their owners, and therefore compensation ought to be made to the owners for the loss of their service, —

It is further Voted and Resolved, That there be allowed and paid by this State to the owners, for every such slave so enlisting, a sum according to his worth, at a price not exceeding one hundred and twenty pounds for the most valuable slave, and in proportion for a slave of less value, — provided the owner of said slave shall deliver up to the officer who shall enlist him the clothes of the said slave, or otherwise he shall not be entitled to said sum.

And for settling and ascertaining the value of such slaves, it is further Voted and Resolved, That a committee of five shall be appointed, to wit, — one from each county, any three of whom to be a quorum, — to examine the slaves who shall be so enlisted, after they shall have passed muster, and to set a price upon each slave, according to his value as aforesaid.

It is further Voted and Resolved, That upon any able-bodied negro, mulatto or Indian slave enlisting as aforesaid, the officer who shall so enlist him, after he has passed muster as aforesaid, shall deliver a certificate thereof to the master or mistress of said negro, mulatto, or Indian slave, which shall discharge him from the service of said master or mistress.

It is further Voted and Resolved, That the committee who shall estimate the value of the slave aforesaid, shall give a certificate of the sum at which he may be valued to the owner of said slave, and the general treasurer of this State is hereby empowered and directed to give unto the owner of said slave his promissory note for the sum of money at which he shall be valued as aforesaid, payable on demand, with interest, — which shall be paid with the money from Congress.

A true copy, examined, HENRY WARD, Sec'y.

In 1782, a female slave named BELINDA presented a petition to the Legislature, in which she says: — "Although I have been servant to a Colonel forty years, my labors have not procured me any comfort. I have not yet enjoyed the benefits of creation. With my poor daughter, I fear I shall pass the remainder of my days in slavery and misery. For her and myself, I beg freedom."

MUM BETT.

I extract the following account of this remarkable woman from an Address delivered in Stockbridge, Mass., February, 1831, by THEODORE SEDGWICK, Esq., a son of Judge Sedgwick, who had the honor of judicially pronouncing the doom of slavery in Massachusetts, under her Bill of Rights: —

"We have arrived, by imperceptible degrees, to a point of elevation from which we look down and around, with a sense of superiority, as if the height had been attained by our unaided efforts, and without remembering or regarding the means whereby we ascended. We despise the abject African, because he does not at once leap up to the ascent upon which we have been placed by circumstances, which we could no more control than he could have controlled his destiny.

"We should look at the subject in a different aspect. We should make all allowances for the different condition of the Africans and ourselves; give them credit for what they have done, and not reproach them for not doing what they had no means of doing. They have the same principle of buoyancy with ourselves, and the instant that the weight which depresses their level in society is taken off, they will rise and occupy the space which is left vacant for them.

"Such has been my acquaintance with individuals of this race, that I regard the pretence of original and natural superiority in the whites, very much as I regard the tales of ancient fables, setting forth the superior bodily strength of heroes. But for the care of one of this calumniated race, I should not now, probably, be living to give this testimony.

"A very slight sketch of the history of the person to whom I refer may serve to illustrate this argument. Elizabeth Freeman (known afterwards by the name of Mum Bett) was born a slave, and lived in that condition thirty or forty years. She first lived in Claverac, Columbia county, in the State of New York, in the family of a Mr. Hogeboom. She was purchased at an early age by Col. Ashley, of Sheffield, in the county of Berkshire, in the now Commonwealth of Massachusetts. In both these States, and I believe every where in the Northern States, slavery existed in a very mitigated form. This is not so much to be ascribed to the superior humanity of the people, as to the circumstances of the case. The slaves were comparatively few. Society, except, perhaps, in the capitals, was in a state nearly primitive. The slaves were precluded from the table in but few families. Their masters and mistresses wrought with the slaves. A great degree of familiarity necessarily resulted from this mode of life. Slavery in New York and New England was so marked, that but a slight difference could be perceived in the condition of slaves and hired servants. The character of the slaves was moulded accordingly. Sales were very rare. The same feeling which induces a father to retain a child in his family, or at least under his control, disinclined him from parting with his slave. There was little distinction of rank in the country. The younger slaves not only ate and drank, but played with the children. They thus became familiar companions with each other. The black women were cooks and nurses, and, as such, assisted by their mistresses. There was no great difference between the fare or clothing of black and white laborers.

"In this state of familiar intercourse, instances of cruelty were uncommon, and the minds of the slaves were not so much subdued but that they caused a degree of indignation not much less than if committed upon a freeman.

"Under this condition of society, while Mum Bett resided in the family of Col. Ashley, she received a severe wound in a generous attempt to shield her sister. Her mistress, in a fit of passion, resorted to a degree and mode of violence very uncommon in this country: she struck at the weak and timid girl with a heated kitchen shovel; Mum Bett interposed her arm, and received the blow; and she bore the honorable scar it left to the day of her death. The spirit of Mum Bett had not been broken down by ill usage — she resented the insult and outrage as a white person would have done. She left the house, and neither commands nor entreaties could induce her to return. Her master, Col. Ashley, resorted to the law to regain possession of his slave. This was shortly after the adoption of the Constitution of Massachusetts. The case was tried at Great Barrington. Mum Bett was declared free; it being, I believe, the first instance (or among the first instances) of the practical application of the declaration in the Massachusetts Bill of Rights, that 'all men are born free and equal.'

The late Judge Sedgwick had the principal agency in her deliverance. She attached herself to his family as a servant. In that station she remained for many years, and was never entirely disconnected from his family.

"She was married when young; her husband died soon after, in the continental service of the Revolutionary War, leaving her with one child. During the residue of her life, she remained a widow. She died in December, 1829, at a very advanced age. She supposed herself to be nearly a hundred years old.

"If there could be a practical refutation of the imagined natural superiority of our race to hers, the life and character of this woman would afford that refutation. She knew her station, and perfectly observed its decorum; yet she had nothing of the submissive or the subdued character, which succumbs to superior force, and is the usual result of the state of slavery. On the contrary, without ever claiming superiority, she uniformly, in every case, obtained an ascendency over all those with whom she was associated in service. Her spirit of fidelity to her employers was such as has never been surpassed. This was exemplified in her whole life. I can convey an idea of it only by the relation of a single incident.

"The house of Mr. Sedgwick, in this town, (Stockbridge,) was attacked by a body of insurgents, during the Shay's war, so well remembered in this vicinity. Mr. Sedgwick was then absent in Boston, and Mum Bett was the only guardian of the house. She assured the party that Mr. Sedgwick was absent, but suffered them to search the house to find him, which they did, by feeling under the beds and other places of concealment, with the points of their bayonets. She did not attempt to resist, by direct force, the rifling of property, which was one of the objects of the insurgents. She, however, assumed a degree of authority; told the plunderers that they 'dare not strike a woman,' and attended them in their exploring the house, to prevent wanton destruction. She escorted them into the cellar with a large kitchen shovel in her hand, which she intimated that she would use in case of necessity. One of the party broke off the neck of a bottle of porter. She told him that if he or his companions desired to drink porter, she would fetch a corkscrew, and draw a cork, and they might drink like gentlemen; but that, if the neck of another bottle should be broken, she would lay the man that broke it flat with her shovel. Upon tasting the liquor, the party decided that 'if gentlemen loved such cursed bitter stuff, they might keep it.'

"Understanding, from the conversation of the party, that they intended to take with them, in their retreat, a very fine gray mare that was in the stable, which she had been in the riding, she left the house and went directly to the stable. Before the rioters were apprised of her intention, she led the animal to a gate that opened upon the street, stripped off the halter, and, by a blow with it, incited the mare to a degree of speed that soon put her out of danger from the pursuit of the marauders.

"Even in her humble station, she had, when occasion required it, an air of command which conferred a degree of dignity, and gave her an ascendency over those of her rank, which is very unusual in persons of any rank or color. Her determined and resolute character, which enabled her to limit the ravages of a Shay's mob, was manifested in her conduct and deportment, during her whole life. She claimed no distinction; but it was yielded to her from her superior experience, energy, skill, and sagacity. In her sphere, she had no superior, nor any equal. In the latter part of her life, she was much employed as a nurse. Here she had no competitor. I believe she never lost a child, when she had the care of its mother, at its birth.

When a child, wailing in the arms of its mother, heard her steps on the stairway, or approaching the door, it ceased to cry.

"This woman, by her extreme industry and economy, supported a large family of grand-children and great-grand-children. She could neither read nor write; yet her conversation was instructive, and her society was much sought. She received many visits at her own house, and very frequently received and accepted invitations to pass considerble intervals of time in the families of her friends. Her death, notwithstanding her great age, was deeply lamented.

"Having known this woman as familiarly as I knew either of my parents, I cannot believe in the moral or physical inferiority of the race to which she belonged. The degradation of the African must have been otherwise caused than by natural inferiority. Civilization has made slow progress in every portion of the earth; where it has made progress, it proceeds in an accelerated ratio."

In 1795, Judge Tucker, of Virginia, propounded to Rev. Dr. Belknap, of Massachusetts, eleven queries respecting the slavery and emancipation of negroes in Massachusetts, which were answered by Dr. Belknap in a very intelligent manner. The queries and replies may be found in the fourth volume of the Collections of the Massachusetts Historical Society. In one of his letters, Dr. Belknap says: — "The present Constitution of Massachusetts was established in 1780. The first article of the Declaration of Rights asserts that 'all men are born free and equal.' This was inserted not merely as a moral or political truth, but with a particular view to establish the liberation of the negroes on a general principle, and so it was understood by the people at large: but some doubted whether this was sufficient. Many of the blacks, taking advantage of the public opinion and of this general assertion in the Bill of Rights, asked their freedom and obtained it. Others took it without leave. In 1781, at the Court in Worcester County, an indictment was found against a white man for assaulting, beating and imprisoning a black. He was tried at the Supreme Judicial Court in 1783. His defence was that the black (Walker) was his slave, and that the beating, &c., was the necessary restraint and correction by the master.

"The judges and jury were of opinion that he had no right to beat or imprison him. He was found guilty, and fined forty shillings. This decision was a mortal wound to slavery in Massachusetts."

There is no specific record of the Abolition of slavery in Massachusetts; and, of course, different versions are given concerning it. John Quincy Adams, in reply to a question put by J. C. Spencer, stated that "a note had been given for the price of a slave in 1787. This note was sued, and the Court ruled that the maker had received no consideration, as man could not be sold. From that time forward, slavery died in the Old Bay State."

I find, in Dr. Belknap's letters, the following account of an early kidnapping enterprise in the city of Boston. The kidnappers were not so successful as others of a more recent date, since they do not seem to have had the State authorities on their side. "In the month of February, 1788," says Dr. Belknap, "just after the adoption of the present Federal Constitution by the Convention of Massachusetts, a most flagrant violation of the laws of society and humanity was perpetrated in Boston, by one Avery, of Connecticut. By the assistance of another infamous fellow, he decoyed three unsuspecting black men on board a vessel, which he had chartered, and sent them down into the hold to work. Whilst they were there employed, the vessel came to sail and went to sea, having been previously cleared out for Martinice.

"As soon as this infamous transaction was known, Governor Hancock and M. L. Etombe, the French consul, wrote letters to the governors of all the islands in the West Indies, in favor of the decoyed blacks. The public indignation being greatly excited against the actors in this affair, and against others who had been concerned in the traffic of slaves, it was thought proper to take advantage of the ferment, and bring good out of evil.

"The three blacks who were decoyed were offered for sale at the Danish island of St. Bartholomew. They told their story publicly, which coming to the ears of the governor, he prevented the sale. A Mr. Atherton, of the island, generously became bound for their good behavior for six months, in which time letters came, informing of their case, and they were permitted to return.

"They arrived in Boston on the 20th of July following; and it was a day of jubilee, not only among their countrymen, but among, all the friends of justice and humanity."

Extract from a charge delivered to the African Lodge, June 24th, 1797, at Menotomy, (now West Cambridge,) Mass., by the Right Worshipful PRINCE HALL.

"Beloved Brethren of the African Lodge:

"It is now five years since I delivered a charge to you on some parts and points of masonry. As one branch or superstructure of the foundation, I endeavored to show you the duty of a mason to a mason, and of charity and love to all mankind, as the work and image of the great God and the Father of the human race. I shall now attempt to show you that it is our duty to sympathise with our fellow-men under their troubles, and with the families of our brethren who are gone, we hope, to the Grand Lodge above.

"We are to have sympathy," said he, "but this, after all, is not to be confined to parties or colors, nor to towns or states, nor to a kingdom, but to the kingdoms of the whole earth, over whom Christ the King is head and grand master for all in distress.

"Among these numerous sons and daughters of distress, let us see our friends and brethren; and first let us see them dragged from their native country, by the iron hand of tyranny and oppression, from their dear friends and connections, with weeping eyes and aching hearts, to a strange land, and among, a strange people, whose tender mercies are cruel, — and there to bear the iron yoke of slavery and cruelty, till death, as a friend, shall relieve them. And must not the unhappy condition of these, our fellow-men, draw forth our hearty prayers and wishes for their deliverance from those merchants and traders, whose characters you have described in Revelations xviii. 11-13? And who knows but these same sort of traders may, in a short time, in like manner bewail the loss of the African traffic, to their shame and confusion? The day dawns now in some of the West India Islands. God can and will change their condition and their hearts, too, and let Boston and the world know that He hath no respect of persons, and that that bulwark of envy, pride, scorn and contempt, which is so visible in some, shall fall.

"Jethro, an Ethiopian, gave instructions to his son-in-law, Moses, in establishing government. Exodus xviii. 22-24. Thus, Moses was not ashamed to be instructed by a black man. Philip was not ashamed to take a seat beside the Ethiopian Eunuch, and to instruct him in the gospel. The Grand Master Solomon was not ashamed to hold conference with the Queen of Sheba. Our Grand Master Solomon did not divide the living child, whatever he might do with the dead one; neither did he pretend to make a law to forbid the parties from having free intercourse with one another, without the fear of censure, or be turned out of the synagogue.

Now, my brethren, nothing is stable; all things are changeable. Let us seek those things which are sure and steadfast, and let us pray God that, while we remain here, he would give us the grace of patience, and strength to bear up under all our troubles, which, at this day, God knows, we have our share of. Patience, I say; for were we not possessed of a great measure of it, we could not bear up under the daily insults we meet with in the streets of Boston, much more on public days of recreation. How, at such times, are we shamefully abused, and that to such a degree, that we may truly be said to carry our lives in our hands, and the arrows of death are flying about our heads. Helpless women have their clothes torn from their backs. . . . And by whom are these disgraceful and abusive actions committed? Not by the men born and bred in Boston, — they are better bred; but by a mob or horde of shameless, low-lived, envious, spiteful persons — some of them, not long since, servants in gentlemen's kitchens, scouring knives, horse-tenders, chaise-drivers. I was told by a gentleman who saw the filthy behavior in the Common, that, in all places he had been in, he never saw so cruel behavior in all his life; and that a slave in the West Indies, on Sundays, or holidays, enjoys himself and friends without molestation. Not only this man, but many in town, who have seen their behavior to us, and that, without provocation, twenty or thirty cowards have fallen upon one man. (O, the patience of the blacks!) 'T is not for want of courage in you, for they know that they do not face you man for man but in a mob, which we despise, and would rather suffer wrong than to do wrong, to the disturbance of the community, and the disgrace of our reputation; for every good citizen doth honor to the laws of the State where he resides.

"My brethren, let us not be cast down under these and many other abuses we at present are laboring under, — for the darkest hour is just before the break of day. My brethren, let us remember what a dark day it was with our African brethren, six years ago, in the French West Indies. Nothing but the snap of the whip was heard, from morning to evening. Hanging, breaking on the wheel, burning, and all manner of tortures, were inflicted on those unhappy people. But, blessed be God, the scene is changed. They now confess that God hath no respect of persons, and, therefore, receive them as their friends, and treat them as brothers. Thus doth Ethiopia stretch forth her hand from slavery, to freedom and equality."

About this time, the celebrated Prince Sanders was teaching in Boston. He subsequently prepared a compilation of Haytien documents, and presented, December 11, 1818, to the American Convention, a memorial for the abolition of slavery, and improving the condition of the African race.

PHILLIS WHEATLY.

PHILLIS WHEATLY was a native of Africa, and was brought to this country in the year 1761, and sold as a slave. She was purchased by Mr. John Wheatly, a respectable citizen of Boston. This gentleman, at the time of the purchase, was already the owner of several slaves; but the females in his possession were getting something beyond the active periods of life, and Mrs. Wheatly wished to obtain a young negress, with the view of training her up under her own eye, that she might, by, gentle usage, secure to herself a faithful domestic in her old age. She visited the slave-market, that she might make a personal selection form the group of unfortunates for sale. There she found several robust, healthy females, exhibited at the same time with Phillis, who was of a slender frame, and evidently suffering from change of climate. She was, however, the choice of the lady, who acknowledged herself influenced to this decision by the humble and modest demeanor, and the interesting features, of the little stranger.

The poor, naked child (for she had no other covering than a quantity of dirty carpet about her, like a "fillibeg") was taken home in the chaise of her mistress, and comfortably attired. She is supposed to have been about seven years old, at this time, from the circumstance of shedding her front teeth. She soon gave indications of uncommon intelligence, and was frequently seen endeavoring to make letters upon the wall with a piece of chalk or charcoal.

A daughter of Mrs. Wheatly, not long after the child's first introduction to the family, undertook to learn her to read and write; and, while she astonished her instructress by her rapid progress, she won the good-will of her kind mistress by her amiable disposition and the propriety of her behavior. She was not devoted to menial occupations, as was at first intended; nor was she allowed to associate with the other domestics of the family, who were of her own color and condition, but was kept constantly about the person of her mistress.

She does not seem to have preserved any remembrance of the place of her nativity, or of her parents, excepting the simple circumstance, that her mother poured out water before the sun at its rising — in reference, no doubt, to an ancient African custom.

As Phillis increased in years, the development of her mind realized the promise of her childhood; and she soon attracted the attention of the literati of the day, many of whom furnished her with books. These enabled her to make considerable progress in belles-lettres; but such gratification seems only to have increased her thirst after knowledge, as is the case with most gifted minds, not misled by vanity; and we soon find her endeavoring to roaster the Latin tongue.

She was now frequently visited by clergymen, and other individuals of high standing in society; but, notwithstanding the attention she received, and the distinction with which she was treated, she never for a moment lost sight of that modest, unassuming demeanor, which first won the heart of her mistress in the slave-market. Indeed, we consider the strongest proof of her worth to have been the earnest affection of this excellent woman, who admitted her to her own board. Phillis ate of her bread, and drank of her cup, and was to her as a daughter; for she returned her affection with unbounded gratitude, and was so devoted to her interests as to have no will in opposition to that of her benefactress.

In 1770, at the age of sixteen, Phillis was received as a member of the church worshipping in the Old South Meeting House, then under the pastoral charge of the Rev. Dr. Sewall. She became an ornament to her profession; for she possessed that meekness of spirit, which, in the language of inspiration, is said to be above all price. She was very gentle-tempered, extremely affectionate, and altogether free from that most despicable foible, which might naturally have been her besetting sin, — literary vanity.

The little poem, commencing,

"It was mercy brought me from my heathen land,"

will be found to be a beautiful expression of her religious sentiments, and a noble vindication of the claims of her race. We can hardly suppose any one, reflecting by whom it was written — an African and a slave — to read it, without emotions both of regret and admiration.

Phillis never indulged her muse in any fits of sullenness or caprice. She was at all times accessible. If any one requested her to write upon any particular subject or event, she immediately set herself to the task, and produced something upon the given theme. This is probably the reason why so many of her pieces are funeral poems, many of them, no doubt, being written at the request of friends. Still, the variety of her compositions affords sufficient proof of the versatility of her genius. We find her, at one time, occupied in contemplation of an event affecting the condition of a whole people, and pouring forth her thoughts in a lofty strain. Then the song sinks to the soft tones of sympathy, in the affliction occasioned by domestic bereavement. Again, we see her seeking inspiration from the sacred volume, or from the tomes of heathen lore; now excited by the beauties of art, and now hymning the praises of Nature to "Nature's God." On one occasion, we notice her — a girl of but fourteen years — recognizing a political event, and endeavoring to express the grateful loyalty of subjects to their rightful king — not as one, indeed, who had been trained to note the events of nations, by a course of historical studies, but one whose habits, taste and opinions, were peculiarly her own; for in Phillis, we have an example of originality of no ordinary character. She was allowed, and even encouraged, to follow the leading of her own genius; but nothing was forced upon her, nothing suggested or placed before her as a lure; her literary efforts were altogether the natural workings of her own mind.

There is another circumstance respecting her habits of composition which peculiarly claims our attention. She did not seem to have the power of retaining the creations of her own fancy, for a long time, in her own mind. If, during the vigil of a wakeful night, she amused herself by weaving a tale, she knew nothing of it in the morning — it had vanished in the land of dreams. Her kind mistress indulged her with a light, and, in the cold season, with a fire, in her apartment, during the night. The light was placed upon a table at her bedside, with writing materials, that, if any thing occurred to her after she had retired, she might, without rising or taking cold, secure the swift-wing fancy ere it fled.

By comparing the accounts we have of Phillis's progress with the dates of her earliest poems, we find that she must have commenced her career as an authoress as soon as she could write a legible hand, and without being acquainted with the rules of composition. Indeed, we very much doubt if she ever had any grammatical instruction, or any knowledge of the structure or idiom of the English language, except what she imbibed from the perusal of the best English writers, and from mingling in polite circles, where, fortunately, she was encouraged to converse freely with the wise and the learned.

We gather, from her writings, that she was acquainted with astronomy, ancient and modern geography, and ancient history: and that she was well versed in the scriptures of the Old and New Testament. She discovered a decided taste for the stories of Heathen Mythology, and Pope's Homer seems to have been a great favorite with her.

The reader is already aware of the delicate constitution and frail health of Phillis. During the winter of 1773, the indications of disease had so much increased, that her physician advised a sea voyage. This was earnestly seconded by her friends; and a son of Mr. and Mrs. Wheatly, being about to make a voyage to England, to arrange a mercantile correspondence, it was settled that Phillis should accompany him, and she accordingly embarked in the summer of the same year.

She was at this time but nineteen years old, and was at the highest point of her short and brilliant career. It is with emotions of sorrow that we approach the strange and splendid scenes which were now about to open upon her — to be succeeded by grief and desolation.

Phillis was well received in England, and was presented to Lady Huntingdon, Lord Dartmouth, Mr. Thornton, and many other individuals of distinction; but, says our informant, "not all the attention she received, nor all the honors that were heaped upon her, had the slightest influence upon her temper or deportment. She was still the same single-hearted, unsophisticated being."

During her stay in England, her poems were given to the world., dedicated to the Countess of Huntingdon, and embellished with an engraving, which is said to have been a striking representation of the original. It is supposed that one of these impressions was forwarded to her mistress, as soon as they were struck off; for a grand niece of Mrs. Wheatly informs us that, during the absence of Phillis, she one day called upon her relative, who immediately directed her attention to a picture over the fire-place, exclaiming, — "See! look at my Phillis! Does she not seem as though she would speak to me?"

Phillis arrived in London so late in the season, that the great mart of fashion was deserted. She was, therefore, urgently pressed, by her distinguished friends, to remain until the Court returned to St. James, that she might be presented to the young monarch, George III. She would probably have consented to this arrangement, had not letters from America informed her of the declining health of her mistress, who entreated her to return, that she might once more behold her beloved protegé. Phillis waited not a second bidding, but immediately reëmbarked for that once happy home, soon after made desolate by the death of her affectionate mistress.

She soon after received an offer of marriage from a respectable colored man, of Boston, The name of this individual was Peters. He kept a grocery in Court street, and was a man of handsome person. He wore a wig, carried a cane, and quite acted out "the gentleman." In an evil hour, he was accepted; and, though he was a man of talents and information, — writing with fluency and propriety, and, at one period, reading law, — he proved utterly unworthy of the distinguished woman who honored him by her alliance.

The following letter, written by General Washington in reply to a communication sent to him by Phillis, will be read with the deepest interest. The letter may be found in Spark's Life of Washington.

CAMBRIDGE, Mass., Feb. 28, 1776.

Miss PHILLIS —

Your favor of the 26th of October did not reach my hands till the middle of December. Time enough, you will say, to have given an answer ere this. Granted. But a variety of important occurrences, continually interposing to distract the mind and withdraw the attention, I hope will apologize for the delay, and plead my excuse for the seeming, but not real, neglect. I thank you most sincerely for your polite notice of me, in the elegant lines you enclosed: and, however undeserving I may be of such encomium, and panegyric, the style and manner exhibit a striking proof of your poetical talents; in honor of which, and as a tribute justly due to you, I would have published the poem, had I not been apprehensive that, while I only meant to give the world this new instance of your genius, I might have incurred the imputation of vanity. This, and nothing else, determined me not to give it place in the public prints.

If you should ever come to Cambridge, or near head-quarters, I should be happy to see a person so favored by the Muses, and to whom Nature has been so liberal and beneficent in her dispensations.

I am, with great respect, your obedient, humble servant,

GEORGE WASHINGTON.

As a preface to the edition of Miss Wheatly's poems published in Boston about 1770, I find this card from the publisher: —

TO THE PUBLIC.

As it has been repeatedly suggested to the publisher, by persons who have seen the manuscript, that numbers would be ready to suspect they were not really the writings of PHILLIS, he has procured the following attestation, from the most respectable characters in Boston, that none might have the least ground for disputing their Original.

We whose Names are under-written, do assure the World, that the Poems specified in the following page were (as we verily believe) written by PHILLIS, a young Negro Girl, who was, but a few years since, brought, an uncultivated Barbarian, from Africa, and has ever since been, and now is, under the disadvantage of serving as a Slave in a family in this town. She has been examined by some of the best judges, and is thought qualified to write them.

His Excellency THOMAS HUTCHINSON, Governor,
The Hon. ANDREW OLIVER, Lieutenant Governor,
Hon. Thomas Hubbard,
Hon. John Erving,
Hon. James Pitts,
Hon. Harrison Gray,
Hon. James Bowdoin,
John Hancock, Esq.
Joseph Green, Esq.
Richard Cary, Esq.
Rev. Charles Chauncy,
Rev. Mather Byles,
Rev. Ed. Pemberton,
Rev. Andrew Elliot,
Rev. Samuel Cooper,
Rev. Samuel Mather,
Rev. John Moorhead,
Mr. John Wheatly, her master.

PAUL CUFFE.

PAUL CUFFE'S father was a native of Africa, whence, at an early age, he was dragged by the unfeeling hand of avarice from his home and connections; torn from the parental roof and every thing in this world that was near and dear to him; transported over the wide and trackless ocean, many thousand miles from the land of his birth, to be for ever consigned to rigorous and cruel bondage:

"To increase a stranger's treasures,
 O'er the raging billows borne."

He was purchased as a slave by a person named Slocum, residing in Massachusetts, one of the United States of North America, by whom he was kept in slavery a considerable portion of his life; and there is no reason to doubt, had it not been for his laudable enterprise, aided by great perseverance, he would have worn out his life in perpetual bondage, and ended his days, like many of his degraded and unjustly oppressed fellow-countrymen, under the galling yoke of fetters and chains, or the smart inflicted by the whip of the unrelenting driver. Being possessed, however, of a mind far superior to his degraded and unhappy condition, he was always diligent in his master's business, and proved himself in numerous instances faithful to his interests; so that, by unremitting industry and economy, he was enabled, after a considerable length of time, under the blessing of a kind Providence, to procure the means for purchasing his personal liberty, of which he had been deprived, as already stated, in very early life.

According to the custom of the country into which he was transported, Cuffe also received the name of Slocum, as expressing to whom he belonged; though it appears in after life he was known by the name of John Cuffe. Soon after the happy period in which Cuffe effected his emancipation, and succeeded in releasing himself from the bonds of slavery and unjust oppression, he became acquainted with Ruth Moses, an honorable woman, descended from one of the Indian tribes residing in Massachusetts.

Cuffe's acquaintance with Ruth Moses ended in their taking each other in marriage; and continuing in his praise-worthy habits of industry and frugality, be was enabled, soon after this occurrence, to purchase a farm of 100 acres of land, in Westport, Massachusetts. Cuffe and Ruth continued to live happily together, and brought up a family of ten children — four sons, and six daughters. Three of the former, David, Jonathan and John, were farmers in the neighborhood of Westport, filled respectable stations in society, and were endowed with good intellectual capacities. They all married well, and gave their children a good education.

Cuffe died in 1745, leaving behind him a considerable property in land, the fruits of his industry.

PAUL, the youngest son of Cuffe, and the interesting subject of the present memoir, was born on Cutterhunker, one of the Elizabeth Islands, near New Bedford, in the year 1759; so that, when his father died, he was about fourteen years of age, at which time he had learned but little more than the letters of the alphabet. The land which his father had left behind him proving unproductive, afforded but little provision for the numerous family; so that the care of supporting his mother and sisters devolved jointly upon himself and his brothers. Thus he labored under great disadvantages, being deprived of the means and opportunity for acquiring even the rudiments of a good education. He was not, however, easily to be discouraged, and found opportunities of improving himself in various ways, and cultivating his mind. Having never received the benefits of an education, the knowledge he possessed was obtained entirely by his own indefatigable exertions, and the little assistance which he occasionally received from persons who were friendly disposed towards him. Aided by these means, he soon learned to read and write, and he also attained to a considerable proficiency in arithmetic, and skill in navigation; and we may form some estimate of the natural talent with which he was endowed for the speedy reception of learning, from the fact that, with the assistance of a friend, he acquired such a knowledge of the latter science, in the short space of two weeks, as enabled him to command the vessel, in the voyages which he subsequently made to England, to Russia, to Africa, and to the West Indies, as well as to several different ports in the southern section of the United States.

It has already been stated that his three brothers were respectable farmers in the neighborhood of Westport. The mind of Paul, however, was early inclined to the pursuits of commerce. Conceiving that they furnished to industry more ample rewards than agriculture, and conscious that he possessed qualities which, under proper culture, would enable him to pursue commercial employments with prospects of success, he entered, at the age of sixteen, as a common hand, on board of a vessel destined to the Bay of Mexico, on a whaling expedition. His second voyage was to the West Indies; but on his third, which was during the American war, about the year 1776, he was captured by a British ship. After three months' detention as a prisoner at New York, he was permitted to return home to Westport, where, owing to the unfortunate continuance of hostilities, he spent about two years in agricultural pursuits. During this interval, Paul and his brother, John Cuffe, were called on by the collector of the district in which they resided for the payment of a personal tax. It appeared to them that, by the laws and the Constitution of Massachusetts, taxation and the whole rights of citizenship were united. If the laws demanded of them the payment of personal taxes, the same laws must necessarily and constitutionally invest them with the rights of representing, and being represented, in the State Legislature. But they had never been considered as entitled to the privilege of voting at elections, or of being elected to places of trust and honor. Under these circumstances, they refused to comply. The collector resorted to the force of the laws; and after many delays and vexations, Paul and his brother deemed it most prudent to silence the suit by payment of the demands, which were only small. But they resolved, if it were possible, to obtain the rights which they believed to be connected with taxation. In pursuance of this resolution, they presented a respectful petition to the State Legislature, which met with a warm and almost indignant opposition from some in authority. A considerable majority, however, perceiving the propriety and justness of the petition, were favorable to the object, and, with an honorable magnanimity, in defiance of the prejudice of the times, a law was enacted by them, rendering all free persons of color liable to taxation, according to the ratio established for white men, and granting them all the privileges belonging to other citizens. This was a day equally honorable to the petitioners and to the Legislature; a day in which justice and humanity triumphed over prejudice and oppression; and a day which ought to be gratefully remembered by every person of color within the boundaries of Massachusetts, and the names of John and Paul Cuffe should always be united with its recollection.

Paul, being at this time about twenty years of age, thought himself sufficiently skilled to enter into business on his own account, and laid before his brother David a plan for opening a commercial intercourse with the State of Connecticut. His brother was pleased with the prospect, and they built an open boat and proceeded to sea.

They encountered such numerous and untoward discomfitures, as would have caused the courage of most persons to fail. But Paul's dispositions were not of that yielding nature. He possessed that inflexible spirit of perseverance and firmness of mind, which entitled him to a more successful issue of his endeavors and he believed that, while be maintained integrity of heart and conduct, he might humbly hope for the protection of Providence. Under these impressions, he prepared for another voyage. In his open boat, with a small cargo, he again directed his course towards the island of Nantucket. The weather was favorable, and he arrived in safety at the destined port, and disposed of his little cargo to advantage. The profits of this voyage, by strengthening the confidence of his friends, enabled him further to enlarge his plans, and by a steady perseverance, he was at length enabled, under Divine assistance, to overcome obstacles apparently insurmountable.

Having become master of a small covered vessel, of about twelve tons burthen, he hired a person to assist him as a seaman, and made many advantageous voyages to different parts of the State of Connecticut; and, when about twenty-five years of age, he married a native of the country, and a descendant of the same tribe to which his mother belonged. For some time after his marriage, he attended chiefly to his agricultural concerns; but from an increase of family, he at length deemed it necessary to pursue his commercial undertakings more extensively than he had before done. He arranged his affairs for a new expedition, and hired a small house on Westport river, to which he removed his family. A vessel of eighteen tons was now procured, in which he sailed to the banks of St. George, in quest of codfish, and returned home with a valuable cargo. This important adventure was the foundation of an extensive and profitable fishing establishment from Westport river, which continued for a considerable time, and was the source of an honest and comfortable living to many of the inhabitants of that district.

At this period, Paul formed a connection with his brother-in-law, Michael Wainer, who had several sons well qualified for the sea service, four of whom, subsequently, laudably filled responsible situations as captains and first mates. A vessel of twenty-five tons was built, and in two voyages to the Straits of Bellisle and Newfoundland, he met with such success as enabled him, in conjunction with another person, to build a vessel of forty-two tons burthen, in which he made several profitable voyages.

Paul had experienced the many disadvantages of his very limited education, and he resolved, as far as it was practicable, to relieve his children from similar embarrassments. The neighborhood had neither a tutor nor a school for the instruction of youth, though many of the citizens were desirous that such an institution should be established. About 1797, Paul proposed convening a meeting of the inhabitants, for the purpose of making such arrangements as should accomplish the desired object, the great utility and necessity of which was undeniable. The collision of opinion, however, respecting mode and place, occasioned the meeting to separate without arriving at any conclusion. Several meetings of the same nature were held, but all were alike unsuccessful in their issue. Perceiving that all efforts to procure a union of sentiment were fruitless, Paul, by no means disheartened, set himself to work in earnest, and had a suitable house built on his own ground, and entirely at his own expense, which he freely offered for the use of the public, without requiring any pecuniary remuneration, feeling himself fully compensated in the satisfaction he derived in seeing it occupied for so useful and excellent a purpose; and the school was opened to all who pleased to send their children.

How gratifying to humanity is this anecdote! and who, that justly appreciates human character, would not prefer Paul Cuffe, the offspring of an African slave, to the proudest statesman that ever dealt out destruction amongst mankind?

About this time, Paul proceeded on a whaling voyage to the Straits of Bellisle, where he met with four other vessels, completely equipped with boats and harpoons, for capturing whales. Paul discovered that he had not made proper preparations for the business, having only ten hands on board, and two boats, one of which was old and almost useless. When the masters of the other vessels discovered his situation, they refused to comply with the customary practices adopted on such voyages, and refused to mate with his crew. In this emergency, Paul resolved to prosecute his undertaking alone, till, at length, the other masters thought it most prudent to accede to the usual practice, apprehending his crew, by their ignorance, might alarm and drive the whales from their reach, and thus defeat the object of their voyage. During the season, they took seven whales. The circumstances which had taken place roused the ambition of Paul and his crew; they were diligent and enterprising, and had the honor of killing six of the seven whales, two of which fell by Paul's own hands.

He returned home in due season, heavily freighted with oil and bone, and arrived in the autumn of 1793, being then about his thirty-fourth year. He went to Philadelphia to dispose of his cargo, and found his pecuniary circumstances were by this time in a flourishing train. When in Philadelphia, he purchased iron necessary for bolts, and other work suitable for a schooner of sixty or seventy tons, and, soon after his return to Westport, the keel for a new vessel was laid. In 1795, his schooner, of sixty tons burthen, was launched, and called "The Ranger."

He also possessed two small fishing boats; but his money was exhausted, and the cargo of his new vessel would require a considerable sum beyond his present stock. He now sold his two boats, and was enabled to place on board his schooner a cargo valued at two thousand dollars; with this he sailed to Norfolk, on the Chesapeake Bay, and there learned, that a very plentiful crop of Indian corn had been gathered that year on the eastern shore of Maryland, and that he could procure a schooner-load, for a low price, at Vienna, on the Nantcoke river. Thither he sailed, but, on his arrival, the people were filled with astonishment and alarm. A vessel, owned and commanded by a black man, and manned with a crew of the same complexion, was unprecedented and surprising.

The white inhabitants were struck with apprehensions of the injurious effects which such circumstance would have on the minds of their slaves, suspecting that he wished secretly to kindle the spirit of rebellion, and excite a destructive revolt among them. Under these notions, several persons associated themselves, for the purpose of preventing Paul from entering his vessel or remaining among them. On examination, his papers proved to be correct, and the custom-house officers could not legally refuse the entry of his vessel. Paul combined prudence with resolution; and, on this occasion, conducted himself with candor, modesty, and firmness; and his crew behaved, not only inoffensively, but with a conciliating propriety, In a few days, the inimical association vanished, and the inhabitants treated him and his crew with respect, and even kindness. Many of the principal people visited his vessel, and, in consequence of the pressing invitation of one of them, Paul dined with his family in the town.

During the year 1797, after his return home, he purchased the house in which his family resided, and the adjoining farm. For the latter, including improvements, he paid $3500, and placed it under the management of his brother, who, as before stated, was a farmer.

By judicious plans, and diligence in their execution, Paul gradually increased his property, (one farm covered a hundred acres,) and by the integrity and consistency of his conduct, he gained the esteem and regard of his fellow-citizens. In the year 1800, he, was concerned in one-half of the expenses of building and equipping a brig of 162 tons burthen. One fourth belonged to his brother, and the other fourth was owned by persons not related to his family. The brig was commanded by Thomas Wainer, Paul Cuffe's nephew, whose talents and character were perfectly adapted to such a situation.

The ship "Alpha," of 268 tons, carpenter's measure, of which Paul owned three fourths, was built in 1806. Of this vessel, he was the commander; the rest of the crew consisting of seven men of color. The ship performed a voyage, under his command, from Wilmington to Savannah thence to Gottenburg, and thence to Philadelphia. After Paul's return, in

1806, the brig "Traveller," of 109 tons burthen, was built at Westport, of one half of which he was the owner. After this period, being extensively engaged in his mercantile and agricultural pursuits he resided at Westport.

In his person, Paul Cuffe was tall, well-formed, and athletic; his deportment conciliating, yet dignified and prepossessing; his countenance blending gravity with modesty and sweetness, and firmness with gentleness and humanity; in speech and habit, plain and unostentatious. His whole exterior indicated a man of respectability and piety, and such would a stranger have supposed him to be at first view. His prudence, strengthened by parental care and example, was, no doubt, a safeguard to him in his youth, when exposed to the dissolute company which unavoidably attends a seafaring life; whilst the religion of Jesus Christ, influencing his mind, under the secret guidance of the Holy Spirit of Truth, in silent reflection, added, in advancing manhood, to the brightness of his character, and instituted or confirmed his disposition to practical good.

He became fully convinced of the principles of truth, as held by the Society of Friends, and, uniting himself in membership with them, it pleased the great Head of the Church, in whom are hid all the treasures of wisdom and knowledge, who respecteth not the persons of men, in his own due time, to entrust him with a gift in the ministry, which he frequently exercised, to the comfort and edification of his friends and brethren.

When he was prevented from going abroad, as, usual, in the pursuit of his business, on account of the rigors of the winter, he often devoted a considerable portion of his time in teaching navigation to his own sons, and to the young men in the neighborhood in which he resided. And even on his voyages, when opportunities occurred, he employed himself in imparting a knowledge of this invaluable science to those under him, so that he had the honor of training up, both amongst the white and colored population, a considerable number of skilful navigators.

He was careful to maintain a strict integrity and uprightness in all his transactions in trade, and, believing himself to be accountable to God for the mode of using and acquiring his possessions, he was at all times willing, and conceived it to be his bounden duty, as a humble follower of a crucified Lord, to sacrifice his private interests, rather than engage in any enterprise, however lawful in the eyes of the world, or however profitable, that might have a tendency, in the smallest degree, either directly or indirectly, to injure his fellowmen. On these grounds, he would not deal in intoxicating liquors, or in slaves, though he might have done either, without violating the laws of his country, and with great prospects of pecuniary gain.

He turned his attention to the British settlement at Sierra Leone, being induced to believe, from various communications he had received from Europe and other sources, that his endeavors to contribute to its welfare, and to that of his fellow-men, might not be ineffectual. On examination, he found his affairs were in so prosperous and flourishing a state as to warrant the undertaking; and, being fully convinced that he was called upon to appropriate a portion of what he had freely received from the hands of an ever bountiful Providence, to the benefit of his unhappy race, he embarked, in the commencement of 1811, in his own brig "Traveller," manned entirely by persons of color, his nephew, Thomas Wainer, being the captain. After a passage of about two months, they arrived at Sierra Leone, where Paul remained about the same length of time, during which interval he made himself acquainted with the real state and condition of the colony. He had frequent conversations with the Governor and principal inhabitants, during which opportunities he suggested several important improvements. Amongst other things, he recommended the formation of a society, for the purpose of promoting the interests of its members and the colonists in general; which measure was immediately acceded to and adopted, and the society named, "The Friendly Society of Sierra Leone," composed principally of respectable men of color.

Paul Cuffe terminated his labors and his life, which he departed in peace, the 7th of the 9th mo., 1817, being then in the fifty-ninth year of his age.

Joseph Congdon, Esq., of New Bedford, has kindly obtained for me the following valuable documents, bearing on PAUL CUFFF'S exertions in behalf of equal suffrage: —

To the Honorable Council and House of Representatives, in General Court assembled, for the State of the Massachusetts Bay, in New England:

The petition of several poor negroes and mulattoes, who are inhabitants of the town of Dartmouth, humbly showeth, —

That we being chiefly of the African extract, and by reason of long bondage and hard slavery, we have been deprived of enjoying the profits of our labor or the advantage of inheriting estates from our parents, as our neighbors the white people do, having some of us not long enjoyed our own freedom; yet of late, contrary to the invariable custom and practice of the country, we have been, and now are, taxed both in our polls and that small pittance of estate which, through much hard labor and industry, we have got together to sustain ourselves and families withall. We apprehend it, therefore, to be hard usage, and will doubtless (if continued) reduce us to a state of beggary, whereby we shall become a burthen to others, if not timely prevented by the interposition of your justice and your power.

Your petitioners further show, that we apprehend ourselves to be aggrieved, in that, while we are not allowed the privilege of freemen of the State, having no vote or influence in the election of those that tax us, yet many of our colour (as is well known) have cheerfully entered the field of battle in the defence of the common cause, and that (as we conceive) against a similar exertion of power (in regard to taxation), too well known to need a recital in this place.

We most humbly request, therefore, that you would take our unhappy case into your serious consideration, and, in your wisdom and power, grant us relief from taxation, while under our present depressed circumstances; and your poor petitioners, as in duty bound, shall ever pray, &c.

JOHN CUFFE,

ADVENTUR CHILD,

PAUL CUFFE,

SAMUEL GRAY, X his mark.

PERO HOWLAND, X his mark.

PERO RUSSELL, X his mark.

PERO COGGESHALL.

Dated at Dartmouth, the 10th of February, 1780.

Memorandum in the hand-writing of John Cuffe: —

"This is the copy of the petition which we did deliver unto the Honorable Council and House, for relief from taxation in the days of our distress. But we received none. JOHN CUFFE."

There is also a copy of the petition, with the date, "January 22d, 1781," not signed, by which it would appear that they intended to renew their application to the government for relief.

[From the Records of Dartmouth, May 10, 1780]

"The town [Dartmouth] took in consideration the form of Government, &c.

"The Committee recommend that in the 4th article, 25th page, the words 'sui juris and that pays a poll tax, except such who, from their respective offices and age, are exempted by law,' be added after the words, 'every male person'; and to expunge the following clause in said article, namely,

— 'having a freehold estate within the same town of the annual income of three pounds, or any estate of the value of sixty pounds,' — for the following reason: such qualification appears to your Committee to be inconsistent with the liberty we are contending for, so long, especially, as any subject, who is not a qualified voter, is obliged to pay a poll tax.

"(Signed,) EDWARD POPE, Chairman.

"The report was accepted by an unanimous vote of one hundred and fifty persons present."

Extract from the Town Warrant of Dartmouth, dated February 20, 1781:

"To choose an agent or agents to defend an action against John and Paul Cuff, at the next Court to be holden at Taunton."

At the meeting, March 8, 1781, — "The Honorable Walter Spooner, Esquire, chosen agent, in behalf of the town, to make answer to John and Paul Cuff at the next Inferior Court to be held at Taunton."

"A REQUEST.

"To the Selectmen of the Town of Dartmouth, Greeting:

"We the subscribers, your humble petitioners, desire that you would, in your capacity, put a stroke in your next warrant for calling a town meeting, so that it may legally be laid before said town, by way of vote, to know the mind of said town, whether all free negroes and mulattoes shall have the same privileges in this said Town of Dartmouth as the white people have, respecting places of profit, choosing of officers, and the like, together with all other privileges in all cases that shall or may happen or be brought in this our said Town of Dartmouth. We, your petitioners, as in duty bound, shall ever pray.

(Signed,) JOHN CUFFE, PAUL CUFFE.

"Dated at Dartmouth, the 22d of the 4th mo., 1781."

This "Request" bears the following endorsement: —

"A true copy of the request which John Cuffe and Paul Cuffe delivered unto the Selectmen of the Town of Dartmouth, for to have all free negroes and mulattoes to be entered equally with the white people, or to have relief granted us jointly from taxation, &c.

"Given under my hand,
JOHN CUFFE."

"DARTMOUTH, June 11, 1781.

"Then received of John Cuffe, eight pounds twelve shillings silver money, in full for all John Cuffe's and Paul Cuffe's Rates, until this date; also, for all my Court charges. Received by me,

"RICHARD COLLENS, Constable."

"John and Paul Cuff, of Dartmouth, Dr., to Elijah Dean, of Taunton, —
To summoning the assessors of Dartmouth to Taunton Court, 21. £140
[On the back.]
"Rec'd of John Cuff twenty-four shillings, being the contents of the within acc't, in behalf of Elijah Dean.

"(Signed) EDWARD POPE."

It was ascertained by these proceedings, that taxes must be paid, the receipts being forwarded; and this case, although no action followed in Court, settled the right of the colored man to the elective franchise in the State of Massachusetts.

RICHARD JOHNSON, who married a daughter of Paul Cuffe, resided at New Bedford nearly fifty years. In early life, he was engaged as a mariner, and filled every capacity, from a cabin boy to a captain.

During the war of 1812, he was taken prisoner, but was released, after having been confined six months.

He was distinguished for prudence and sagacity in his business operations, and, despite the obstacles that prejudice against color so constantly strewed in his path, he succeeded in his mercantile affairs, accumulated a competency, and retired from business several years since.

Mr. Johnson was always ready to extend the hand of relief to his enslaved countrymen, and no one was more ready to assist, according to his ability, in the elevation of his people.

He was one of the earliest friends of Mr. Garrison; a subscriber to his paper, from the time the first number was issued in Baltimore, and for several years an efficient agent for the Liberator; and very active in circulating Mr. Garrison's "Thoughts on Colonization," in 1832. In all the vicissitudes through which the anti-slavery cause has been called to pass, Mr. J. always maintained a straight-forward, consistent course, firmly adhering to the pioneer who first sounded the alarm.

He died in peace, February 15, 1853, aged seventy-seven; and the funeral service of himself and wife (whose death preceded his one day) was numerously attended by New Bedford citizens.

RICHARD POTTER.

On the Northern New Hampshire Railroad, some thirty miles from Concord, in the town of Andover, is a station called Potter's Place. This little village derives its name from RICHARD POTTER, the celebrated Ventriloquist and Professor of Legerdemain. Within twenty rods of the track stands a neat white, one-story building, with two projecting wings, all of Grecian architecture. From this extends, south-westerly, a fine expanse of level meadow. This house, and the adjacent two hundred acres, were owned by RICHARD POTTER. There once stood, on pillars before the house, two graven images, taken from Lord Timothy Dexter's place, in Newburyport. Potter built the house and cultivated the farm, which were estimated in the days of Potter, and long before the railroad was built, to be worth $5000. This Potter owned in fee simple, unincumbered, the fruits of his successful illusions, optical and auricular.

Potter was a colored man, half-way between fair and black. He for a long time monopolized the market for such wares as sleight of hand, and "laborious speaking from the stomach." Says one writer in the Boston Traveller, of November 6, 1851: —

"We well remember how our astonished eyes first beheld his debut upon the stage, — a portentous-looking magician from India. And then to see him perform; eat tow, spit fire, and draw form his mouth yards and yards of ribbon, all made out of tow; far down in his crop to hear him command an egg to all over him, from head to foot, from foot to head, etc., etc. And then his comic songs! Donning another attire, he would hobble around the stage, an old woman; and the old woman would tell over her various troubles, in successive stanzas, always concluding with the cheerful refrain — 'Howsever, I keep up a pretty good heart.'"

Richard was born in the town of Hopkinton, Mass., and, when quite a boy, was prevailed upon to engage himself in the service of Samuel Dillaway, Esq., of Boston, — a relative of the family being on a wedding tour to that pleasant town. After being 'brought up' by Mr. Dillaway, he became a valued and esteemed servant in the family of Rev. Daniel Oliver, of Boston; and in his kitchen, he studied out the theory and began the practice of legerdemain. Mr. Oliver's son, late Adjutant General of Massachusetts, often alludes to the winter evening amusements afforded to the children at home by the tricks and pranks of Potter.

He, who was so successful in these, his first efforts, and so able to set up business on his own account, could not long be retained as a servant. He followed his vocation, ever after, till death arrested him in his course. Columbian Hall, and Concert Hall, in the olden time, were the prominent places, in Boston, for Potter's levees.

Potter was temperate, steady, attentive to his business, and his business was his delight. He took as much pleasure in pleasing others, as others did in being pleased. I have never heard a lisp against his character for honesty and fair dealing. He was once the victim of persecution from a Mr. Fitch, who had him arrested as a juggler. Potter plead his own case, and secured an equittal.

Close by Potter's house, in a small enclosure, stands two monumental slabs, of white marble; one, for his wife, Sally H., — the other,

In Memory of
RICHARD POTTER,
THE CELEBRATED VENTRILOQUIST,
Who died
Sept. 20, 1835,
Aged 52 years.

THE MARSHPEE INDIANS.

The Marshpee Indians also did noble service in our revolutionary struggle. During the discussion of the subject of the militia laws before the Massachusetts Constitutional Convention of 1853, it was stated that the practice of excluding colored men from the militia did not exist previous to the United States Militia Law of 1792, which first introduced the word "white"; and in confirmation of this statement, the following interesting fact in our own State history was mentioned. During the War of the Revolution, when the county of Barnstable was required to raise a regiment of four hundred men in the Continental army, the Indian district of Marshpee, in that county, furnished twenty-seven colored soldiers, who fought in the battles, and all but one of them perished, and he died a pensioner a few years ago. At that time, (1776,) Marshpee had a population of three hundred and twenty-seven colored persons, of whom fourteen were negroes married to Indian women. There were sixty-four married couples and thirty-three widows on the plantation; so that, in proportion to adult male population, Marshpee furnished a larger quota for that regiment than any white town in the county. A census taken after the Revolutionary

War, showed that there were seventy-three colored widows in Marshpee, whose husbands had been slain or died in the service of their country during that war.

And yet, the Legislature of Massachusetts, in 1788-89, treated these Indians with extreme rigor, by abolishing their charter — under which, in 1763, they had been incorporated into a district, with right to choose their selectmen — and putting them under guardians, who had power to take all their lands and income, and treat the proprietors as paupers. Under these laws, the Indians could make no contract and hold no property, and the overseers could take all their earnings, bind out their children without their parents' consent; and, still further, by a subsequent act, these overseers, from whose decision there was no appeal, could sell the proprietors, male or female adults, to service, for three years at a term, and renew it at pleasure.

These laws, and worse, against these poor Indians, who all the time were sole owners of ten thousand acres of land, were continued in force until 1834, when, principally by the efforts of Benj. F. Hallett, Esq., as their counsel, in exposing their injustice, the system was broken up, and the district of Marshpee was incorporated under free laws, and the property divided among the proprietors in fee. They are now a very prosperous and thriving community, deserving the interest and encouragement of every wise statesman or true philanthropist.

Among the Marshpee volunteers in the War of the Revolution were the following: — Francis Websquish, Samuel Moses, Demps Squibs, Mark Negro Tom Cæsar, Joseph Ashur, James Keeter, Joseph Keeter, Daniel Pocknit, Job Rimmon, George Shaun, Castel Barnet, Joshua Pognit, James Rimmon, David Hatch, James No Cake, Abel Hoswitt, Elisha Keeter, John Pearce, John Mapix, Amos Babcock, Hosea Pognit, Church Ashur, Gideon Turnpum.

In 1783, Parson Holly presented a memorial to the Legislature, in behalf of the seventy-three widows whose husbands had died in their country's service.

PATRIOTS OF THE OLDEN TIME.

The wife of Samuel Adams, of revolutionary celebrity, one day informed her husband that a friend had made her a present of a female slave. Mr. Adams replied, in a very decided manner, "She may come, but not as a slave; for a slave cannot breathe in my house. If she comes, she, must come free." The woman took up her abode with the family of this champion of liberty; and there she lived free and died free.

LOYALTY OF AN AFRICAN BENEVOLENT SOCIETY.

Some of the colored citizens, in 1796, instituted at Boston the African Society. Its objects were benevolent ones, as set forth in the preamble, which also expressed its loyalty as follows: — "Behaving ourselves, at the same time, as true and faithful citizens of the commonwealth in which we live, and that we take no one into the Society who shall commit any injustice or outrage against the laws of their country."

I subjoin the names of the members of the "African Society."

PLATO ALDERSON,
HANNIBAL ALLEN,
THOMAS BURDINE,
PETER BAILEY,
JOSEPH BALL,
PETER BRANCH,
PRINCE BROWN,
BOSTON BALLARD,
ANTHONY BATTIS,
SERICO COLLENS,
RUFUS CALLEHORN,
JOHN CLARK,
SCIPIO DALTON,
ARTHUR DAVIS,
JOHN DECRUSE,
HAMLET EARL,
CÆSAR FAYERWEATHER,
MINGO FREEMAN,
CATO GARDNER,
JEREMIAH GREEN,
JAMES HAWKINS,
JOHN HARRISON,
GLOSASTER HASKINS,
PRINCE M. HARRIS,
JUBER HOLLAND,
RICHARD HOLSTED,
THOMAS JACKSON,

GEORGE JACKSON,
LEWIS JONES,
ISAAC JOHNSON,
JOHN JOHNSON,
SEAR KIMBALL,
THOMAS LEWIS,
JOSEPH LOW,
GEORGE MIDDLETON,
DERBY MILLER,
CATO MOREY,
RICHARD MARSHALL,
JOSEPH OCRUMAN,
JOHN PHILLIPS,
CATO RAWSON,
RICHARD STANDLEY,
CYRUS VASSALL,
DERBY VASSALL.

ISAAC WOODLAND.

The following obituary of one who will be long remembered in Boston is inserted here as connected with the associations of by-gone days.

ISAAC WOODLAND was a native of Maryland, but many years since, he adopted for his home the State of Massachusetts. His life here was marked with an active zeal for the fugitive from Southern bondage. His money was always generously appropriated for their aid and comfort. At one of the meetings in Belknap Street Church, when the question whether Boston jail should longer confine George Latimer as a slave was the theme of discussion in every gathering, I well remember Isaac Woodland walking up the aisle, and placing upon the table a handful of silver, with the remark that he had more shot in the locker, if by that means the man could be kept from slavery. In the olden time, when the abolitionists of Boston celebrated the 14th of July, commemorative of the abolition of slavery in the State, (the day was not historical, for no special act of emancipation had taken place, but the grateful heart of the colored man thus wished to signalize the fact that slavery had departed from the old Bay State,) in their processions, his towering and manly form was always the observed of all observers. And when that was superseded by the glorious First of August, the Jubilee of British West India Emancipation, no one name was more sure of appointment as Marshal than his; and, surely, but few, if any, could better adorn the office.

His occupation was that of grain inspector, and by his application and integrity in business, he won the respect and patronage of a large circle of Boston merchants.

He was genial and mirthful, fond of children and friends, but yet had that in him which, when roused in defence of his race, was not easily subdued. This last trait was fully illustrated in an encounter on one of the wharves, several years since, between a party of white and colored laborers, when, but for his prowess and Herculean strength, the fate of his companions would have been much worse than the event proved. He was "in war a tiger chafed by the hunter's spear; but in peace, more gentle than the unweaned lamb." His death took place in Boston, May 24, 1853, aged 68.

EPITAPHS ON SLAVES.

The following celebrated epitaph from the old burial ground of Concord, Mass., although it has been often published, will bear to be reprinted here. It is understood to have been written by Daniel Bliss, Esq., a lawyer at Concord, before the Revolutionary War. He was the son of a minister of that place, whose name and history occupy a large space in the ecclesiastical annals of the town. This single production will secure to its author for ever the credit of taste, ingenuity, and an enlightened moral sense; and proves that sound abolition sentiments were cherished then as strongly as at the present day.

GOD
Wills us free.
MAN
Wills us slaves
I will as God wills.
God's will be done.
Here lies the body of John Jack, a native of Africa,
who died March, 1773, aged about 60 years.
Though born in a land of slaves,
He was born free.
Though he lived in a land of liberty,
He lived a slave;
Till, by his honest, though stolen labors,
He acquired the source of Slavery,

Which gave him his freedom.
Though not long before
Death, the grand tyrant,
Gave him his final emancipation,
And set him upon a footing with kings.
Tho' a slave to vice,
He practiced those virtues
Without which, kings are but slaves.

The following inscription is taken from a gravestone in a burying-ground in the town of North Attleboro', Mass., near what was formerly called "Hatch's Tavern." It is an interesting memento of what the state of things was in this commonwealth seventy years ago. The testimony thus borne to the goodness of "Cæsar's" heart certainly reflects but little credit on the person who could make him or keep him a slave.

"Here lies the best of slaves,
Now turning into dust;
Cæsar, the Ethiopian, craves,
A place among the just.
His faithful soul is fled,
To realms of heavenly light,
And, by the blood that Jesus shed,
Is changed from black to white.
Jan. 15th he quitted the stage,
In the 77th year of his age,
1780."

THE EQUAL RIGHTS MOVEMENT.

A number of the chivalric portion of the colored Bostonians, having taken the initiatory steps for a military company, petitioned the Legislature, in the year 1852, for a charter, the claims of which were advocated by Charles Lenox Remond and Robert Morris, Esqs.; but, like the Attucks petitioners, they, too, "had leave to withdraw." In February, 1853, the subject was again presented to the Constitutional Convention, and Robert Morris, Esq., before a committee of that body, alluded to an old law of the Massachusetts colony, which called upon all negroes, inhabitants of the colony, of the age of sixteen and upwards, to make their appearance in case of alarm, armed and equipped, in connection with the regularly enrolled militia company, under a penalty of twenty shillings. And they always did appear, and performed efficient service. He further remarked, that a charter had been lately granted to an Irish company, and said that the colored citizens, who are native born, desired the same rights which were given to our adopted brethren. "We do not want," said he, "a step-mother in the case, who will butter the bread for one, and sand it for another. We hunger and thirst for prosperity and advancement, and, so far as in your power lies, we wish you to do all you can to aid us in our endeavors. We wish you to make us feel that we are of some use and advantage, in this our day and generation."

William J. Watkins, Esq., concluded an able argument as follows: —

"We love Massachusetts; if she reciprocates that love, let her show forth her love by her works. Let her throw around us the mantle of her protection, and then, O Massachusetts, if we forget thee, "may our right hand forget its cunning, and our tongue cleave to the roof of our mouth."

Yes! let the old Bay State treat us as men, and she shall elicit our undying, indissoluble attachment; and neither height, nor depth, nor principalities, nor powers, nor things present, nor things to come, shall ever be able to alienate our affection from her. We will be with her in the sixth trouble, and in the seventh; we will neither leave nor forsake her. Amid the angry howling of the tempest, as well as in the cheering sunshine, we shall be ever found, a faithful few, indomitable, unterrified, who know their friends to love them with that affection which nought but the destroying angel can annihilate.

"Again, grant us this petition, and it will induce in us a determination to surmount every obstacle calculated to impede our progress; to rise higher, and higher, and HIGHER, until we scale the Mount of Heaven, and look down, from our lofty and commanding position, upon our revilers and persecutors. Yes, sir; it will incite us to renewed diligence, and cause our arid desert to rejoice and blossom as the rose. It will inspire us with confidence, and encourage us to hope, amid the almost tangible darkness that envelopes us. We care not for the hoarse, rough thunder's voice, nor the lightning's lurid gleamings, if we are yet to be a people; if we are yet to behold the superstructure of our liberties consummated amid paeans of thanksgiving, and shouts from millions, redeemed, regenerated, and disenthralled."

Sixty-five colored citizens of Boston petitioned the Massachusetts Constitutional Convention, in June, 1853, — "That the Constitution be so amended as to remove the disabilities of colored citizens from holding military commissions and serving in the militia."

An amendment was offered, "That it is inexpedient to act thereon;" when Henry Wilson, Charles Sumner, E. L. Keyes, D. S. Whitney, and others, advocated the colored man's equality. The following are extract is from the speech of Hon. Henry Wilson, in support of his amendment, viz.:

"Resolved, That no distinction shall ever hereafter be made, in organizing the volunteer militia of the Commonwealth, by reason of color or race."

"If it be true," said Mr. Wilson, that our 'volunteer system' is 'not contemplated by the laws of the United States,' — that it is the creature of Massachusetts law — that 'no reference in the law is made to color' — that the 'officers' authorized 'to grant petitions for raising companies' have 'control and authority' over the 'whole subject' — and that they may grant petitions for companies without distinction of color, — then it is in accordance with the ideas, and sentiments of the people, to declare in the fundamental law of the Commonwealth, that in the organization of these volunteer companies, no distinction on account of color or race shall ever be made by those 'officers' having 'control and authority over the whole subject.' This is my proposition — nothing more, nothing less. If our voluntary militia system is the creature of local law, purely a Massachusetts system, 'not contemplated by the laws of the United States,' no distinction on account of race or color should be allowed. The Constitution of this Commonwealth knows no distinction of color or race. A colored man may fill any office in the gift of the people. A colored man may be the 'Supreme Executive Magistrate' of Massachusetts, and 'Commander-in-chief of the army and navy, and of the military forces of the State by sea and land,' and he 'shall have full power from time to time to train, instruct, exercise, and govern the militia,' and 'to lead and conduct them, and with them to encounter, repel, resist, expel and pursue,' 'and also to kill, slay and destroy' the invading enemies of the Commonwealth. If a colored man may be by the Constitution 'Captain General and Commander-in-chief and Admiral' of the Commonwealth, should he be denied admission into the ranks of her volunteer militia? The colored men of Massachusetts have been denied admission into the volunteer militia, although the Committee tell us that 'no reference is made by law to color or race.' If 'officers,' who are authorized by law 'to grant petitions for companies,' and who have 'control and authority over the whole subject,' have made distinctions on account of color or race, when 'no reference is made to color' in the laws, then they should be compelled by constitutional authority to abandon the position they have without law assumed, and to carry out the idea which pervades our Constitution, that all men, of every race, are equal before the laws of this Commonwealth. The democratic idea of the equality before the law of all men, no matter where they were born or from what race they sprung, is the sentiment of the people.

"This right, claimed by the colored men of Massachusetts, to become members of the volunteer militia, is of little practical importance to them or to the public. They feel the exclusion as an indignity to their race. If we have the power to remove that unjust exclusion, we are false to the principles and ideas upon which our Constitution is founded, if we do not do so. If we have not the power, or if its exercise would bring us in conflict with the laws of the United States, which we acknowledge to be the supreme laws of the land, we must submit to the necessity imposed upon us, and bow to what we cannot control. I have said, Sir, that the question was of little practical importance, whether the right of the colored men of Massachusetts to become members of the volunteer militia was admitted or not. To them, it can be of little practical value, although they have wives, children and homes, and a country, to defend. To the country, it is of little practical importance. We are strong and powerful now, able to drive into the ocean any power on earth that should step with hostile foot upon the soil of the Republic. But it was not always so. In our days of weakness, the men of this wronged race gave their blood freely for the defence and liberties of the country.

"The first victim of the Boston massacre, on the 5th of March, 1770, which made the fires of resistance burn more intensely, was a colored man. Hundreds of colored men entered the ranks and fought bravely on all the fields of the Revolution. Graydon, of Pennsylvania, in his Memoirs, informs us that many of the Southern officers disliked the New England regiments, because so many colored men were in their ranks. When the country has required their blood in days of trial and conflict, they have given it freely, and we have accepted it; but in times of peace, when their blood is not needed, we spurn and trample them under foot. I have no part in this great wrong to a race. Wherever and whenever we have the power to do it, I would give to all men, of every clime and race, of every faith and creed, freedom and equality before the law. My voice and my vote shall ever be given for the equality of all the children of men before the laws of the Commonwealth of Massachusetts and the United States."

The petition was received, referred, and finally rejected, on the ground that it could not be granted without bringing Massachusetts into conflict with the United States Constitution and the laws of the land.

On the last day of the Convention, the following petition was presented by the Hon. E. L. Keyes, of Dedham: —

To the Convention for revising and amending the Constitution of Massachusetts:

The undersigned, acknowledged citizens of this Commonwealth, (notwithstanding their complexional differences,) and therefore citizens of the United States, with the feeling and spirit becoming freemen, and with the deepest solicitude, respectfully submit —

That having petitioned your honorable body for such a modification of the laws as that no able-bodied male citizen shall be forbidden or prevented from serving, or holding office or commission, in the militia, on account of his color, their petition was duly referred and considered, but not granted, and therefore they are still a proscribed and injured class. The reason assigned for the rejection of their request, in the report submitted by the Committee to whom the subject was referred, was, "that this Convention cannot incorporate into the Constitution of Massachusetts any provision which shall conflict with THE LAWS of the United States." In the course of the debate that ensued upon this report, the Attorney General of Massachusetts [Hon. Rufus Choate] said, — "You caw raise no colored regiment, or part of a regiment, that shall be of the militia of the United States — none whatever. . . . It is certain that, if they were to go upon parade, and to win Bunker Hills, yet they never can be part of the militia of the United States. . . . Nay, more; he did not see how he could do any thing for this colored race, by putting them in one of the high places of the Commonwealth, with weapons in their hands, and allow our glorious banner to throw around them all the pomp and parade and condition of war; the color cleaves to them there, and on parade is only the more conspicuous."

Another distinguished member of the Convention [Hon. Benj. F. Hallett] said, — "If Massachusetts should send a colored commander-in-chief at the head of her militia, the United States would not recognise his authority, and would at once supersede him."

Your petitioners feel bound to protest, (in behalf of the colored citizens of Massachusetts,) that all such opinions and declarations constitute —

(1) A denial of their equality as citizens of this Commonwealth, and are clearly at variance with the Constitution of this State, which knows nothing of the complexion of the people, and which asserts [Art. I.] that "all men are born free and EQUAL, and have certain natural, essential and inalienable rights; among which may be reckoned the right of enjoying and DEFENDING their lives and liberties; that of acquiring, possessing and protecting property; in fine, that of seeking and obtaining their safety and happiness." It would be absurd to say that the General Government, or that Congress, has the constitutional right to declare, if it think proper, that the white citizen of Massachusetts shall not be enrolled in the militia of the country; and it is not to be supposed, for a moment, that, if such a proscriptive edict were to be issued, it would be tamely submitted to. It is, surely, just as great an absurdity, just as glaring an insult, to assume that colored citizens may be legally excluded from the national militia.

(2) In the Constitution of the United States, not a sentence or a syllable can be found, recognising any distinctions among the citizens of the States, collectively or individually, but they are all placed on the same equality. Article IV., Section 2d, declares — "The citizens of each State shall be entitled to all the privileges and immunities of citizens in the several States." It is not possible to make a more unequivocal recognition of the equality of all citizens; and, therefore, whatever contravenes or denies it, in the shape of legislation, is manifestly unconstitutional. Whatever may have been the compromises of the Constitution, in regard to those held in bondage as chattel slaves, none were ever made, or proposed, respecting the rights and liberties of citizens.

(3) It is true that, by the United States Constitution, Congress is empowered "to provide for organizing, arming and disciplining the militia"; it is also true, that Congress, in "organizing" the militia, has authorised none but "white" citizens to be enrolled therein; nevertheless, it is not less true, that the law of Congress, making this unnatural distinction, is, in this particular, unconstitutional, and therefore ought to exert no controlling force over the legislation of any of the States. To organize the militia of the country is one thing; to dishonor and outrage a portion of the citizens, on any ground, is a very different thing. To do the former, Congress is clothed with ample constitutional authority; to accomplish the

latter, it has no power to legislate, and resort must be had, and has been had, to usurpation and tyranny.

Your petitioners, therefore, earnestly entreat the Convention, by every consideration of justice and righteousness, not to adjourn without asserting and vindicating the entire fitness and equal right of the colored citizens of Massachusetts to be enrolled in the national militia; or, if this be not granted, then they respectfully ask that this protest may be placed on the records of the Convention, and published with the official proceedings, that the stigma may not rest upon their memories of having tamely acquiesced in a proscription, equally at war with the American Constitution, the Massachusetts Bill of Rights, and the claims of human nature.

WILLIAM C. NELL,
JONAS W. CLARK,
EDWARD GRAY,
JOHN THOMPSON,
ENOCH L. STALLAD
JOHN WRIGHT,
JOHN P. COBURN,
THOMAS BROWN,
JOHN LOCKLEY,
IRA S. GRAY
BENJAMIN P. BASSETT
BENJAMIN WEEDEN,
WILLIAM J. WATKINS,
ISAAC H. SNOWDEN,
SIMPSON H. LEWIS,
JOHN J. FATAL,
LEMUEL BURR,
THOMAS CUMMINGS,
N. L. PERKINS,
JOHN OLIVER,
H. L. W. THACKER,
GEORGE WASHINGTON,
JAMES SCOTT.

This petition having been read, it was ordered to be entered upon the records, by a vote of 97 to 66; but subsequently, on motion of Mr. Stetson, of Braintree, the vote was reconsidered.

Hon. B. F. Hallett, for Wilbraham, upon a question of privilege, spoke at some length in defence of his action in the matter, and in favor of reconsideration, which, under the previous question, was carried — 97 to 57; and, on motion of Mr. Bird, of Walpole, the whole question was laid on the table without dissent. This final action was highly discreditable to the Convention; for the petitioners, having been virtually excluded from the pale of American citizenship by that body, had a right at least to have their protest against such an exclusion placed on the records of the Convention; nor was there a sentence or word in their petition uncalled for or offensively used.

The limits of this work will not allow of an elaborate or statistical report of the present condition of the colored Americans, though very much that is encouraging is at the compiler's disposal. It will be found that, throughout the book, references are made to representative cases of individual enterprise and genius, sufficient, it is presumed, to convey a general idea of the improvements daily developed by that class, which has commonly been stigmatized as incapable of mental and social elevation.

So far as Massachusetts is concerned, it is safe to say that, in many respects, her record is one to be proud of. Her colored citizens (in all but the militia clause in the Constitution) stand, before the law, on an equality with the whites. Her public schools are accessible to all, irrespective of complexion, — prophetic of the day, soon, I hope, to be ushered in, when the mechanic's shop and the merchant's counting-room will be alike ready to extend to them equal facilities with those of another and more favored race.

New Bedford occupies a very prominent position in all that contributes to the prosperity of the colored American, in general intelligence, business, enterprise, and public spirit; much of which is justly attributable to the impetus given by Paul Cuffe's efforts for the. franchise. Some of his descendants yet live in New Bedford. The colored voters there hold the balance of power, and hence exert a potent on election day. The faithful Friends, or Quakers, have always borne such a testimony at New Bedford, as materially to have aided the progress of the colored citizens.

Worcester can boast, among her colored mechanics, Wm. H. Brown, whose well-established reputation as an upholsterer reflects great credit upon the large firm in Boston with whom he served a faithful apprenticeship.

Salem, Springfield, and Lowell, together with many smaller localities, have good and true colored men among their inhabitants, sustaining creditable business relations, and the owners of real estate in a fair proportion with their white fellow-citizens.

Boston compares favorably, in this respect, with larger cities in the United States. Several causes have combined to retard the progress of colored mechanics; but these are being removed, and, in a few years, the results will be manifest. Business and professional men are continually increasing. In addition to the mechanical, artistical, and professional colored men in Boston, elsewhere mentioned, it may be noted, that the two most popular gymnasium galleries are in the proprietorship of J. B. Bailey and Peyton Stewart; the prince of caterers is J. B. Smith; a dentist highly recommended is J. S. Rock; a young artist in crayon portraits is winning his way to excellence and reputation; and other equally meritorious aspirants, — women included, — are soaring to those heights that challenge the ambition of earth's gifted children. Real estate to the value of, at least, $200,000, is in the. hands of our colored citizens. During the struggle for equal school rights, many of the largest tax payers removed into the neighboring towns, and withdrew their investments from Boston real estate.

American colorphobia is never more rampant towards its victims, than when one would avail himself of the facilities for mental improvement, in common with the more favored dominant party, — as if his complexion was, indeed, prima facie evidence that he was an intruder within the sacred portals of knowledge. In Boston, the so-called "Athens of America," large audiences have been thrown almost into spasms by the presence of one colored man in their midst; and, on one occasion, (in the writer's experience,) a mob grossly insulted a gentleman and two ladies, who did not happen to exhibit the Anglo-Saxon (constitutional) complexion.

But, within a few years past, this spirit of caste has lost much of its virulence, owing somewhat to the efforts put forth by the colored people themselves. For ten years, they sustained the Adelphic Union Library Association, and were generally fortunate in securing the most talented and distinguished gentlemen as lecturers. Though proscribed themselves, they removed from the colored locality, opened a hall in the central part of the city, and magnanimously invited all to avail themselves of its benefits. A number of white young men associated themselves with this Society, and participated in several public elocutionary exhibitions; and their lecture-room was usually visited by representatives from all classes of the community, which has had a tendency to excite something of a reciprocal feeling on the part of other association's, — now extending itself through all the ramifications of society; so that the presence of colored persons at popular lectures is now a matter of common occurrence, and excites scarcely any notice or remark. This agreeable state of things superseded the necessity of an exclusive organization, though social literary clubs, mostly composed of colored members, have continued to exist.

In New Bedford, a deserved rebuke was administered to colorphobia, which grew out of an attempt to prescribe colored patrons of the Lyceum from the privileges heretofore shared by them in common with others. This persecution aroused the indignation of those ever-to-be-honored friends of equal rights, CHARLES SUMNER and RALPH WALDO EMERSON. They were both announced to lecture, but, on learning the proceedings, they immediately recalled their engagements, rather than sanction, by their presence on the rostrum, such an outrage on the rights of man. This noble deed was not without its effect, and, as a legitimate consequence, prompted the freemen of New Bedford to establish an independent Lyceum, where men, irrespective of accidental differences, could freely assemble, and have dispensed to them the precious stores of knowledge. Various circumstances combined to create an impetus in favor of the free Lyceum, which completely superseded the other, and thus a victory was achieved in humanity's behalf. A similar triumph, in many respects, was also won in Lynn, where opposition was manifested to a Lyceum lecture by Charles Lenox Remond. A majority united in the formation of another institution, thus proving that, where there is a will, a way can always be found for united hearts to bear a faithful and effective testimony against proscription and tyranny.

Since then, Samuel R. Ward, Frederick Douglass, and other distinguished colored lecturers, have been welcomed to Lyceum platforms in different parts of the country.

To Raynal, who expressed surprise that America had not produced any celebrated man, Jefferson replied, — "When we shall have existed as a nation as long as the Greeks before they had a Homer, the Romans a Virgil, or the French a Racine, there will be room for inquiry;" and I would say, Let the evil spirit of American pro-slavery and prejudice only remove its feet from the neck of its outraged victims, and if improvement be not made commensurate with the means afforded, then, — but not till then, —

will we admit the truth of the gratuitous assertion, that the Author of the universe has stamped upon the brow of the colored American a mark of inferiority.

This feeling must have moved C. V. Caples, a colored teacher, when he uttered the following eloquent words at an early Anti-Slavery Convention in Boston: — "I am pained," said he, "when I think of the condition of colored men in the United States. My blood is as warm as yours, Mr. President, or that of any patriot; and when I behold the finger of scorn pointed at my brethren, and the curled lip, my soul weeps. I think, there may be thus insulted one possessing the highest attributes of man; a mind, perhaps, that, if trained like other minds, might lead to great deeds, — some Cincinnatus, capable of influencing the destinies of a nation, a Hampden, to inspire patriotism, or a Milton, 'pregnant with celestial fire.'"

The colored man's friends are constantly claiming for him an equality of privileges, based on his nativity, loyalty, and the immutable law of God. There have been those, however, sometimes found deficient in a trying hour. Such "fallings from grace" doubtless occur in the ranks of every reform; for all who profess are not always fully imbued with the principle, thereby losing opportunities of squaring their practice with their preaching. To those colored friends, however, who constantly harp upon real or supposed derelictions of white Abolitionists, it is but seasonable to hint, that some of their own number are very indifferent to practical Anti-Slavery, and that, at the South, there are black, as well as white, slaveholders, — a fact teaching humility to both classes, while, at the same time, it proves the identity of both with the human family. These Anti-Slavery tests are presented in the every-day routine of business and social life, and ofttimes prove severe trials, except to those of the genuine radical stamp. All reformers owe it to their high calling to be consistent; not to place their light under a bushel but to let its rays be conspicuous, as a direct means of influencing public sentiment.

A few years since, when the State of Massachusetts was agitated, from Cape Cod to Berkshire, with the exclusion of colored passengers from equal railroad privileges, many an instance occurred where Abolitionists wholly identified themselves with the proscribed, — "remembering those in bonds as bound with them;" and, on some occasions, encountering peril of life and limb, and sharing indignities equally with those whose sin was the "texture of hair and hue of the skin."

It is with the most grateful emotions that I would here record the names of WILLIAM LLOYD GARRISON and WENDELL PHILLIPS, both of whom, on separate occasions, remonstrated against the colonization of colored friends from the cars, and, in the crisis, exiled themselves to the "Jim-Crow car," rather than remain in comfort with the oppressor. Such exhibitions of fidelity to principle were not lost upon their fellow-passengers.

There is abundant reason to believe that these and-similar incidents, in connection with the eloquent appeals of CHARLES LENOX REMOND and other Anti-Slavery lecturers, were instrumental in removing all odious restrictions from the Eastern Railroad; and, at this day, who ventures to exclude a colored passenger, in this section of country? The idea has been consigned to the tomb of the capulets, from whence we do not anticipate a resurrection. Until within a few years, the Boston Directory had a Liberia department for persons of color; but it luckily fell into the hands of an Anti-Slavery man, GEORGE ADAMS, Esq., who, to his honor be it remembered, abolished this inglorious distinction, inserted the names of colored citizens among "the rest of mankind," and, to this day, no orb has been so eccentric as to wander from its sphere in consequence thereof. "So shines a good deed in a naughty world." Live the true life, speak the true word, and God will bless the effort.

There is a sun-dial in Italy, with the inscription, "I mark only the hours that shine," — inculcating the lesson, that though this life is not all happy and beautiful, yet we should not dwell always upon the darker portion of the picture, but remember to look also upon the bright side. What a satisfaction to the proscribed colored American is the fact, that, in this slavery-cursed land, there are those true hearts ready to accord the rights and privileges to others so prized by themselves; that, in the highways and byways of life, on the railroad car and in the steamboat, in the lyceum and college, in the street, the store, and the parlor, a noble band is found, united in purpose, uncompromising in principle, fearless in action, whose examples are like specks of verdure amidst universal barrenness, — as scattered lights amidst thick and prevailing darkness.

CHAPTER II: NEW HAMPSHIRE.

JUDE HALL was born at Exeter, N. H., and was a soldier in the Revolutionary War, under General Poor. He served faithfully eight years, and fought in most all the battles, beginning at Bunker Hill. He was called a great soldier, and was known in New Hampshire to the day of his death by the name of "Old Rock."

Singular to relate, three of his sons have been kidnapped at different times, and reduced to slavery. James was put on board a New Orleans vessel; Aaron was stolen from Providence, in 1807; William went to sea in the bark Hannibal, from Newburyport, and was sold in the West Indies, from whence he escaped after ten years of slavery, and sailed as captain of a collier from Newcastle to London.

The anecdote of the slave of Gen. Sullivan, of New Hampshire, is well known. When his master told him that they were on the point of starting for the army, to fight for liberty, he shrewdly suggested, that it would be a great satisfaction to know that he was indeed going to fight for his liberty. Struck with the reasonableness and justice of this suggestion, Gen. S. at once gave him his freedom.

It is not very surprising, that in the time of the Revolutionary War, when so much was said of freedom, equality, and the rights of man, the poor African should think that he had some rights, and should seek that freedom which others valued so highly. There were slaves then, even in New Hampshire, and their owners, like the Egyptians of old, and the Carolinians now, were unwilling to "let them go." Here is an extract from the Journal of New Hampshire, touching this matter, showing how justice and humanity were postponed, as repentance often is, to a more convenient opportunity: —

"JUNE 9, 1780. Agreeable to order of the day, the petition of Negro Brewster and others, negro slaves, praying to be set free from slavery, being read, considered, and argued by counsel for petitioners before this House, it appears that at this time this House is not ripe for a determination in this matter. Therefore, ordered, That the further consideration of the matter be postponed till a more convenient opportunity."

Senator Morrill, of New Hampshire, in his speech at Washington, in 1820, on the Missouri question, alluded to a colored man in his own State, by the name of CHESWELL, who, with his family, were respectable in point of property, ability, and character. He held some of the first offices of the town in which he resided, was appointed Justice of the Peace for the county, and was perfectly competent to perform all the duties of his various offices in the most prompt, accurate, and acceptable manner.

"In New Hampshire," says Dr. Belknap, in 1795, "those blacks who enlisted into the army for three years, were entitled to the same bounty as the whites. This bounty their masters received as the price of their liberty, and then delivered up their bills of sale, and gave them a certificate of manumission. Several of these bills and certificates were deposited in my hands; and those who survived the three years' service were free."

New Hampshire papers of a quite recent date record the death, at Hanover, of Mrs. JANE E. WENTWORTH, a colored woman, at the age of three score and ten. Graduates at Dartmouth will recollect her as Aunt Jenny, the wash-woman, and nurse in sickness. Her parents were slaves, kidnapped when very young, and came by inheritance in possession of the family of Mrs. House, of Hanover. They were subsequently sold to a gentleman in Salem, N. H., where they remained until they were emancipated by the laws of the State. Jenny was born in Hanover, in 1777, was sold with her parents, and upon becoming free, she married Charles Wentworth, a slave of Gov. Wentworth. They then removed to Hanover, where they remained till their death. Jenny outlived her husband several years, and was one of the last of the African race who in our early history were held in bondage in New England.

CHAPTER III: VERMONT.

AUGUST 16th, 1777, the Green Mountain Boys, aided by troops from New Hampshire, and some few from Berkshire County, Massachusetts, under the command of Gen. Stark, captured the left wing of the British army near Bennington. As soon as arrangements could be made, after the prisoners were all collected, — something more than seven hundred, — they were tied to a rope, one on each side. The rope not being long enough, Gen. Stark called for more; when Mrs. Robinson, wife of Hon. Moses Robinson, said to the General, "I will take down the last bedstead in the house, and present the rope to you, on one condition. When the prisoners are all tied to the rope, you shall permit my negro man to harness up my old mare, and hitch the rope to the whiffletree, mount the mare, and conduct the British and tory prisoners out of town." The General willingly accepted Mrs. Robinson's proposition. The negro mounted the mare, and thus conducted the left wing of the British army into Massachusetts, on their way to Boston.

Gen. Schuyler writes from Saratoga, July 23, 1777, to the President of Massachusetts Bay, "That of the few continental troops we have had to the Northward, one third part is composed of men too far advanced in years for field service, of boys, or rather, children, and, mortifying barely to mention, of negroes."

The General also addressed a similar letter to John Hancock, and again to the Provincial Congress, in which he stated that the foregoing were facts which were altogether incontrovertible.

LEMUEL HAYNES was born in Hartford, Conn., July 18, 1753. His father was an African, his mother, white. It was his good fortune to fall into kind hands, and he enjoyed excellent advantages of education, both before and after the Revolution. He ultimately became a ripe scholar, and, in 1804, received the honorary degree of A. M. from Middlebury College, Vt. After completing a theological course of study, he preached in various places in Connecticut, until the year 1788, when he made a permanent settlement in West Rutland, Vt., and remained there thirty years, being one of the most popular preachers in the State.

In 1805, Mr. Haynes preached his noted sermon from Gen. iii. 4, the fame of which, and his discussion with the venerable Hosea Ballou, was world-wide.

He was no less distinguished for his patriotism than for his theological attainments. He enlisted as a minute man in 1774, and became connected with the American army. After the battle of Lexington, in 1775, be joined the army at Roxbury. Two years after, he was a volunteer in the expedition to Ticonderoga, to stop the inroads of Burgoyne's Northern army. His neighbors and friends often heard him describe his sufferings while engaged in that campaign.

His social qualities were of a high order. He was a somewhat eccentric man, very musical, and full of wit and anecdote, but serious and reverent when the occasion demanded. He was a kind neighbor and a warm friend. He lived to the age of 81, dying on the 28th of September, 1833.

The opinion of Judge Harrington, of Vermont, in the case of a person claimed as a fugitive slave, is probably familiar to most Abolitionists. In answer to some inquiries with regard to the particulars of the case, by Hon. Samuel E. Sewall, of Massachusetts, the Hon. Dorastus Wooster, of Middlebury, Vt., says: —

"The transaction to which you allude is somewhat an ancient one. The case occurred before my time; but I have the history of it from the lips of an eye-witness, who was present at the time, — the Hon. Horatio Seymour, formerly a Senator from this State in Congress. There was a person of color in Middlebury, who was claimed as a slave by his master, from the State of New York. He was brought before two Justices of the Peace, and they decided to surrender him. Loyal Case, Esq., counsel for the slave, brought him up, on a habeas corpus, to the Supreme Court, then in session, for his liberation. The master brought forward documentary and other evidence to show his title to the slave. Judge Harrington, who was then on the bench, gave the opinion of the Court. He said that the evidence of title was good, as far as it went, but the chain had some of its links broken. The evidence did not go far enough. If the master could show a bill of sale, or grant, from the Almighty, then his title to him would be complete: otherwise, it would not. And as he had not shown such evidence, the Court refused to surrender him, and discharged him. This is the opinion of the Court, as delivered by Judge Harrington, as well as can be recollected after such a lapse of time. The transaction took place about the year 1807. Judge Harrington is now dead. He possessed a powerful mind, not fond of technicalities: had a strong sense of justice, and was a great friend to liberty."

Two points in this case merit particular attention: —

1. The decision was made only about seventeen years after the Constitution of the United States went into operation.

2. It was the solemn and deliberate decision of the Supreme Court of Vermont, not the opinion of Judge Harrington alone. As such, it becomes of great weight as a legal authority, and should be cited whenever a person, claimed as a fugitive slave, is brought before any Court.

CHAPTER IV: RHODE ISLAND.

Tim Hon. Tristam Burges, of Rhode Island, in a speech in Congress, January, 1828, said: — "At the commencement of the Revolutionary War, Rhode Island had a number of slaves. A regiment of them were enlisted into the Continental service, and no braver men met the enemy in battle; but not one of them was permitted to be a soldier until he had first been made a freeman."

"In Rhode Island," says Governor Eustis, in his able speech against slavery in Missouri, 12th December, 1820, "the blacks formed an entire regiment, and they discharged their duty with zeal and fidelity. The gallant defence of Red Bank, in which the black regiment bore a part, is among the proofs of their valor." In this contest, it will be recollected that four hundred men met and repulsed, after a terrible and sanguinary struggle, fifteen hundred Hessian troops, headed by Count Donop. The glory of the defence of Red Bank, which has been pronounced one of the most heroic actions of the war, belongs in reality to black men; yet who now hears them spoken of in connection with it? Among the traits which distinguished the black regiment, was devotion to their officers. In the attack made upon the American lines, near Croton river, on the 13th of May, 1781, Colonel Greene, the commander of the regiment, was cut down and mortally wounded but the sabres of the enemy only reached him through the bodies of his faithful guard of blacks, who hovered over him to protect him, and every one of whom was killed.

Lieu tenant-Colonel Barton, of the Rhode Island militia, planned a bold exploit for the purpose of surprising and taking Major-General Prescott, the commanding officer of the royal army at Newport. Taking with him, in the night, about forty men, in two boats, with ours muffled, he had the address to elude the vigilance of the ships of war and guard boats, and, having arrived undiscovered at the General's quarters, they were taken for the sentinels, and the General was not alarmed till his captors were at the door of his lodging chamber, which was fast closed. A negro man, named Prince, instantly thrust his head through the panel door and seized the victim while in bed. The General's aid-decamp leaped from a window undressed, and attempted to escape, but was taken, and, with the General, brought off in safety.

I have received from Mr. George E. Willis, of Providence, the following list of names, as among the colored soldiers in the Rhode Island Regiment during the Revolutionary War: —

SCIPIO BROWN,
PRINCE VAUGHN,
GUY WATSON,
PRIMUS RHODES,
PRINCE GREENE,
HENRY TABOR,
REUBEN ROBERTS,
CÆSAR POWER,
THOMAS BROWN,
SAMSON HAZZARD,
RICHARD RHODES,
CUFF GREENE,
CATO GREENE,
PRINCE JENKS,
PHILO PHILLIPS,
YORK CHAMPLIN,
ICHABOD NORTHUP.

RICHARD COZZENS, a fifer in the Rhode Island Regiment, was born in Africa, and died in Providence. in 1829.

In this connection, the following extracts from an address delivered, in 1842, before the Congregational and Presbyterian Anti-Slavery Society, at Francestown, N. H., by Dr. HARRIS, a Revolutionary veteran, will be read with great interest: —

"I sympathize deeply," said Dr. Harris, "in the objects of this Society. I fought, my hearers, for the liberty which you enjoy. It surprises me that every man does not rally at the sound of liberty, and array himself with those who are laboring to abolish slavery in our country. The very mention of it warms the blood in my veins, and, old as I am, makes me feel something of the spirit and impulses of '76.

"Then liberty meant something. Then, liberty, independence, freedom, were in every man's mouth. They were the sounds at which they rallied, and under which they fought and bled. They were the words which encouraged and cheered them through their hunger, and nakedness, and fatigue, in cold and in heat. The word slavery then filled their hearts with horror. They fought because they would not be slaves. Those whom liberty has cost nothing, do not know how to prize it.

"I served in the Revolution, in General Washington's army, three years under one enlistment. I have stood in battle, where balls, like hail, were flying all around me. The man standing next to me was shot by my side — his blood spouted upon my clothes, which I wore for weeks. My nearest blood, except that which runs in my veins, was shed for liberty. My only brother was shot dead instantly in the Revolution. Liberty is dear to my heart — I cannot endure the thought, that my countrymen should be slaves.

"When stationed in the State of Rhode Island, the regiment to which I belonged was once ordered to what was called a flanking position, — that is, upon a place which the enemy must pass in order to come round in our rear, to drive us from the fort. This pass was every thing, both to them and to us; of course, it was a post of imminent danger. They attacked us with great fury, but were repulsed. They reinforced, and attacked us again, with more vigor and determination, and again were repulsed. Again they reinforced, and attacked us the third time, with the most desperate courage and resolution, but a third time were repulsed. The contest was fearful. Our position was hotly disputed and as hotly maintained.

"But I have another object in view in stating these facts. I would not be trumpeting my own acts; the only reason why I have named myself in connection with this transaction is, to show that I know whereof I affirm. There was a black regiment in the same situation. Yes, a regiment of negroes, fighting for our liberty and independence, — not a white man among them but the officers, — stationed in this same dangerous and responsible position. Had they been unfaithful, or given way before the enemy, all would have been lost. Three times in succession were they attacked, with most desperate valor and fury, by well disciplined and veteran troops, and three times did they successfully repel the assault, and thus preserve our army from capture. They fought through the war. They were brave, hardy troops. They helped to gain our liberty and independence.

"Now, the war is over, our freedom is gained — what is to be done with these colored soldiers, who have shed their best blood in its defence? Must they be sent off out of the country, because they are black? or must they be sent back into slavery, now they have risked their lives and shed their blood to secure the freedom of their masters? I ask, what became of these noble colored soldiers? Many of them, I fear, were taken back to the South, and doomed to the fetter and the chain.

"And why is it, that the colored inhabitants of our nation, born in this country, and entitled to all the rights of freemen, are held in slavery? Why, but because they are black? I have often thought, that, should God see fit, by a miracle, to change their color, straighten their hair, and give their features and complexion the appearance of the whites, slavery would not continue a year. No, you would then go and abolish it with the sword, if it were not speedily done without. But is it a suitable cause for making men slaves, because God has given them such a color, such hair and such features, as he saw fit?"

During the Dorr excitement, the colored population of Rhode Island received high encomiums from the papers of the State for their conduct. The New York Courier and Enquirer said: — "The colored people of Rhode Island deserve the good opinion and kind feeling of every citizen of the State, for their conduct during the recent troublous times in Providence. They promptly volunteered their services for any duty to which they might be useful in maintaining law and order. Upwards of a hundred of them organized themselves for the purpose of acting as a city guard for the protection of the city, and to extinguish fires, in case of their occurrence, while the citizens were absent on military duty. The fathers of these people were distinguished for their patriotism and bravery in the war of the Revolution, and the Rhode Island colored regiment fought, on one occasion, until half their number were slain. There was not a regiment in the service which did more soldierly duty, or showed itself more devotedly patriotic."

A colored military company, called the "National Guard," has recently been formed in Providence, using, by special grant, the State arms.

CHAPTER V: CONNECTICUT.

HON. CALVIN GODDARD, of Connecticut, states that in the little circle of his residence, he was instrumental in securing, under the Act of 1818, the pensions of nineteen colored soldiers. "I cannot," he says, "refrain from mentioning one black man, PRIMUS BABCOCK, who proudly presented to me an honorable discharge from service during the war, dated, at the close of it, wholly in the handwriting of George Washington. Nor can I forget the expression of his feelings, when informed, after his discharge had been sent to the War Department, that it could not be returned. At his request, it was written for, as he seemed inclined to spurn the pension and reclaim the discharge."

There is a touching anecdote related of Baron Steuben, on the occasion of the disbandment of the American army. A black soldier, with his wounds unhealed, utterly destitute, stood on the wharf, just as a vessel bound for his distant home was getting under weigh. The poor fellow gazed at the vessel with tears in his eyes, and gave himself up to despair. The warm-hearted foreigner witnessed his emotion, and, inquiring into the cause of it, took his last dollar from his purse, and gave it to him, while tears of sympathy trickled down his cheeks. Overwhelmed with gratitude, the poor wounded soldier hailed the sloop, and was received on board. As it moved out from the wharf, he cried back to his noble friend on shore, "God Almighty bless you, master Baron!"

During the Revolutionary War, and after the sufferings of a protracted contest had rendered it difficult to procure recruits for the army, the Colony of Connecticut adopted the expedient of forming a corps of colored soldiers. A battalion of blacks was soon enlisted, and, throughout the war, conducted themselves with fidelity and efficiency. The late General Humphreys, then a Captain, commanded a company of this corps. It is said that some objections were made, on the part of officers, to accepting the command of the colored troops. In this exigency, Capt. Humphreys, who was attached to the family of Gen. Washington, volunteered his services. His patriotism was rewarded, and his fellow officers were afterwards as desirous to obtain appointments in that corps as they had previously been to avoid them.

The following extract from the pay roll of the second company, fourth regiment, of the Connecticut line of the Revolutionary army, may rescue many gallant names from oblivion: —

Captain,
DAVID HUMPHREYS,
Privates,
JACK ARABUS,
JOHN CLEVELAND,
PHINEAS STRONG,
NED FIELDS,
ISAAC HIGGINS,
LEWIS MARTIN,
CÆSAR CHAPMAN,
PETER MIX,
PHILO FREEMAN,
HECTOR WILLIAMS,
JUBA FREEMAN,
CATO ROBINSON,
PRINCE GEORGE,
PRINCE CROSBEE,
SHUBAEL JOHNSON,
TIM CÆSAR,
JACK LITTLE,
BILL SOWERS,
DICK VIOLET,
BRISTER BAKER,
CÆSAR BAGDON,
GAMALIEL TERRY,
LENT MUNSON,
HEMAN ROGERS,
JOB CÆSAR,
JOHN ROGERS,
NED FREEDOM,
CONGO ZADO,
PETER GIBBS,
PRINCE JOHNSON,
ALEX. JUDD,
POMP LIBERTY,

CUFF LIBERTY,
POMP CYRUS,
HARRY WILLIAMS,
SHARP ROGERS,
JOHN BALL,
JOHN MCLEAN,
JESSE VOSE,
DANIEL BRADLEY,
SHARP CAMP,
JO OTIS,
JAMES DINAH,
SOLOMON SOWTICE,
PETER FREEMAN,
CATO WILBROW,
CUFF FREEMAN,
JUBA DYER,
ANDREW JACK,
PETER MORANDO,
SAMPSON CUFF,
DICK FREEDOM,
POMP MCCUFF.

The Hartford Review for Sept., 1839, gives the following account of a colored man by the name of HAMET, then living in Middletown, who was formerly owned by Washington: — "Hamet is, according to his own account, nearly one hundred years old. He draws a pension for his services in the Revolutionary War, and manufactures toy drums for his support. He has a white wife and one child. His hair is white with age, and hangs matted together in masses over his shoulders. His height is about four feet six inches. He retains a perfect recollection of his massa, and missus Washington, and has several remembrancers of them. Among these, there is a lock of the General's hair, and his (the General's) service sword. He converses in three or four different languages, — the French, Spanish and German, besides his native African tongue."

A clergyman in Connecticut, during the Revolutionary War, manifested, on all occasions, his zeal in the cause of freedom and his country, but, at the same time, held in bondage a colored man named Jack. To contend for liberty, and hold the poor African in slavery, was, according to Jack's conception of right and wrong, a manifest inconsistency. Under this impression, and anxious to obtain that liberty which is the inherent and natural right of man, Jack went to his master one day, and addressed him in the following language: — "Master, I observe you always keep preaching about liberty and praying for liberty, and I love to hear you, sir, for liberty be a good thing. You preach well and you pray well; but one thing you remember, master, — Poor Jack is not free yet." Struck with the propriety and force of Jack's admonition, the clergyman, after a momentary pause, told Jack if he would behave well in his service for one year longer, he should be free. Jack fulfilled the condition, obtained his freedom, and became a man of some property and respectability.

EBENEZER HILLS died at Vienna, New York, August, 1849, aged one hundred and ten. He was born a slave, in Stonington, Connecticut, and became free when twenty-eight years of age. He served through the Revolutionary War, and was at the battles of Saratoga and Stillwater, and was present at the surrender of Burgoyne.

In a letter to the author, Parker Pillsbury, of New Hampshire, says: — "The names of the two brave men of color, who fell, with Ledyard, at the storming of Fort Griswold, were LAMBO LATHAM and JORDAN FREEMAN. All the names of the slain, at that time, are inscribed on a marble tablet, wrought into the monument — the names of the colored soldiers last, — and not only last, but a blank space is left between them and the whites; in genuine keeping with the "Negro Pew" distinction — setting them not only below all others, but by themselves, even after that. And it is difficult to say why. They were not last in the fight. When Major Montgomery, one of the leaders in the expedition against the Americans, was lifted upon the walls of the fort by his soldiers, flourishing his sword and calling on them to follow him, JORDAN FREEMAN received him on the point of a pike, and pinned him dead to the earth. [Vide Hist. Collections of Connecticut.] And the name of JORDAN FREEMAN stands away down, last on the list of heroes, — perhaps the greatest hero of them all."

The seventy-second anniversary of the memorable tragedy at Groton Heights, in 1781, was celebrated by the people of New London and vicinity, on Wednesday, September 7, 1853. Of the address of Hon. Robert C. Winthrop on that occasion, the New York Express says: —

"It was beautifully eloquent and appropriate. His father was born in New London, and his ancestors for a century and a half had lived there. The very name of Groton came from Groton Manor in England, an estate once owned by the Winthrops. The names of New London and the Thames originated in a natural love for the great metropolis of the old world and the river which passed by, for these were once in the neighborhood of the homes of those who planted some of the earliest colonies in America. Mr. W. pictured the events of the 6th of September, the bravery of the volunteers, the shocking murders, the dead and surviving, the sufferings of Ledyard, the revolutionary struggle, and all in letters of gold. His address charmed alike the lettered and unlettered among his hearers, and that is the test of true eloquence."

The orator's omission to make a brief allusion, even, to the two colored soldiers, called out the following tribute from William Anderson, of New London, Connecticut: —

"I stood," he says, "on the heights of Groton, a few days since, listening to the praises of the white heroes, from the lips of Hon. R. C. Winthrop, W. I. Hammersley, Esq., Gov. Seymour, and others. I saw there, on the battle-ground, the descendants of the gallant Ledyard, (or, rather, the connections,) with those of the Averys, the Lathams, the Perkinses, the Baileys, and others, in the full enjoyment of that liberty so dearly bought by their ancestors. I was glad that they were free, and living out their God-given rights. My mind became excited with the scene; but, on reflection, my excitement was calmed down by the sober thought of an unpleasant reality, and you will ask, why was I sad? Well, as Shakespeare says, 'I will to you a tale unfold'; and, while you bear with me in the recital, I know your sympathies will attend me in the sequel.

"September 6th, 1781, New London was taken by the British, under the command of that traitor, Arnold. The small band composing the garrison retreated to the fort opposite, in the town of Groton, and there resolved either to gain a victory or die for their country. The latter pledge was faithfully redeemed, and by none more gallantly than the two colored men; and, if the survivors of that day's carnage tell truly, they fought like tigers, and were butchered after the gates were burst open. One of these men was the brother of my grandmother, by the name of Lambert, but called Lambo, — since chiselled on the marble monument by the American classic appellation of 'Sambo.' The name of the other man was Jordan Freeman. Lambert was living with a gentleman in Groton, by the name of Latham, so, of course, he was called Lambert Latham, Mr. Latham and Lambert, on the day of the massacre, were work in a field, at a distance, from the house. On hearing the alarm upon the approach of the enemy, Mr. Latham started for home, leaving Lambert to drive the team up to the house. On arriving at the house, Lambert was told that Mr. Latham had gone up to the fort. Lambert took the cattle from the team, and, making all secure, started for the point of defence, where he arrived before the British began the attack. And here let me say, my dear friend, that there was not any negro pew in that fort, although there was some praying as well as fighting. But there they stood, side by side, and shoulder to shoulder, and, after a few rounds of firing, each man's visage was so blackened by the smoke of powder, that Lambert and Jordan had but little to boast of on the score of color.

"The assault on the part of the British was a deadly one, and manfully resisted by the Americans, even to the clubbing of their muskets after their ammunition was expended; but finally, the little garrison was overcome, and, on the entrance of the enemy, the British officer inquired, "Who commands this fort?" The gallant Ledyard replied, "I once did; you do now," — at the same time handing his sword, which was immediately run through his body to the hilt by the officer. This was the commencement of an unparalleled slaughter. Lambert, being near Col. Ledyard when he was slain, retaliated upon the officer by thrusting his bayonet through his body. Lambert, in return, received from the enemy thirty-three bayonet wounds, and thus fell, nobly avenging the death of his commander.

These facts were given me on the spot, at the time of the laying of the corner-stone, by two veterans who were present at the battle. And now I would ask, has Connecticut done her duty towards us, while she permits foreigners to exercise the right of suffrage, — yes, even those who were fighting against us in the last war, — while we, "native, and to the manner born," are not allowed to peep into the ballot-box? Among the many great orators at Groton Heights, the last 6th of September, I heard not the first word spoken of our forefathers' valor, or of our present disenfranchisement.

"My dear friend, I well remember the last war between this country and Great Britain. I was then a mere schoolboy. The school where I went was also attended by several hundred boys; and, one day, we were all marshalled out, and under drum and fife, marched down to help construct a battery, near the water's edge, below the mouth of the harbor; and proudly did we feel, that we little fellows could do something for our country, if nothing more than lugging a small turf, or carrying wooden pins for securing the turf. I have often thought of that day's work and of its close, as being so truly in keeping with past and present usage. At the close of the day, we returned to town, treading time to the music, with the promise that we should receive some food — of which we had not tasted any since morning. But, alas! The proverb was verified in that case, "that the last should be first," — for, on arriving at the house, the order was given to open ranks, and those in the rear, being the men, passed up the ranks, filling the house, to the exclusion of the boys, who returned home to a late supper, thinking of ardor, patriotism, and hunger; but nevertheless, ready for another tramp, if called on."

The colored inhabitants of Connecticut assembled in convention, in 1849, to devise means to secure the elective franchise, denied to seven thousand of their number. A gentleman present gives the following incident: — "A young man, Mr. WEST, of Bridgeport, spoke with a great deal of energy, and with a clear and pleasant tone of voice, which many a lawyer, statesman, or clergyman, might covet, nobly vindicating the rights of the brethren. He said that the bones of the colored man had bleached on every battle-field where American valor had contended for national independence. Side by side with the white man, the black man stood and struggled to the last for the inheritance with the white men now enjoy, but deny to us. His father was a soldier slave, and his master said to him, when the liberty of the country was achieved, 'Stephen, we will do something for you.' But what have they ever done for Stephen, or for Stephen's posterity? This orator is evidently a young man of high promise, and better capable of voting intelligently than half of the white men who would deny him a freeman's privilege."

At the Troy Convention, held October, 1847, Rev. Amos G. Beman gave vent to his feelings in a most eloquent speech on the pro-slavery results of the colored suffrage question, in his native State, Connecticut, remarking that nine-tenths of the Irish residents in Connecticut voted against the colored American; and, though he had loved Ireland, revered her great men, sympathized with her present and past afflictions, and some of her blood flowed in his veins, he could not forego administering the burning rebuke which he believed due for their recreancy to the cause of human rights, and to the men who had never done harm to them. He alluded to the conversion of Judge Daggett, which has been graphically delineated by another writer, as follows: —

"While the black laws of Connecticut were in force, Chief Justice Daggett decided that we were not citizens of the United States, and that the colored people there had no claims to the privileges of American citizens. But time rolled on; he had become acquainted with the intelligent and enterprising colored citizens of that State; he had finished his term and retired. But a few years ago, when the question was before the people of Connecticut — Shall the colored people of the State have the right to vote? — while his fellow-citizens were voting, three to one, in the negative, the old gentleman, from his retirement, stepped forth, in his white-topped boots, with his silver locks of eighty winters flowing beneath his venerable brim; leaning upon his staff, he walked to the polls, amid popular excitement, and voted in the affirmative." Not a few great men, on the bench, at the bar, or in the pulpit, have undergone similar changes. These changes will multiply, under the influence of the praiseworthy exertions of her gallant, but proscribed, colored citizens, encouraged by the good and true around them. In the struggle for enfranchisement, victory, at no distant day, is destined to perch upon their banners.

In addition to what Mr. Phillips has said of DAVID RUGGLES, in earlier pages of this book, the following reminiscences of that gifted son of Connecticut are worthy to be recorded here. August 1st, 1841, a complimentary soiree was given to Mr. Ruggles in Boston, at which he made a speech, in the course of which he said: —

"I have had the pleasure of helping six hundred persons in their flight from bonds. In this, I have tried to do my duty, and mean still to persevere, until the last fetter shall be broken, and the last sigh heard from the lips of a slave. But give the praise to Him who sustains us all, who holds up the heart of the laborer in the rice swamp, and cheers him when, by the twinkling of the North Star, he finds his way to liberty. Six hundred in three years I have saved; had it been in one year, I should have been nearer my duty, nearer the duty of every American, when he reflects that it was the blood of colored men, as well as whites, which crimsoned the battle-fields of Bunker Hill and the rest, in the struggle to sustain the principles embodied in our Declaration of Independence."

Mr. Ruggles, for a brief period, successfully edited the Mirror of Liberty. He died in 1849, and highly eulogistic notices of him appeared in the Boston Liberator and the Chronotype, the editors of these papers having long been conversant with the trials, perseverance and martyrdom of this "brave soldier in the battle of life."

Rev. J. C. BEMAN gives the following account of the origin of his name. He says that when his father was presented with manumission papers, he was asked what name he had selected, and replied that he had always loathed slavery, and wanted to be a man; hence he adopted the name, Beman.

At the Colored Men's Convention held at Hartford, in October, 1854, Rev. A. G. BEMAN, of New Haven, made a report on the condition and prospects of the colored people of that city and county. He contrasted their present position with what it was twenty years ago. Then, not a man of them could enter his habitation and say, "This is mine"; not a single church, nor the shadow of any school or other place for the education of their children, was in existence or prospect. To have looked for the strictly temperate, moral and religious, had been as fruitless as to search for hailstones in boiling water. Now, there are about two hundred thousand dollars' worth of real estate, besides bank and railroad stock, four Methodist churches, one Congregational, one Episcopal, and one Baptist, and a Literary Society with a Circulating Library, in possession of the colored people of New Haven city. There are four schools in full and prosperous operation. How can any man, said Mr. B., who has lived in the midst of the one thousand and upwards colored people of New Haven, and witnessed the progress they have made in spite of almost every obstacle, publicly say, as the Hon. H. Olmstead has done, in his report on Colonization to the Legislature of 1851, that "the colored men in this State are dying out, their hopes crushed, their manhood gone"?

EPITAPH FROM THE LIBERTY STREET BURIAL GROUND, MIDDLETOWN.
In Memory of
JENNY,
Servant to the Rev, Enoch Huntington, and Wife Of Mark Winthrop, Who died April 28, 1784.
The day of her death she was Mr. Huntington's Property.

CHAPTER VI: NEW YORK.

As early as 1712, there had been an insurrection of the slaves in New York, and the recollection of this, and a general distrust of the negro population, rendered the citizen of that city peculiarly suspicious of their movements; and when, in 1741, the cry was raised of a "negro plot," there ensued a scene of confusion and alarm, of folly, frenzy and injustice, which scarcely has a parallel in this, or any other, country. It happened that a Spanish vessel, partly manned with negroes, had previously been brought into New York as a prize, and that all the men had been condemned as slaves, in the Court of Admiralty, and were sold at vendue. Now, these men had the impudence to say notwithstanding they were black, that they had been free men in their own country, and to grumble at their hard usage in being sold for slaves. One of them had been bought by the owner of a house in which fire had been discovered, and a cry was raised among the people — "The Spanish negroes!" — "Take up the Spanish negroes!" They were immediately incarcerated, and, a fire occurring in the afternoon of the same day, the rumor became general, that the slaves, in a body, were concerned in these wicked attempts to burn the city.

The negroes were brought to trial, May 29, 1741. The principal evidence against them was one Mary Burton, the common informer, who was rewarded by the sum of one hundred dollars from the city authorities. She continued to implicate parties, until the "people of consequence" began to be annoyed by her, when the prosecutions became unpopular, and the excitement subsided. There was some evidence against them from negroes, as, by a law of the colony, the evidence of slaves was competent against each other, though not allowed to be used against white men. The prisoners had no counsel, while the Attorney General, assisted by two members of the bar, appeared against them. The evidence had little consistency, and was extremely loose and general. The arguments of the lawyers were chiefly declamatory respecting the horrible plot, of the existence of which, however, no sufficient evidence was introduced. "The monstrous ingratitude of the black tribe (was the language of one of them in addressing the jury) is what exceedingly aggravated their guilt; their slavery among us is generally softened with great indulgence." The prisoners were immediately convicted, and were sentenced by the Court, in a brutal address, (which is singularly indicative of the general excitement on the subject,) to be burnt to death. "You, abject wretches," said the Judge, "the outcast of the nations of the earth, are treated here with tenderness and humanity"! The prisoners protested their innocence, and utterly denied any knowledge of any plot whatever; but, when they were taken out to execution, the poor creatures were much terrified; and, when chained to the stake, and the executioner was ready to apply the torch, they admitted all that was required of them. An attempt was then made to procure a reprieve; but a great multitude had assembled to witness the executions, and the excitement was so great, that it was considered impossible to return the prisoners to prison; they were, accordingly, burned at the stake.

John Ury, the son of a former Secretary of the South Sea Company, a non-juring clergyman, and a man of education, was convicted, on the evidence of Mary Burton, though denying all knowledge of any plot, or even of the witnesses who testified against him.

After his execution, a day of thanksgiving to Almighty God was observed by public command, for the delivery from the late execrable conspiracy. But the public mind was at rest for a short time only. A few negroes in Queen's county, on Long Island, having formed themselves into a military company for amusement on the Christmas holidays, a letter was written to the authorities there by the Attorney General, and the slaves were severely chastised for this daring piece of insolence. The cry of a new plot was immediately raised, which resulted in the execution of other slaves. The whole number of persons taken into custody was over one hundred and fifty. Of these, four white persons were hanged; eleven negroes were burnt, eighteen were hanged, and fifty were sold, principally in the West Indies.

Thus ended the famous "Negro Plot" of New York. Upon a review of the evidence, as reported by one who had implicit faith in the existence of a conspiracy, we have no difficulty in pronouncing the whole thing to have been a complete delusion — the natural result of the condition of society at that day. This opinion is confirmed by Bancroft, United States historian, and Dunlap, in the History of New York.

Dr. Clarke, in the Convention which revised the Constitution of New York, in 1821, speaking of the colored inhabitants of the State, said: — My honorable colleague has told us, that, as the colored people are not required to contribute to the protection or defence of the State, they are not entitled to an equal participation in the privileges of its citizens. But, Sir, whose fault is this? Have they ever refused to do military duty when called upon? It is haughtily asked, who will stand in the ranks shoulder to shoulder with a negro? I answer, no one, in time of peace; no one, when your musters and trainings are looked upon as mere pastimes; no one, when your militia will shoulder their muskets and march to their trainings with as much unconcern as they would go to a sumptuous entertainment or a splendid ball. But, Sir, when the hour of danger approaches, your 'white' militia are just as willing that the man of color Should be set up as a mark to be shot at by the enemy, as to be set up themselves. In the War of the Revolution, these people helped to fight your battles by land and by sea. Some of your States were glad to turn out corps of colored men, and to stand 'shoulder to shoulder' with them.

"In your late war, they contributed largely towards some of your most splendid victories. On Lakes Erie and Champlain, where your fleets triumphed over a foe superior in numbers and engines of death, they were manned, in a large proportion, with men of color. And, in this very House, in the fall of 1814, a bill passed, receiving the a probation of all the branches of your government, authorising the Governor to accept the services of a corps of two thousand free people of color. Sir, these were times which tried men's souls. In these times, it was no sporting matter to bear arms. These were times, when a man who shouldered his musket, did not know but he bared his bosom to receive a death wound from the enemy, ere he laid it aside; and, in these times, these people were found as ready and as willing to volunteer in your service as any other. They were not compelled to go; they were not drafted. No; your pride had placed them beyond your compulsory power. But there was no necessity for its exercise; they were volunteers; yes, Sir, volunteers to defend that very country from the inroads and ravages of a ruthless and vindictive foe, which had treated them with insult, degradation, and slavery.

"Volunteers are the best of soldiers. Give me the men, whatever be their complexion, that willingly volunteer, and not those who are compelled to turn out. Such men do not fight from necessity, nor from mercenary motives, but from principle."

Said Martindale, of New York, in Congress, 22d of January, 1828: — "Slaves, or negroes who had been slaves, were enlisted as soldiers in the War of the Revolution; and I myself saw a battalion of them, as fine martial-looking men as I ever saw, attached to the Northern army, in the last war, on its march from Plattsburg to Sackett's Harbor."

During the Revolutionary War, the Legislature of New York passed an Act granting freedom to all slaves who should serve in the army for three years, or until regularly discharged. (See 2 Kent's Com., p. 255.)

The poor requital for the colored man's valor was forcibly alluded to by Henry H. Garnet at the anniversary of the American Anti-Slavery Society, in New York city, May, 1840. "It is with pride," said he, "that I remember, that in the earliest attempts to establish democracy in this hemisphere, colored men stood by the side of your fathers, and shared with them the toils of the Revolution. When Freedom, that had been chased over half the world, at last thought she had here found a shelter, and held out her hands for protection, the tearful eye of the colored man, in many instances, gazed with pity upon her tattered garments, and ran to her relief. Many fell in her defence, and the grateful soil received them affectionately into its bosom. No monumental piles distinguish their 'dreamless beds'; scarcely an inch on the page of history has been appropriated to their memory; yet truth will give them a share of the fame that was reaped upon the fields of Lexington and Bunker Hill; truth will affirm that they participated in the immortal honor that adorned the brow of the illustrious Washington."

I am indebted to Rev. Theodore Parker, of Boston, for the following historical sketch of the New York colored soldiery: —

"Not long ago, while the excavations for the vaults of the great retail dry goods store of New York were going on, a gentleman from Boston noticed a large quantity of human bones thrown up by the workmen. Every body knows the African countenance: the skulls also bore unmistakable marks of the race they belonged to. They were shovelled up with the earth which they had rested in, carted off and emptied into the sea to fill up a chasm, and make the foundation of a warehouse.

"On inquiry, the Bostonian learned that these were the bones of colored American soldiers, who fell in the disastrous battles of Long Island, in 1776, and of such as died of the wounds then received. At that day, as at this, spite of the declaration that 'all men are created equal,' the prejudice against the colored man was intensely strong. The black and the white had fought against the same enemy, under the same banner, contending for the same 'unalienable right' to life, liberty, and the pursuit of happiness. The same shot with promiscuous slaughter had mowed down Africans and Americans. But in the grave, they must be divided. On the battle-field, the blacks and whites had mixed their bravery and their blood, but their ashes must not mingle in the bosom of their common mother. The white Saxon, exclusive and haughty even in his burial, must have his place of rest proudly apart from the grave of the African he had once enslaved.

"Now, after seventy-five years have passed by, the bones of these forgotten victims of the Revolution are shovelled up by Irish laborers, carted off, and shot into the sea, as the rubbish of the town. Had they been white men's relics, how would they have been honored with sumptuous burial anew, and the purchased prayers and preaching of Christian divines! Now, they are the rubbish of the street!

"True, they were the bones of Revolutionary soldiers, — but they were black men; and shall a city that kidnaps its citizens, honor a negro with a grave? What boots it that he fought for our freedom; that he bled for our liberty; that he died for you and me? Does the 'nigger' deserve a tomb? Ask the American State — the American Church!

Three quarters of a century have passed by since the retreat from Long Island. What a change since then! From the Washington of that day to the world's Washington of this, what a change! In America, what alterations! What a change in England! The Briton has emancipated every bondman; slavery no longer burns his soil on either Continent, the East or West. America has a population of slaves greater than the people of all England in the reign of Elizabeth. Under the pavement of Broadway, beneath the walls of the Bazaar, there still lie the bones of the colored martyrs to American Independence. Dandies of either sex swarm gaily over the threshhold, heedless of the dead African, contemptuous of the living. And while these faithful bones were getting shovelled up and carted to the sea, there was a great slave-hunt in New York: a man was kidnapped and carried off to bondage by the citizens, at the instigation of politicians, and to the sacramental delight of 'divines.'

"Happy are the dead Africans, whom British shot mowed down! They did not live to see a man kidnapped in the city which their blood helped free."

Within a recent period, several military companies have been formed in New York city, exclusively of colored men. They have been organized, in part, through the exertions of Captains Simmons and Hawkins, and are designated as the "Hannibal Guards," the "Free Soil Guards," and the "Attucks Guards." The New York Tribune says of one of these companies, in announcing their parade, "They looked like men, handled their arms like men, and, should occasion demand, we presume would fight like men."

At the New York State Convention of the Soldiers of 1812, held at Syracuse, June 21, 1854, the following resolutions were adopted: —

Resolved, That in view of the resulting benefits to the nation at large, and in view of the dangers and hardships encountered by the soldiers of the war of 1812, — in view of the state of our finances, and especially in view of the fact that the soldiers of that war are now aged and rapidly dropping away, — and in view of the precedent established by Congress in reference to the soldiers of the Revolutionary War, — all officers and soldiers in the war of 1812, now living, and the widows of such as are deceased, should be provided for by a liberal annuity, to be continued during their natural lives, and that such provisions should extend to and include both the Indian and African race, for services either on sea or land, who enlisted or served in that war, and who joined with the white man in defending our rights and maintaining our independence.

Resolved, That we cordially invite the coöperation of the officers and soldiers of the war of 1812, in all the other States of the Union; that they be respectfully and earnestly requested to hold similar Conventions in their own States, to call upon their respective Legislatures to instruct their members in Congress to make just and ample provision, by grants of land and annuities, for the officers and soldiers of 1812, and for the widows of such as are deceased; and that without distinction of race or color.

LEWIS and MILTON CLARKE several years since made their escape from Kentucky slavery, and have distinguished themselves by their public advocacy of human rights. Their father was a Scotchman, who came to this country in time to be in the earliest scenes of the American Revolution. He was at the battle of Bunker Hill, and continued in the army to the close of the war. When his children were about being sold at auction, the venerable father, though debilitated from the effects of the wounds received in the war, was nevertheless roused by this outrage upon his rights and upon those of his children. "He had never expected," he said, "when fighting for the liberties of this country, to see his own wife and children sold in it to the highest bidder." But what were the entreaties of an agonized old man in the sight of eight or ten hungry heirs?

CYRUS CLARKE, brother to Lewis and Milton, became a resident of Hamilton Village, N. Y., and, possessing all the necessary qualifications of white men to vote, went to the polls and presented his ballot, when he was challenged, and told that, being a colored man, he could not vote unless possessed of two hundred and fifty dollars' worth of real estate. Clark replied to the challenger, "I am as white as you, and don't you vote?" Friends and foes warmly contested what constituted a colored man under the New York statute. The officers finally came to the conclusion that to be a colored man, an individual must be at least one half blood African. Mr. Clarke, the Kentucky slave, then voted, he being nearly full white.

It is believed that the debate on the military services of colored men had great influence in obtaining for them the right of suffrage; though it must also be recorded, that colored citizens were ungenerously made subject to a property qualification of two hundred and fifty dollars. Plutus must be highly esteemed where his rod can change even a negro into a man. If two hundred and fifty dollars will perform this miracle, what would it require to elevate a monkey to the enviable distinction? The friends of freedom are now attempting to remove this restriction, and we feel assured the right will triumph in the Empire State.

In Watkins, Schuyler county, on the 13th of August, 1855, a colored man (John D. Berry, Esq.) was chosen to sit as a juror in a criminal trial, and the citizens appeared very well satisfied.

JAMES M. WHITFIELD, the colored poet, is a resident of Buffalo. His time is almost constantly occupied in his business as a hair-dresser, and he writes in such intervals of leisure as he is able to realize. He is uneducated, — not entirely, but substantially; his genius is native and uncultivated, and yet his verse possesses much of the finish of experienced authorship. The following is an extract from poem by him on the Fourth of July:

"Another year has passed away,
And brings again the glorious day,
When Freedom from her slumber woke,
And broke the British tyrant's yoke —
Unfurled her standard to the air,
In gorgeous beauty, bright and fair —
Pealed forth the sound of war's alarms,
And called her patriot sons to arms!

May those great truths which they maintained
Through years of deadly strife and toil,
Be by their children well sustained,
Till slavery ceases on our soil!"

I have taken great pleasure in visiting, in New York city, the Apothecary's Hall of Dr. J. M'Cune Smith, and also hat of Philip J. White. (Since then, several accomplished colored physicians have been added to the list.) I found Drs. Smith and White practical men, conducting their business and preparing medicines with as much readiness and skill as any other disciples of Galen and Hippocrates. I was also introduced to a colored carpenter, — not a practical one, but a master workman, and contractor for buildings.

Among the enterprising Albanians, may be mentioned William H. Topp, a merchant tailor, and a perfect gentleman, winning golden opinions from all who, in the course of business or otherwise, become acquainted with him. His store, in Broadway, will not suffer by comparison with the best in any of the Atlantic cities. He has long been interested in the ways and means of elevating his oppressed brethren, and, in their hearts' best affections, evidently stands a-Topp of the fraternity.

It is a fault, with many colored men, that they do not aim at perfection in a knowledge of their business, whereas, they should all aim for the highest pinnacle of merit. As a friend once said to a musical aspirant, "You should strive to be something more than a superficial scraper of catgut." Policy and principle alike demand this at the hands of colored Americans.

From an elaborate and very encouraging statistical report, embracing the real estate owned by the colored citizens of New York, the amount invested by them in business enterprises, and their general prosperity, as a class, prepared by Dr. J. M'Cune Smith, I copy the following statements.

The Colored Home and Orphan Asylum contain all the colored poor, dependent on public support, with a very few exceptions. In New York city, the colored population to the white, fairly estimated, is as one to twenty-five; hence, the colored population of that city is twenty-seven per centum less burdensome, than is the white population, to the poor fund. And this happy state of things has arisen, in part, from the fact, that the former class have mutual benefit societies, with a cash capital of $30,000, from which they take care of their sick and bury their dead.

The sending of children to school is a fair test of the intelligence of a people. During the year 1850, there were 3,393 colored children in attendance in common schools, in New York city, which is nearly the same proportion as there were white children attending the same class of schools.

In reviewing these facts, it must be borne in mind, that but one quarter of a century has elapsed since a large portion of the colored population of New York has been freed from slavery; and that, during the earlier portion of this time, the very possession of the newly-gotten freedom had in it an enjoyment so full and perfect, that the getting of money became a secondary consideration, to say nothing of the dependent and thriftless habits which slavery had engendered. Nor should it be forgotten, that, during the same fourth of a century, we have borne the brunt of competition with a flood of emigrants from the old world; for nearly all such emigrants were immediate and direct competitors in our callings, having on their side the odds of complexional sympathy and political influence, from the moment their landing upon our shores.

The following business card is inserted for its historical significance, having a two-fold application to the purposes of this book. This example supersedes the necessity of exclusive colored action, and, at the same time, is an exhibition of practical anti-slavery. May such instances speedily multiplied!

WILLIAMS, PLUMB & CO., IMPORTERS AND WHOLESALE DEALERS IN CHINA, GLASS AND EARTHEN WARE, No. 71 BARCLAY STREET.

ONE of the partners (Mr. WILLIAMS) is a COLORED MAN, has been connected with the CROCKERY TRADE of New York for twenty years, and for several years has conducted the business on his own account. A leading object in establishing the present firm, both by the parties themselves and their friends and advisers, having been to contribute to the SOCIAL ELEVATION OF THE COLORED PEOPLE, they feel warranted in making an appeal for patronage, as they now do, to all that class of merchants throughout the country who sympathise with the object now expressed, and who would gladly avail themselves of so direct a method and so favorable an opportunity to subserve it. We hope to see all such in our establishment, and we express the confidence that the favors bestowed upon us by our friends will be the interest of themselves as well as us.

JAMES WILLIAMS,
DAVID PLUMB,
JAMES J. ACHESON.

CHAPTER VII: NEW JERSEY.

THE Burlington Gazette gives the following account of an aged colored resident of that city, which will be read with much interest: —

"The attention of many of our citizens has, doubtless, been arrested by the appearance of an old colored man, who might have been seen, sitting in front of his residence, in East Union street, respectfully raising his hat to those who might be passing by. His attenuated frame, his silvered head, his feeble movements, combine to prove that he is very aged; and yet, comparatively few are aware that he is among the survivors of the gallant army who fought for the liberties of our country, 'in the days which tried men's souls.'

"On Monday last, we stopped to speak to him, and asked him how old he was. He asked the day of the month, and, upon being told that it was the 24th of May, replied, with trembling lips, 'I am very old — I am a hundred years old to-day.'

"His name is OLIVER CROMWELL, and he says that he was born at the Black Horse, (now Columbus,) in this county, in the family of John Hutchin. He enlisted in company commanded by Capt. Lowery, attached to the Second New Jersey Regiment, under the command of Col. Israel Shreve. He was at the battles of Trenton, Princeton, Brandywine, Monmouth, and Yorktown, at which latter place, he told us, he saw the last man killed. Although his faculties are failing, yet he relates many interesting reminiscences the Revolution. He was with the army at the retreat of the Delaware, on the memorable crossing of the 25th of December, 1776, and relates the story of the battles on the succeeding days with enthusiasm. He gives the details of the march from Trenton to Princeton, and told us, with much humor, that they 'knocked the British about lively' at the latter place. He was also at the battle of Springfield, and says that he saw the house burning in which Mrs. Caldwell was shot, at Connecticut Farms."

I further learn, that Cromwell was brought up a farmer, having served his time with Thomas Hutchins, Esq., his maternal uncle. He was, for six years and nine months, under the immediate command of Washington, whom he loved affectionately. "His discharge," (says Dr. M'Cune Smith,) "at the close of the war, was in Washington's own hand-writing, of which he was very proud, often speaking of it. He received, annually, ninety-six dollars pension. He lived a long and honorable life. Had he been of a little lighter complexion, (he was just half white,) every newspaper in the land would have been eloquent in praise of many virtues." He left three sons and three daughters; had fourteen children who reached the age of maturity — seven sons and seven daughters. He saw his grand-children to the third generation. He was a man of strong natural powers — never chewed tobacco nor drank a glass of ardent spirit. He died, in the town of his birth, January 24th, 1853, and now sleeps in the church-yard of the Broad street Methodist Church.

"SAMUEL CHARLTON," says Mr. McDougal, "was born in the State of New Jersey, a slave, in the family of Mr. M., who owned, also, other members belonging to his family — all residing in the English neighborhood. During the progress of the war, he was placed by his master, (as a substitute for himself,) in the army then in New Jersey, as a teamster in the baggage train. He was in active service at the battle of Monmouth, not only witnessing, but taking a part in, the struggle of that day. He was, also, in several other engagements in different sections of that part of the State. He was a great admirer of General Washington, and was, at one time, attached to his baggage train, and received the General's commendation for his courage and devotion to the cause of liberty. Mr. Charlton was about fifteen or seventeen years of age when placed in the army, for which his master rewarded him with a silver dollar. At the expiration of his time, he returned to his master, to serve again in bondage, after having toiled, fought and bled for liberty, in common with the regular soldiery. Mr. M., at his death, by will, liberated his slaves, and provided a pension for Charlton, to be paid during his lifetime. Mr. Charlton then, with his wife, took up his residence in New York city, with his son, Charles Charlton. He died twelve years since, being about eighty years of age. He and his partner were both honored and worthy members of the Dutch Reformed Church.

"An old colored woman," says the Stamford Advocate, "familiarly known as HAGAR, died in this village, on Saturday last. Her age is not exactly known, but, from the most reliable data at our command, we infer that she must have been upward of a hundred years old. She was born a slave, in Newark, New Jersey, and was brought to Stamford when she was five or six years old, and lived here until the day of her death. A lady, Mrs.

Knapp, now living, aged ninety-six years, remembers that Hagar used to carry her when a child. Assuming that Mrs. Knapp must have been three years old at the time to which her recollection extends, and that Hagar must have been thirteen to be charged with the care of children, it will make her, at the time of her death, one hundred and six years old. Another circumstance confirms this view of the case. During the Revolutionary War, Hagar was a cook in Weed's Tavern, and her husband, George Dykins, was hostler in the same establishment. Hagar used to relate, that she once cooked a dinner for General Washington, when he stopped at the tavern, on his way to Cambridge, Massachusetts, the head-quarters of the American army, in June, 1775. On the same occasion, Washington presented to her husband a silver dollar for his name's sake. Supposing Hagar to have been twenty-seven at that time, it would make her age one hundred and six, as is the case of the first supposition. In all probability, this is very nearly her age."

The Newark Eagle published, some time ago, the following account of a consistent celebration of the Fourth of July, in Woodbridge: —

"We have recently had an interview with a person who was present at the first abolition meeting ever held in the United States. It took place in the township of Woodbridge, County of Middlesex, in this State, on the Fourth of July, 1783, being the first anniversary of our Independence, after the close of the Revolutionary War. Great preparations had been made — an ox was roasted, and an immense number had assembled on the memorable occasion. A platform was erected, just above the heads of the spectators, and, at a given signal, Dr. Bloomfield, father of the late Governor Bloomfield, of this State, mounted the platform, followed by his fourteen slaves, male and female, seven taking their stations on his right hand, and seven on his left. Being thus arranged, he advanced somewhat in front of his slaves, and addressed the multitude on the subject of slavery and its evils, and, in conclusion, pointing to those on his right and left, 'As a nation,' said he, 'we are free and independent, — all men are created equal, and why should these, my fellow citizens, my equals, be held in bondage? From this day, they are emancipated; and I here declare them free, and absolved from all servitude to me or my posterity.' Then, calling up before him one somewhat advanced in years — 'Hector,' said the Doctor, 'whenever you become too old or infirm to support yourself, you are entitled to your maintenance from me or my property. How long do you suppose it will be before you will require that maintenance?' Hector held up his left hand, and, with his right, drew a line across the middle joints of his fingers, saying — 'Never, never, massa, so long as any of these fingers remain below these joints.' Then, turning to the audience, the Doctor remarked, — 'There, fellow-citizens, you see that liberty is as dear to the man of color as to you or me.' The air now rung with shouts of applause, and thus the scene ended.

"Dr. Bloomfield immediately procured for Hector, either by purchase or setting off from his own farm, three acres of land, and built him a small house, where he resided and cultivated his little farm until the day of his death; and it was a common remark with the neighbors, that Hector's hay, when he took it to Amboy to sell, would always command a better price than their own."

CHAPTER VIII: PENNSYLVANIA.

JAMES FORTEN.

JAMES FORTEN was born on the second day of September, 1766, and died on the Ides of March, 1842. He was the son of Thomas Forten, who died when James was but seven years old. His mother survived long after he had reached the years of maturity. In early life, he was marked for great sprightliness and energy of character, a generous disposition, and indomitable courage, always frank, kind, courteous, and disinterested. In the year 1775, he left school, being then about nine years of age, having received a very limited education (and he never went to school afterwards) from that early, devoted, and worldwide known philanthropist, ANTHONY BENEZET. He was then employed at a grocery store and at home, when his mother, yielding to the earnest and unceasing solicitations of her son, whose young heart fired with the enthusiasm and feeling of the patriots and revolutionists of that day, with the firmness and devotion of a Roman matron, but with a heart then truly deemed American, gave the boy of her promise, the child of her heart and her hopes, to his country; upon the altar of its liberties she laid the apple of her eye, the jewel of her soul.

In 1780, then in his fourteenth year, he embarked board the "Royal Louis," Stephen Decatur, Senr., Commander, in the capacity of "powder-boy." Scarce waft from his native shore, and perilled upon the dark blue sea than he found himself amid the roar of cannon, the smoke of blood, the dying and the dead. Their ship was so brought into action with an English vessel, the Lawrence, which, after a severe fight, in which great loss was sustain on both sides, and leaving every man wounded on board the "Louis" but himself, they succeeded in capturing, and brought her into port amid the loud huzzas and acclamations of the crowds that assembled upon the occasion. Forten, sharing largely in the feeling which so brilliant a victory had inspired, with fresh courage, and an unquenchable devotion to the interests of his native land, soon reëmbarked in the same vessel. In this cruise, however, they were unfortunate; for, falling in with three of the enemy's vessels, — the Amphyon, Nymph, and Pomona, — they were forced to strike their colors, and become prisoners of war. It was at this juncture that his mind was harassed with the most painful forebodings, from a knowledge of the fact that rarely, if ever, were prisoners of his complexion exchanged; they were sent to the West Indies, and there doomed to a life of slavery. But his destiny, by a kind Providence, was otherwise. He was placed on board the Amphyon, Captain Beasly, who, struck with his open and honest countenance, made him the companion of his son. During one of those dull and monotonous periods which frequently occur on ship-board, young Beasly and Forten were engaged in a game at marbles, when, with signal dexterity and skill, the marbles were upon every trial successively displaced by the unerring hand of Forten. This excited the surprise and admiration of his young companion, who, hastening to his father, called his attention to it. Upon being questioned as to the truth of the matter, and assuring the Captain that nothing was easier for him to accomplish, the marbles were again placed in the ring, and in rapid succession he redeemed his word.

A fresh and deeper interest was from that moment taken in his behalf. Captain Beasly proffered him a passage to England, tempted him with the allurements of wealth, under the patronage of his son, who was heir to a large estate there, the advantages of a good education, and freedom, equality and happiness, for ever. "No, No!," was the invariable reply; "I am here a prisoner for the liberties of my country; I never, NEVER, shall prove a traitor to her interests!" What sentiment more exalted! What patriotism more lofty, devoted, and self-sacrificing! Indeed, with him, the feeling was, "America, with all thy faults, I love thee still"; for, with a full knowledge of the wrongs and outrages which she was then inflicting upon his brethren and by the "ties of consanguinity and of wrong," we see this by the persecuted and valiant son of hers, in the very darkest hour of his existence, when hope seemed to have departed from him, when the horrors of a hopeless West India slavery, with its whips for his shrinking flesh, and its chains for hi free-born soul could only be dissipated by severing that tie, which, by the strongest cords of love, bound him to his native land, we see him standing up in the spirit of martyrdom, with a constancy of affection, and an invincibility of purpose, for the honor of his country, that place him above the noblest of the C'sars, and entitle him to a monument towering above that which a Bonaparte erected at the Place Vendome. Beasly, having failed in inducing him to go to England, soon had him consigned to that floating and pestilential hell, the frigate "Old Jersey," — giving him, however, as a token of his regard and friendship, a letter to the Commander of the prison-ship, highly commendatory of him, and also requesting that

Forten should not be forgotten on the list of exchanges. Thus (as he frequently remarked in after life) did a game of marbles save him from a life of West India servitude. In the mean while, his mother, at home, was in a state of mind bordering upon distraction, having learned that her son had been shot from the foretop of the Royal Louis; but her mind was relieved, after he had been absent nearly eight months, by his appearing in person.

To return. While on board the "Old Jersey," amid the privations and horrors incident to that receiving ship of disease and death, no less than three thousand five hundred persons died; and, according to a statement of Edwards, eleven thousand in all perished, while she remained the receptacle of the American prisoners. And here we have an instance to record of the most thrilling and stupendous exhibition of his generous and benevolent heart. Amid all that would make escape from his confinement desirable, when disease the most loathsome, death the most horrible, was around him, he was willing to and did endure all. He stifled the longings of his heart for the enjoyments of home, and for the embraces of his widowed and adored mother; yes, at a time when, if ever, self would lay in contribution every feeling of the heart, and every avenue of a generous out-going spirit be smothered, when the instincts and impulses of nature would unerringly covet in the closest scrutiny and watchfulness its own interests, JAMES FORTEN, in the ardor of his own high-toned beneficence, performed an act, which, in my humble opinion, is unexcelled, perhaps without a parallel, in the annals of our country's history. It was this: An officer of the American navy was about to be exchanged for a British prisoner, when the thoughtful mind of Forten conceived the idea of an easy escape for himself in the officer's chest; but, when about to avail himself of this opportunity, a fellow-prisoner, a youth, his junior in years, his companion and associate in suffering, was thought of. He immediately urged upon him to avail himself of the chances of an escape so easy. The offer was accepted, and Forten had the satisfaction of assisting in taking down the "chest of old clothes," as it was then called, from the side of the prison ship. The individual thus fortunately rescued was Captain Daniel Brewton, — the present incumbent in the Stewardship at the Lazaretto. I will read the certificate of Mr. Brewton in regard to this matter: —

"I do hereby certify, that James Forten was one who participated in the Revolution, in the year of our Lord one thousand seven hundred and seventy-six, and was a prisoner on board of the prison-ship, 'Old Jersey' in the year of our Lord one thousand seven hundred and eighty, with me.

(Signed,) DANIEL BREWTON."
PHILADELPHIA, March 15th, 1837.
Acknowledged before Alderman
J. W. PALMER.

It was my great privilege to see, but a short time ago, this venerable and grateful friend of JAMES FORTEN; to hear from his own lips a strict confirmation of the facts stated, as well as to witness the solemn scene which ensued, in his taking for the last time the hand of his dying benefactor. The old man's tears fell like rain; his stifled utterance marked the deep emotions of his almost bursting heart. Sad and dejected, with feelings that made him more ready to die than to live, he silently retired, stayed with the hope that they would soon meet in a better and a happier world.

After remaining seven months a prisoner on board this ship, young Forten obtained his release, and, without shoes upon his feet, (until he reached Trenton, where he was generously supplied,) arrived home in a wretchedly bad condition, having, among other evidences of great hardships endured, his hair nearly entirely worn from his head. He remained but a short time at home, when, in company with his brother-in-law, he sailed, in the ship Commerce, for London. He arrived there at a period of the greatest excitement. The great struggle between liberty and slavery had already been settled by the decision in the noted case of Somersett, when it was decreed, that the moment a slave trod the soil of Britain, "no matter in what language his doom may have been pronounced, — no matter what complexion incompatible with freedom an Indian or an African sun may have burnt upon him, — no matter in what disastrous battle his liberty may have been cloven down, — no matter with what solemnities he may have been devoted upon the altar of slavery, the first moment he touches the sacred soil of Britain, the altar and the god sink together in the dust; his body swells beyond the measure of his chains that burst from around him, and he stands redeemed, regenerated and disenthralled, by the irresistible Genius of Universal Emancipation."

But the accursed slave trade was still glutting in the blood and sinews of Afric's helpless children, and that mighty man, that prince of philanthropists, GRANVILLE SHARPE, was directing his benevolent efforts to its overthrow. At this time, the Christian feeling had awakened up an indignant nation to a determination for its destruction; and no small interest was taken in the discussions, both in and out of Parliament, by our deceased friend. It was among the many pleasing reminiscences of his life to refer to those scenes, so strikingly analogous to the trials and persecution of the friends of freedom here, and the hypocritical sophisms of their opponents. After remaining in London about a year, he returned home, and was apprenticed, with hi own consent, to Mr. Robert Bridges, sail-maker. He was not long at his trade, when his great skill, energy, diligence, and good conduct, commended him to his master, who, neither discriminating nor appreciating a man by the mere color of the skin in which he may be born, served his own interest in doing an act commensurate to the merits of young Forten, in promoting him foreman in his business. This was in his twentieth year. He continued in this capacity until 1798, when, upon the retirement of Mr. Bridges, he assumed the entire control and responsibility of the establishment. Having formed for himself a reputation for capability and industry, he found it no difficult task to secure the friendship of those, who, perceiving qualities it him which ever adorn and beautify the human character gave him their countenance and patronage; for although it was by the force of his own unassisted genius and energy of character that he rose above those depressing influences which have ever operated against those

"Whose hue makes a brother hate

A brother mortal here," —

yet he was indebted to some few stanch friends, of whose encouragement and kindness he was ever wont to speak in terms of gratitude. He continued, with great consistency of conduct, in prosecuting his business, offering up, on the altar of filial and fraternal regard, the first fruits of his labor, in purchasing a house for his mother and widowed sister, which sheltered the one until the period of her death, and now affords protection and support to the other in her declining years. With undiminished vigor of mind and body, enjoying the very best of health, he continued to give personal attention to his business until confined to his house from that disease, which, in a few months, proved fatal to him. It was during the long period of his active business life that he acquired that reputation, which ever remained unclouded, shedding abroad in its own, clear sky the brightest and noblest qualities of the human heart; so courteous, polished and gentlemanly in his manners, — so intelligent, social, and interesting, — so honest, just and true in his dealings, — so kind and benevolent in his actions, — so noble and lofty in his bearing, — that none knew him but to admire, to speak of him but in praise. He lived but to cherish those noble properties of his soul, and those exalted principles of action, which ever prompted him to deeds of benevolence, patriotism and honor. Perhaps one of the strongest traits in his character was that of benevolence. With him, it was no occasional or fitful impulse, but a living principle of action. Wherever suffering humanity presented itself, a glow of generous and brotherly sympathy was excited in his heart; and not bestowing nor graduating his gifts by the mere color of the skin, his open hand was ever ready to administer to the wants of all. Nor was this feeling confined to the giving of his worldly substance. No danger could appal him, no hindrance prevent, even at the greatest personal risk, in relieving from danger and death his fellow-man. No less than seven persons were at different times rescued from drowning by his promptness, energy and benevolence. From the Humane Society he obtained this certificate: —

"The Managers of the Humane Society of Philadelphia, entertaining a grateful sense of the benevolent and successful exertions of JAMES FORTEN in rescuing, at the imminent hazard of his life, four persons from drowning in the river Delaware at different times, to wit: one on the — day, 11th mo., 1805; a second on the — day of 1st mo., 1807; a third on the — day of 4th mo., 1810; and on the — day of 4th mo., 1821, present this Honorary Certificate as a testimony of their approbation of his meritorious conduct.

By order of the Managers,

JOSEPH CRUKESHANK, President.

PHILADELPHIA, Fifth mo., 9th, 1821."

Of his patriotism, who doubts? He gave the best evidence of his love for his country by consecrating his life, in "the times that tried men's souls," to her liberties; and when urged by an honorable gentleman to petition his government for a pension, he promptly declined, saying, "I was a volunteer, sir." In the last war, when an invasion was threatened by the British upon our city, he was found, with twenty of his journeymen, and with hundreds of his persecuted and oppressed brethren, throwing up the redoubts on the west bank of the Schuylkill. Indeed, his interest was so strong in any matter connected with his country, that we would sometimes express our surprise at this. He would reply, "that he had drawn the spirit of her free institutions from his mother's breast, and that he had fought for her independence." With all this, however, his sensitive mind was but too truly pained at her ingratitude, in the wrongs she continued to inflict upon her unoffending and unfortunate children; believing, as he often expressed it, that she would bring down the vengeance of Heaven upon her, and quoting the fearful lines of Jefferson, "I tremble for my country when I remember that God is just, and that his justice will not sleep for ever." Perhaps no instance gave greater poignancy to his feelings than the late atrocious act of the miscalled Reform Convention. For this State, his attachments were peculiar and strong. Here he was born, — his ancestors were residents for upwards of one hundred and seventy years. He had paid a large amount of taxes, and contributed to almost every institution which adorned and beautified this large city. Here had lived a Franklin, Rush, Rawle, Wistar, Vaux, Parrish, and Shipley, the very brightest ornaments of Christian love and philanthropy. Yet no recollection of their principles, no regard for the true policy of this State, or for justice, humanity, or God, could stay the ruthless arms of those marauders upon human liberty from striking down the rights of forty thousand of her tax-paying citizens.

In the year 1800, Mr. Forten addressed a letter to Hon. George Thatcher, in reference to the law of Congress '93, authorising the seizure of fugitive slaves. The letter was intended as an acknowledgment for Mr. Thacher's advocacy of the petition of Mr. Forten and others, remonstrating against the iniquitous law.

In the year 1817, this good man's principles were put the test. Having, at this time, an extended influence, a being prominent in the eyes of the community as a man of singular probity and worth, extorting, even from the jaundiced heart of prejudice, involuntary respect, he was marked by the enemies of freedom, and every device, which the scheme of colonization could invent, was attempted to blind and mislead him. It was about this time, that this society of innate wickedness, mantled in the cloak benevolence, came stalking over the land, so specious and whining in its tone, so soft and insinuating in its low breathings, that many were deceived. But the discriminating mind of JAMES FORTEN penetrated the veil that covered deformed and damning features. The clique of clerical wolves, who had besieged him in tones of flattery, assuring him that he would become the Lord Mansfield of their "Heaven-born republic" on the. western coast of Africa, was told, in the simplicity of truth, but with sarcasm the more cutting because unaffected, "That he would rather remain as James Forten, sail-maker, in Philadelphia, than enjoy the highest offices in the gift of their society." The matter, however, did not rest here with him. He foresaw what would be the evil tendencies and effects of this infamous institution, and the necessity of frustrating the designs of the leagued spirits of this dark crusade against the rapidly improving condition of his people, and of incorporating, at once and for ever, the idea in the public mind, that we were fixtures in this our native country, — "that here we were born, here we would live, and here die." With this view, and having the coöperation of some of the most intelligent of his brethren, among whom were our sterling and inflexible friend to human rights, Robert Douglass, Senr., the good-hearted Absalom Jones, and last, though not least, the founder of your church, that extraordinary man, the Rt. Rev. Bishop Allen, a meeting was called in this church, in the month of January, 1817. The house, upon the occasion, was literally crammed. Mr. Forten presided as chairman, and a beautiful preamble and resolutions, which had been previously prepared, went down, in an unanimous vote, as the death-knell to colonization. Of these resolutions, two were from the pen of Mr. Forten.

[After detailing Mr. F.'s efforts against colonization, Mr. Purvis continues:]

His hand was promptly extended to that pure Christian and exalted philanthropist, WILLIAM, LLOYD GARRISON. He saw in him all those qualities necessary as a leader in the great enterprise; and, in his own language, considered him as a chosen instrument, in the Divine hand, to accomplish the great work of the abolition of American slavery. Indeed, such was his confidence (and justly so) in the principles of the American Anti-Slavery Society, and of the men and women who advocated them, that nothing was ever more painful to his feelings, nothing sooner excited his indignation, than the attempt to cast reproach upon them. The course pursued by Mr. Garrison he ever thought conformable to the true anti-slavery principles; and those principles, founded upon the immutability of eternal truth, had thrown around him, and all others who acted with him, the influences of its divinity. Hence, no difficulties nor dangers have intimidated them, — they have gone on, conquering and to conquer. In no restricted sense, but in its proper signification and application, he was a friend to human rights. The doctrine of "Woman's Rights," as it is called, found in him a zealous friend. He believed that those doctrines would be acknowledged universally, because, as he would say, we live in an enlightened age, — an age which tolerates a free expression of opinion, and leaves the mind to the guidance of its own inwardly revealing light, to the enjoyment of its own individuality; and, setting aside the dogmas and creeds of established usage and custom, unshackles the immortal mind, leaving it free and independent, as it was designed by its bountiful Creator. Yet, while truth, bright, eternal truth, is rising in all the gorgeousness of her transcendental supremacy, there are those who, not more egregiously than pertinaciously, cling to their blindness, their infatuation, meanness, and despotism. But woman is not a mere dependant upon man. The relation is perfectly reciprocal. God has given to both man and woman the same intellectual capacities, and made them subjects alike to the same moral government. He was a man of religion, but no bigot; the last survivor of the founders of St. Thomas's Episcopal Church, and its most liberal patron and friend; and, though connected with this institution for more than fifty years — in close communion with its ordinances for many years back, — he ever valued the spirit of Christianity, exemplified in the character of men, as being of infinitely more importance than a mere unity in doctrinal views and creeds. As a business man, none were more honest and fair — no overreaching, misrepresentations, or deceiving; and, as a remarkable fact in his history, as well as a lesson to others, he never had, as I have often heard him declare, been guilty of that genteel kind of swindling, which all sorts of professedly good people practice, under the gloss of the name of note-shaving.

Temperate in habits, and, more especially, an enemy to all intoxicating drinks, having never taken a glass of ardent spirit in his life, nor permitted its introduction into the premises among those he employed, he was a ready advocate of the blessed cause of temperance, and of all other great moral enterprises which are now so rife in our land. He was a member and the presiding officer of the American Moral Reform Society, from its origin to the time of his death. In a word, whatever was right, useful and patriotic, secured in him a friend, advocate and patron. In the social relations, he was the most affectionate of husbands, and the most indulgent of parents; as a friend, unwavering and steadfast in his attachments.

He was a model, not, as some flippant scribbler asserts, for what are called "colored men," but for all men. His example will ever be worthy of emulation, his virtues never forgotten in the community in which he lived.

Three or four thousand persons, it was believed, attended the funeral of Mr. Forten, one half of whom were white.

Among other reminiscences connected with the Revolution, Mr. Forten often alluded to the part taken by colored men in the war. He saw the regiments from Rhode Island, Connecticut and Massachusetts, when they marched through Philadelphia, to meet Cornwallis, who was then overrunning the South, and said that one or two companies of colored men were attached to each. The vessels of war of that period were all, to a greater or less extent, manned by colored men. On board the Royal Louis, in which Mr. Forten enlisted, there were twenty colored seamen; the Alliance, of thirty-six guns, Commodore Barry, the Trumbull, of thirty-two guns, Captain Nicholson, and the ships South Carolina, Confederacy, and Randolph, were all manned, in part, by colored men.

JOHN B. VASHON.

JOHN BATHAN VASHON was born in Norfolk, Va., in 1792. His mother was a mulatto; his father, Capt. George Vashon, a white man of French ancestry, who was appointed Indian Agent under General Jackson, and retained his office under President Van Buren. Being a colored child, though the offspring of a white man of standing, there was probably no other care taken of his education than is usual for one of his class in the United States, under such circumstances. But John continued to grow a boy of observation, and, as was inseparable from his nature, to be "interested in whatever was interesting to man."

In 1812, during the struggle in which Europe was engaged to avert the danger threatened by the usurpation of Napoleon, and the disturbance of the amicable relations which, for a time, had seemed to exist between the United States and Great Britain, young Vashon, being now twenty years of age, and full of that curiosity which the ardor and romance of youth so naturally inspires, without even the poor consolation, as the only hope for an escape with life or liberty, that he was an acknowledged American citizen, embarked as a common seaman and soldier on board of the old war ship "Revenge," destined to cruise through the West Indies and on the coast of South America. In an engagement on the coast of Brazil, Mr. Vashon, with others, was made prisoner of war by the English. Among his fellow-prisoners was young Henry Bears, now Major Henry Bears, a prominent and affluent old citizen of Pittsburg, Pa., to whom any reference may be made concerning this statement. The prisoners were all released on exchange. On Mr. Vashon's return to Virginia, he settled in Fredericksburg, from whence he removed to Dumfries, and subsequently to Leesburg. While a resident of the latter place, he volunteered in the land service, at a time when the colored people of that neighborhood were called upon to aid in the defence of their country, and prevent the British fleet from ascending the Potomac.

In 1822, he left Leesburg, with his family, (an amiable wife and two children,) and resided in Carlisle, Penn., for seven years. Here he was much respected as a useful member of the community; he was the proprietor of a public saloon, a place of general resort and accommodation for the students of Dickinson College, and the first gentlemen of the town; an extensive livery stable was also a part of the establishment.

He was not content with having served his country, but was desirous of becoming especially useful to his brethren. In 1823, but one year subsequent to his settlement in the town, he assisted in the formation of a mutual improvement association, and was immediately chosen Treasurer, in coöperation with his friend and very useful fellow-citizen, John Peck, as President. This institution was known as the "Lay Benevolent Society."

In 1829, he removed, with his family, (which now had an addition of a son,) to Pittsburg, Pa. Here, also, Mr. Vashon made himself much respected in the community, and quite useful among his brethren. The first public baths in Pittsburg, and probably the first public baths for ladies established west of the mountains, were the result of his exertions. He was among the first to promote the assembling of colored men in National Conventions; and was a prominent advocate of the equality of the white and colored races, always claiming to be an American, — a name which he appeared to love but little less than that of liberty, which it seemed to imply.

Immediately after the National Convention of Colored Men had been field in Philadelphia, Garrison's "Thoughts on Colonization" made its appearance, for which Mr. Vashon was appointed by the author an agent. Through his influence, and that of the book itself, the late Robert Bruce, D. D., then President of the University of Western Pennsylvania, and several other prominent citizens of Pittsburg, formerly earnest advocates of the Colonization Society, were happily converted to anti-slavery views. Mr. Vashon was also a faithful agent for the Liberator in the same district.

In 1833, the first Anti-Slavery Society west of the mountains was organized by him in the front parlor of his homestead. He also promoted the formation of an Educational Institution, and was its first President. Through his efforts, the handsome sum of twelve hundred dollars was contributed in its support, he himself giving, at one time, fifty dollars from his own purse. In 1834, he was elected President of a Temperance Society, and also of a Moral Reform Society, as a testimony to his devoted and assiduous labors in behalf of those movements.

In 1835, being in Boston when the infuriated mob attacked Mr. Garrison, dragging him like a felon through the streets, Mr. Vashon was an eye-witness to the terrible scene, which was heart-rending beyond his ability ever afterwards to express, as, of all living men, JOHN B. VASHON loved WILLIAM LLOYD GARRISON most; and this feeling of affection toward him continued, for aught that is known, till the day of his death. When the mob passed along Washington street, shouting and yelling like madmen the apprehensions of Mr. Vashon became fearfully aroused. Presently there approached a group which appeared even more infuriated than the rest, and he beheld, in the midst of this furious throng, Garrison himself, with a rope round his neck, led on like a beast to the slaughter. He had been on the field of battle, had faced the cannon's mouth, seen its lightnings flash and heard its thunders roar, but such a sight as this was more than the old citizen-soldier could bear, without giving vent to a flood of tears.

The next day, the old soldier, who had helped to preserve his country's liberty on the plighted faith of security to his own, but who had lived to witness freedom of speech and of the press stricken down by mob violence, and life itself in jeopardy, because that liberty was asked for him and his, with spirits crushed and faltering hopes, called to administer a word of consolation to the bold and courageous young advocate of immediate and universal emancipation. Mr. Garrison subsequently thus referred to this circumstance in his paper: — "On the day of the riot in Boston, he dined at my house, and the next morning called to see me in prison, bringing with him a new hat for me, in the place of one that was cut by the knives of the 'men of property and standing from all parts of the city.'" In this, he proved a "ministering angel" to the philanthropist in time of trouble.

Mr. Vashon was zealous in promoting the education of his children. One daughter was sent to the excellent Female Academy of Miss Sarah M. Douglass, in Philadelphia, and his son to the Oberlin Collegiate Institute, where he graduated with the first honors of his class, and delivered the valedictory. He subsequently studied in the law office of the late Hon. Walter Forward, ex-Secretary of the U. S. Treasury, and more recently Presiding Judge in the Western District of Pennsylvania.

A circumstance well worthy of record took place during the exemplary efforts of this good old American patriot in preparing his children to fill useful positions in society. During the collegiate course of his son, (his daughter having previously finished her education,) a change in his circumstances induced a friend to propose recalling his son George from college.

"I will never do it!" was the positive reply.

"How can you do otherwise? you must live," said his adviser.

"I will stint my market basket," rejoined the old gentleman.

"Yes, but you can't do without eating," continued his friend.

"No, but I can eat less, and economise by selecting cheaper articles of food," replied the devoted father.

"That will do well enough to talk about, friend Vashon, but when it comes to the test, that's another thing."

"Friend J.," replied the old gentleman, with feeling, "as God is my judge, I will live on potatoes and herring, and see the last piece of furniture sold out of my house, before my son shall be left without an education. When he come from that school, he will have finished his education."

Finding that it was in vain to attempt to advise so contrary to his feelings and designs, his friend left him. His son did return, indeed, a scholar of the highest order, and is now Professor of Belles Lettres in Central College, McGrawville, N. Y. When he applied for admission to the bar, it was granted, after a successful examination in open Court in New York city.

Mr. Vashon was one of the Vice Presidents of the National Convention of Colored Men, held at Rochester, July, 1853, and was subsequently chosen a member of the Pennsylvania State Council. On the 8th of January, 1854, National Convention of the old soldiers of 1812 was held in the city of Philadelphia. This gathering of veterans aroused the military fire in the old man's breast, and, never having received a pension, nor government lands, for his services, he determined on taking his seat, as a soldier delegate, among the defenders of his country. He was amply supplied with letters and certificates from distinguished gentlemen in his adopted city. In the best of spirits and hopes, he set out on his mission to the State Council and the Military Convention. He had proceeded as far as the depot, when, (he was of corpulent person,) resting on his trunk for relief from his fatigue, Death, that untiring, but ever certain messenger, unexpectedly summoned him home to his fathers.

Thus departed the good old citizen-soldier, clothed in the vesture of peace and war. In the language of one of his friends, in an editorial column, "he fell with his harness on, and died in the last act of service to his brethren, and in obedience to the summons of his country, in the person of one of her delegated warriors."

MAJOR JEFFREY.

Among the brave blacks who fought in the battle for American liberty was one whose name stands at the head of this brief notice. Major Jeffrey was a Tennesseean, and, during the campaign of Major-General Andrew Jackson in Mobile, filled the place of "regular" among the soldiers. In the charge made by General Stump against the enemy, the Americans were repulsed and thrown into disorder, — Major Stump being forced to retire, in a manner by no means desirable, under the circumstances. Major Jeffrey, who was but a common soldier, seeing the condition of his comrades, and comprehending the disastrous results about to befall them, rushed forward, mounted a horse, took command of the troops, and, by an heroic effort, rallied them to the charge, — completely routing the enemy, who left the Americans masters of the field. He at once received from the General the title of "Major," though he could not, according to the American policy, so commission him. To the day of his death, he was known by that title in Nashville, where he resided, and the circumstances which entitled him to it were constantly the subject of popular conversation.

Major Jeffrey was highly respected by the whites generally, and revered, in his own neighborhood, by all the colored people who knew him.

A few years ago, receiving an indignity from a common ruffian, he was forced to strike him in self-defence; for which act, in accordance with the laws of slavery in that, as well as in many other of the slave States, he was compelled to receive, on his naked person, nine and thirty lashes with a raw hide! This, at the age of seventy odd, after the distinguished services rendered his country, — probably when the white ruffian for whom he was tortured was unable to raise an arm in its defence, — was more than he could bear; it broke his heart, and he sank to rise no more, till summoned by the blast of the last trumpet to stand on the battle-field of the general resurrection.

JOHNSON AND DAVIS.

The names of these brave heroes, JOHNSON and DAVIS, have no where appeared in American history, though, in reality, a part of the history of the times in which they lived. The Pittsburg Dispatch, a daily independent paper, of December 19, 1854, has the following notice of them: —

"We are indebted to a friend for a copy of the Pittsburg Mercury, of March 9, 1814 — nearly forty-one years old. The paper was in its second year, published by John M. Snowden, Esq. Pittsburg was then a borough. The war between England and this country was raging, and the paper is chiefly filled with reports of land and naval operations. General Hull's trial for the surrender of Detroit was then pending. The frigate President had just returned from a cruise, in which she had run past the blockading fleet, succeeded in destroying a number of English merchant vessels, and rescued the American schooner Comet, which had been captured by the enemy; the privateer Governor Tompkins had also returned home, after escaping from an English frigate, from which she had 'caught a tartar,' having mistaken her for a merchantman. The only persons killed on board the General Tompkins were two colored seamen, JOHN JOHNSON and JOHN DAVIS, of whom Captain Shaler makes this mention: —

"The name of one of my poor fellows who was killed ought to be registered in the books of Fame, and remembered with reverence as long as bravery is considered a virtue. He was a black man by the name of JOHN JOHNSON. A twenty-four pound shot struck him in the hip, and took away all the lower part; of his body. In this state, the poor, brave fellow lay on the deck, and several times exclaimed to his shipmates, "Fire away, my boys! — No haul a color down!"

"'The other was also a black man, by the name of JOHN DAVIS, and was struck in much the same way. He fell near me, and several times requested to be thrown overboard, saying he was only in the way of others. While America has such tars, she has little to fear from the tyrants of Europe.'"

On the capture of Washington by the British forces, it was judged expedient to fortify, without delay, the principal towns and cities exposed to similar attacks. The Vigilance Committee of Philadelphia waited upon three of the principal colored citizens, namely, JAMES FORTEN, BISHOP ALLEN, and ABSALOM JONES, soliciting the aid of the people of color in erecting suitable defences for the city. Accordingly, two thousand five hundred colored men assembled in the State House yard, and from thence marched to Gray's ferry where they labored for two days, almost without intermission. Their labors were so faithful and efficient, that a vote of thanks was tendered them by the Committee. A battalion of colored troops was at the same time organized in the city, under an officer of the United States army; and they were on the point of marching to the frontier, when peace was proclaimed.

In a letter written during the week of the mob against the colored people, August, 1842, Henry C. Wright, says: —

"A colored man, whom I visited in the hospital, called to see me to-day. He had just got out, and looked very pitiful. His head was bent down; he said he could not erect it, his neck was so injured. He is a very intelligent man, and can read and write. His name is CHARLES BLACK and he resides in Lombard street. He was at home, with his little boy, unconscious of what was transpiring without. Suddenly, the mob rushed into his room, dragged him down stairs, and beat him so unmercifully, that he would have been killed, had not some humane individuals interposed, and prevented further violence. He was an impressed seaman on board an English sixty-four gun-ship, in the beginning of the war of 1812. When he heard of the war, he refused to fight against his country, although he had nine hundred dollars prize-money coming to him from the ship. He was, therefore placed in irons, and kept a prisoner on board some time, and then sent to the well-known Dartmoor prison. He was exchanged, and shipped for France. Shortly afterwards, he was taken and sent back to Dartmoor — was exchanged a second time, and succeeded in reaching the United States. He soon joined the fleet on Lake Champlain, under M'Donough; was with him in the celebrated battle which gave honor (?) to the American arms. He was wounded, but never received a pension. His father was in the battle of Bunker Hill, and his grandfather fought in the old French War."

JAMES DERHAM, originally a slave in Philadelphia, was transferred by his master to a physician, who gave him a subordinate employment as preparer of drugs. During the American War, he was sold by this physician to a surgeon, and by the surgeon to Robert Dove, of New Orleans. Learned in the languages, he speaks with facility English, French and Spanish. In 1778, at the age of twenty-one, he became the most distinguished physician at New Orleans. "I conversed with him on medicine,", says Dr. Rush, "and found him very learned. I thought I could give him information concerning the treatment of diseases, but I learned more from him than he could expect from me."

WILLIAM BURLEIGH was a soldier in the war of 1812, and fought in the battle of North Point. He was recognised by the proper authorities, and participated in the Anniversary of Veterans, celebrated at Philadelphia, December, 1853.

A digression from the military services of colored men those rendered voluntarily, by the same despised and persecuted class, in a time of pestilence, seems to me warrantable in this connection.

In the autumn of 1793, the yellow fever broke out in Philadelphia with peculiar malignity. The insolent and unnatural distinctions of caste were overturned, and the colored people were solicited, in the public papers, to come forward and assist the perishing sick. The same mouth which had gloried against them in prosperity, in its overwhelming adversity implored their assistance. The colored people of Philadelphia nobly responded. The then Mayor Matthew Clarkson, received their deputation with respect, and commended their course. They appointed ABSALOM JONES and WILLIAM GRAY to superintend the operations, the Mayor advertising the public that, by applying to them, aid could be obtained. This took place about September. Soon afterwards, the sickness increased so dreadfully, that it became next to impossible to remove the corpses. The colored people volunteered this painful and dangerous duty — did it extensively, and hired help in doing it. Dr. Rush instructed the two superintendents in the proper precautions and measures to be used.

A sick white man crept to his chamber window, and entreated the passers-by to bring him a drink of water. Several white men passed but hurried on. A foreigner came up — paused — was afraid to supply with this own hands, but stood and offered eight dollars to whomsoever would. At length, a poor black man appeared; he heard — stopped — ran for water — took it to the sick man; and then stayed by to nurse him, steadily and mildly refusing all pecuniary compensation.

SARAH BOSS, a poor black widow, was active in voluntary and benevolent services.

A poor black man, named SAMPSON, went constantly from house to house, giving assistance every where gratuitously, until he was seized with the fever and died.

MARY SCOTT, a woman of color, attended Mr. Richard Mason and his son so kindly and disinterestedly, that the widow, Mrs. R. Mason, settled an annuity of six pounds upon her for life.

An elderly black nurse, going about most diligently and affectionately, when asked what pay she wished, used to say, "A dinner, massa, some cold winter's day."

A young, black woman was offered any price, if she would attend a white merchant and his wife. She would take no money, but went, saying that, if she went from holy love, she might hope to be preserved, but not if she went for money. She was seized with the fever, but recovered.

A black man, riding through the streets, saw a white man push a white woman out of the house. The woman staggered forward, fell in the gutter, and was too weak to rise. The black man dismounted, and took her gently to the hospital at Bush-Hill.

ABSALOM JONES and WILLIAM GRAY, the colored superintendents, say, — "A white man threatened to shoot us if we passed by his house with a corpse. We buried him three days afterwards."

About twenty times as many black nurses as white were thus employed during the sickness.

The following certificate was subsequently given by the Mayor: —

"Having, during the prevalence of the late malignant disorder, had almost daily opportunities of seeing the conduct of ABSALOM JONES and RICHARD ALLEN, and the people employed by them to bury the dead, I with cheerfulness give this testimony of my approbation of their proceedings, as far as the same came under my notice. Their diligence, attention, and decency of deportment, afforded me, at the time, much satisfaction.

(Signed,) MATTHEW CLARKSON, Mayor.

PHILADELPHIA, Jan. 23, 1794."

Some years since, a singular incident occurred in one of the courts of Philadelphia. When the Sheriff was calling over the names of the jury, he summoned, among others, "George Jones."

"Here, Sir," answered a voice from the crowd, and a colored man came forth and took his seat in the jury-box.

"Here is some mistake," said the Sheriff.

"No mistake at all," replied the juror. "Here is your summons; my name has been regularly drawn, and is on the jury list."

The Judge interfered, — "You may retire," said he.

"I'd rather not, Sir. I am willing to perform my duty."

Here was a dilemma. There was nothing in the law to exclude a colored man from the jury box, and the Court was at a loss what to do. At length, the juryman was challenged by one of the parties, and had to leave the box.

This is, perhaps, the only instance of such an error though it might be supposed that it would be of frequent, occurrence.

The devotion and services of colored Pennsylvanians have been rewarded by the exclusion of fifty-two thousand of their number from the ballot-box. An effort, however, has been recently commenced for restoring to them the franchise, which, we trust, will soon be successful.

In a very neatly printed pamphlet, prepared by a Committee of the Colored Citizens of Philadelphia, asking for the same right of suffrage they enjoyed for forty-seven years prior to the adoption of the present Constitution, in 1838, it is stated, that they number 30,000 persons in Philadelphia; that they possess $2,685,693 of real and personal estate; and have paid $9,766.42 for taxes during the past year, and $392,7792.27 for house, water, and ground rent. Frederick Douglass, in his paper, says of the people of color in Philadelphia, and of the State at large: —

"They buy and sell property, own lumber yards, (two of the most extensive, if not the largest, lumber merchants in the State are colored men,) and till the soil: there are mechanics, professional men, and artists, among them; they are developing, not only their identity, but their equality, with the whites."

We rejoice (says the National Era) in these assurance of the success of the partial freedom enjoyed by the negro race in Pennsylvania, and sincerely hope that every man of them may continue true and steadfast in the judicious defence of their cause, until the justice shall be accorded to industry, intelligence, and wealth, that has been withheld from poverty and ignorance.

CHAPTER IX: DELAWARE.

In the engravings of Washington crossing the Delaware on the evening previous to the battle of Trenton, Dec. 25, 1779, a colored soldier is seen, on horseback, quite prominent, near the Commander-in-Chief, — the same figure that, in other sketches, is seen pulling the stroke oar in that memorable crossing. This colored soldier was PRINCE WHIPPLE, body-guard to Gen. Whipple, of New Hampshire, who was Aid to General Washington.

PRINCE WHIPPLE was born at Amabou, Africa, of comparatively wealthy parents. When about ten years of age, he was sent by them, in company with a cousin, to America, to be educated. An elder brother had returned four years before, and his parents were anxious that their other child should receive the same benefits. The captain who brought the two boys over proved a treacherous villain, and carried them to Baltimore, where he exposed them for sale, and they were both purchased by Portsmouth men, Prince falling to Gen. Whipple. He was emancipated during the war, was much esteemed, and was once entrusted by the General with a large sum of money to carry from Salem to Portsmouth. He was attacked on the road, near Newburyport, by two ruffians; one he struck with a loaded whip, the other he shot, and succeeded in arriving home in safety.

Prince was beloved by all who knew him. He was the "Caleb Quotem" of Portsmouth, where. he died at the age of thirty-two, leaving a widow and children. Their descendants now reside in that place, one being married to Dr. Isaac H. Snowden, son of Rev. Samuel Snowden, of Boston.

Delaware is yet disgraced by a statute forbidding the immigration of free colored persons. Even her own native-born colored citizens, on absenting themselves, cannot return to the State without being liable to fines and imprisonment. A colored man from Columbia, Penn., some six years since, going into the State, was informed against, and fined by a magistrate fifty dollars, after he had been some time in prison. That noble friend of humanity, THOMAS GARRETT, paid his fine and costs, — about eighty-six dollars, (a portion of which was contributed, in Pennsylvania.) The facts were published, when the magistrate sued Mr. Garrett for libel, and he was bound over in the sum of one thousand dollars. The magistrate committed an act of dishonesty, left his family and the State several years to avoid prosecution, and finally his friends obtained a pardon from the Governor, and he returned, and was reappointed magistrate. Mr. Garrett, fearing that, as he had once absented himself, he might do so again, had him bound over in the sum of five hundred dollars to prosecute the charge; but Mr. Garrett has not been troubled on the subject since.

I learn from Mr. Garrett that three arrests have since been made in Newcastle county, but the law was so odious, that the magistrates, fearing their credit would be injured, released the men on their own recognizance, and they left the State. Judge Booth states that a colored girl, in order to obtain better wages, left her parents in Sussex and crossed over to Jersey, where she remained two years. Her mother was then taken ill, and she returned home to nurse her. After she died, before the funeral, some fiend in human shape informed against her. The magistrate issued the writ, and the constable served it before the corpse left the house. Such was the indignation of the neighborhood, however, (slaveholders though they were,) that the informer and constable would have been mobbed if they had not desisted from their attempt. The girl remained at her father's house unmolested.

CHAPTER X: MARYLAND.

A CORRESPONDENT of the New Orleans Picayune gives the following account of THOMAS SAVOY, a "Negro Veteran," as he was called: —

"Few persons, we think, have travelled in Texas, who have not heard of THOMAS SAVOY, alias Black Tom, alias the Special Citizen of Baxar county. He was by trade barber, but by inclination a soldier, and his history is intimately connected with the warlike part of that of Texas. He was much fonder, too, of the company of white men than of that of persons of his own color. Tom was native of Maryland, then a citizen of Washington, D. C., then a resident of Mississippi, whence he emigrated to Texas at the beginning of the Revolution, with a company of Mississippi volunteers, his razor in his pocket, and gun on his shoulder. They joined Gen. Houston shortly after the battle of San Jacinto, but Black Tom's subsequent conduct as a soldier elicited the praise of his hard-fighting comrades and superior officers. The year 1839 was, distinguished in Texan annals by the expedition under Jordan to Saltillo, to assist the treacherous Canales in his armed Federalist attempt against the Mexican Anti-Federalists. He betrayed his little band of Texan allies, but they their gallant leader gave the united Federalists and the State Rights Mexican army two its thorough consecutive drubbings as they ever received, and then returned leisurely home without interruption. Black Tom was one of Jordan's men, and if he had little occasion or time to use his razor, he made up for it by a skilful handling of his offensive weapons. In 1842, Gen. Woll invaded Texas with a Mexican army, and got a good beating at the battle of Salado. Tom was in the midst of it, and was wounded. He participated in several subsequent conflicts with the Indians, fighting bravely as usual. He followed his old Texan comrades under Taylor's banner, and hurried along with them into battle at Monterey. He was also in the memorable struggle of Buena Vista. Black Tom then returned to Texas with the Kentucky volunteers, and after that, San Antonio became his head-quarters. He was, of course, a general favorite, and lived like a lord; but the wandering spirit that ten years in Texas had made second nature with him, would now and then break out, and Black Tom would be missing. The next thing heard of him, he was at a frontier post, or far up in the Indian country, in the midst of danger. On the

15th of July, 1853, the body of a man was found two miles west of San Antonio. A coroner's inquest was held, and a verdict returned of 'Came to his death from cause unknown.' The body was that of old Tom!"

THOMAS HOLLEN, of Dorset county, Maryland, was in the Revolutionary War, attached to the regiment of Col. Charles Gouldsbury, and was wounded by a musket ball in the calf of his leg. He died in 1816, aged seventy-two, at the town of Blackwood, N. J., and was buried in the Snowhill church-yard, east of Woodbury. He had an uncle who fought by his side in the same war. Rev. James Hollen, of the African M. E. Church, is a nephew Thomas Hollen.

JOHN MOORE was skipper of the sloop Roebuck, one hundred and ten tons, which was captured in Chesapeake Bay, between Spry and Poole's Islands, by the British seventy-four Dragon. He was placed on board the brig Bashaw, when, provoked by insolent treatment, he struck an officer with the tiller, for which he was detained prison at Halifax for eighteen months. The sloop and cargo were confiscated. Mr. Moore now resides in Newport, R. I.

BENJAMIN BANNEKER.

BENJAMIN BANNEKER was born in Baltimore county, near the village of Ellicott's Mills, in the year 1732. His father was a native African, and his mother the child natives of Africa; so that, to no admixture of the blood the white man was he indebted for his peculiar and extraordinary abilities. His father was a slave when he married but his wife, who was a free woman, and possessed of great energy and industry, very soon afterwards purchased his freedom. Banneker's mother was named Morton before her marriage, and belonged to a family remarkable for its intelligence. When upwards of seventy, she was still very active; and it is remembered of her, that at this advanced age, she made nothing of catching her chickens, when wanted, by running them down. A nephew of hers, Greenbury Morton, was a person of note, notwithstanding his complexion. Prior to 1809, free people of color, possessed of a certain property qualification, voted in Maryland. In that year, a law was passed, restricting the right of voting to free white males. Morton was ignorant of the law till he offered to vote at the polls in Baltimore county; and it is said, that, when his vote was refused, he addressed the crowd in a strain of pure and impassioned eloquence, which kept the audience, that the election had assembled, the breathless attention while he spoke.

When Benjamin was old enough, he was employed to assist his parents in their labor. This was at an early age, when his destiny seemed nothing better than that of a child of poor and ignorant free negroes, occupying a few acres of land, in a remote and thinly peopled neighborhood; a destiny which, certainly, at this day, is not of very brilliant promise, and which, at the time in question, must been gloomy enough. In the intervals of toil, and when he was approaching, or had attained, manhood, he was scent to an obscure and distant country school, which he attended until he had acquired a knowledge of reading and writing, and had advanced in arithmetic as far as Double Position. In all matters, beyond these rudiments of learning, he was his own instructor. On leaving school, he was obliged to labor for years, almost uninterruptedly, for his support. But his memory being retentive, he lost nothing of the little education he had acquired. On the contrary, although utterly destitute of books, he amplified and improved his stock of arithmetical knowledge by the operation of his mind alone. He was an acute observer of every thing that he saw, or which took place around him in the natural world, and he sought with avidity information from all sources of what was going forward in society; so that he became gradually possessed of a fund of general knowledge which it was difficult to find among those, even, who were far more favored by opportunity and circumstances than he was. At first, his information was a subject of remark and wonder among his illiterate neighbors only; but, by degrees, the reputation of it spread through a wider circle; and Benjamin Banneker, still a young man, came to be thought of as one, who could not only perform all the operations of mental arithmetic with extraordinary facility, but exercise a sound and discriminating judgment upon men and things. It was at this time, when he was about thirty years of age, that he contrived and made a clock, which proved an excellent time-piece. He had seen a watch, but not a clock — such an article not yet having found its way into the quiet and secluded valley in which he lived. The watch was, therefore, his model. It took him a good while to accomplish this feat; his great difficulty, as he often used to say, being to make the hour, minute, and second hands, correspond in their motions. But the clock was finished at last, and raised still higher the credit of Banneker in his neighborhood as an ingenious man, as well as a good arithmetician.

As already stated, the basis of Banneker's arithmetical knowledge was obtained from the school book in which he had advanced as far as Double Position; but, in 1787, Mr. George Ellicott lent him Mayer's Tables,

Ferguson's Astronomy, and Leadbeater's Lunar Tables. Along with these books were some astronomical instruments. Mr. Ellicott was accidentally prevented from giving Banneker any information as to the use of either books or instruments at the time he lent them; but, before he again met him, (and the interval was a brief one,) Banneker was independent of any instruction, and was already absorbed in the contemplation of the new world which was thus opened to his view. From this time, the study of astronomy became the great object of his life, and, for a season, he almost disappeared from the sight of his neighbors.

Very soon after the possession of the books already mentioned had drawn Banneker's attention to astronomy, he determined to compile an almanac, that being the most familiar use that occurred to him of the information he had acquired. Of the labor of the work, few of those can form an estimate, who would at this day commence such a task with all the assistance afforded by accurate tables and well digested rules. Banneker had no such aid; and it is narrated as a well-known fact, that he commenced and had advanced far in the preparation of the logarithms necessary for his purpose, when he was furnished with a set of table by Mr. George Ellicott. About this time, he began the record of his calculations, which is still in existence, and is left with the society for examination.

The first almanac which Banneker prepared, fit for publication, was for the year 1792. By this time, his acquirements had become generally known, and among others who took an interest in him was James McHenry, Esq. Mr. McHenry wrote a letter to Goddard & Angell, then the almanac publishers in Baltimore, which was probably the means of procuring the publication of the first almanac.

In their editorial notice, Messrs. Goddard & Angell say "They feel gratified in the opportunity of presenting to the public, through their press, what must be considered as an extraordinary effort of genius; a complete and accurate Ephemeris for the year 1792, calculated by a sable descendant of Africa," &c. And they further say "That they flatter themselves that a philanthropic public, in this enlightened era, will be induced to give their patronage and support to this work, not only on account of its intrinsic merits, (it having met the approbation of several of the most distinguished astronomers of America, particularly the celebrated Mr. Rittenhouse,) but from similar motives to those which induced the editors to give this calculation the preference, — the ardent desire of drawing modest merit from obscurity, and controverting the long-established illiberal prejudice against the blacks."

The motives alluded to by Goddard & Angell, in the extracts just quoted, of doing justice to the intellect of the colored race, were a prominent object with Banneker himself; and the only occasions when he overstepped a modesty which was his peculiar characteristic, were, when he could, by so doing, "controvert the long-established illiberal prejudice against the blacks." We find him, therefore, sending a copy of his first almanac to Mr. Jefferson, the Secretary of State under General Washington, with an excellent letter, to which Mr. Jefferson made the following reply: —

PHILADELPHIA, Aug. 31, 1791.

Sir, — I thank you sincerely for your letter of the 19th instant, and for the almanac it contained. Nobody wishes more than I do to see such proofs as you exhibit, that Nature has given to our black brethren talents equal to those of the other colors of men, and that the appearance of a want of them is owing only to the degraded condition of their existence, both in Africa and America. I can add, with truth, that no one wishes more ardently to see a good system commenced for raising the condition, both of their body and mind, to what it ought to be, as fast as the imbecility of their present existence, and other circumstances which cannot be neglected, will admit. I have taken the liberty of sending your almanac to Monsieur de Condorcet, Secretary of the Academy of Sciences, at Paris, and members of the Philanthropic Society, because I considered it a document to which your whole color had a right, for their justification against the doubts which have been entertained of them.

I am, with great esteem, sir,

Your most obedient servant,

THO. JEFFERSON.

{Mr. BENJAMIN BANNEKER, near Ellicott's

Lower Mills, Baltimore county.}

When he published his first almanac, Banneker was fifty-nine years old, and had high respect paid to him by all the scientific men of the country, as one whose color did not prevent his belonging to the same class, as far as intellect went, with themselves. After the adoption of the Constitution in 1789, commissioners were appointed to run the lines of the District of Columbia, the ten miles square now occupied by the seat of government, and then called the "Federal Territory." The commissioners invited

Banneker to be present at the runnings, and treated him with much consideration.

Banneker continued to calculate and publish his almanacs until 1802, and the folio already referred to and now before the society, contains the calculations clearly copied, and the figures used by him in his work. The hand-writing, it will be seen, is very good, and remarkably distinct, having a practised look, although evidently that of an old man, who makes his letters and figures slowly and carefully. His letter to Mr. Jefferson gives a very good idea of his style of composition, and his ability as a writer. The title of the almanac is here transcribed at length, as a matter of curious interest at this latter day. If it claims little of the art and elegance and wit of the almanacs of Punch or of Hood, it is, nevertheless, considering its history, a far more surprising production.

"Benjamin Banneker's Pennsylvania, Delaware, Virginia, and Maryland Almanac and Ephemeris, for the year of our Lord 1792, being Bissextile or leap year, and the sixteenth year of American Independence, which commenced July 4, 1776: containing the motions of the Sun and Moon, the true places and aspects of the Planets, the rising and setting of the Sun, and the rising, setting, and southing, place and age of the Moon, &c. The Lunations, Conjunctions, Eclipses, Judgment of the Weather, Festivals, and remarkable days."

In 1804, Banneker died, in the seventy-second year of his age, and his remains are deposited, without a stone to mark the spot, near the dwelling which he occupied during his life-time.

During the whole of his long life, he lived respectably and much esteemed by all who became acquainted with him, but more especially by those who could fully appreciate his genius and the extent of his acquirements. Although his mode of life was regular and extremely retired, living alone, having never married, — cooking his own victuals and washing his own clothes, and scarcely ever being absent from home, — yet there was nothing misanthropic in his character; for a gentleman who knew him, thus speaks of him: — "I recollect him well. He was a brave looking, pleasant man, with something very noble in his appearance. His mind was evidently much engrossed in his calculations; but he was glad always to receive the visits which we often paid to him." Another of Mr. Ellicott's correspondents writes as follows: — "When I was a boy, I became very much interested in him, (Banneker,) as his manners were those of a perfect gentleman; kind, generous, hospitable, humane, dignified and pleasing, abounding in information on all the various subjects and incidents of the day; very modest and unassuming, and delighting in society at his own house. I have seen him frequently. His head was covered with a thick suit of white hair, which gave him a very venerable and dignified appearance. His dress was uniformly of superfine drab broadcloth, made in the old style of a plain coat, with a straight collar and long waistcoat, and a broad-brimmed hat. His color was not jet black, but decidedly negro. In size and personal appearance, the statue of Franklin, at the Library in Philadelphia, as seer from the street, is a perfect likeness of him."

The foregoing account of Mr. Banneker is taken from a Memoir read before the Historical Society of Maryland, by JOHN H. B. LATROBE, which was undoubtedly published to serve the purposes of the American Colonization Society. Rev. JOHN T. RAYMOND, a distinguished colored Baptist clergyman, issued an edition of the pamphlet, in the pre face to which he says: — "I have snatched it from their [the Colonizationists] foul purpose, in order to produce a contrary effect. Our people are now too wise to be entangled in their meshes."

FRANCES ELLEN WATKINS.

Maryland has not only produced gifted colored men but has contributed a fair proportion of women who have proved good their claim to equality. FRANCES ELLEN WATKINS, born in Baltimore, has contended with a thousand disadvantages from early life, and though now a young woman, is actively engaged, on her own responsibility, as an Anti-Slavery lecturer in the Eastern States. She has published a small volume of poems, which certainly are very creditable to her, both in a literary and moral point of view, and indicate the possession of a talent, which, if carefully cultivated, and properly encouraged, cannot fail to secure for herself a poetic reputation, and to deepen the interest already so extensively felt in the liberation and enfranchisement of the entire colored race.

I make the following brief extracts from her book, which is entitled, "Poems and Miscellaneous Writings, by Frances Ellen Watkins."

ELIZA HARRIS.

Like a fawn from the arrow, startled and wild,
A woman swept by us, bearing a child;
In her eye was the night of a settled despair,
And her brow was o'ershaded with anguish and care.

She was nearing the river, — in reaching the brink,
She heeded no danger, she paused not to think
For she is a mother, — her child is a slave, —
And she'll give him his freedom, or find him a grave!

But she's free! — yes, free from the land where the slave
From the hand of oppression must rest in the grave;
Where bondage and torture, where scourges and chains,
Have placed on our banner indelible stains.

The bloodhounds have raised the scent of her way;
The hunter is rifled and foiled of his prey;
Fierce jargon and cursing, with clanking of chains,
Make sounds of strange discord on Liberty's plains.

With the rapture of love and fullness of bliss,
She placed on his brow a mother's fond kiss: —
Oh! poverty, danger and death she can brave,
For the child of her love is no longer a slave!

CHRISTIANITY.

Christianity is a system claiming God for its author and the welfare of man for its object. It is a system so uniform, exalted and pure, that the loftiest intellects have acknowledged its influence, and acquiesced in the justness of its claims. Genius has bent from his erratic course to gather fire from her altars, and pathos from the agony of Gethsemane and the sufferings of Calvary. Philosophy and science have paused amid their speculative researches and wondrous revelations, to gain wisdom from her teachings and knowledge from her precepts. Poetry has culled her fairest flowers and wreathed her softest, to bind her Author's "bleeding brow." Music has strung her sweetest lyres and breathed her noblest strains to celebrate his fame; whilst Learning has bent from her lofty heights to bow at the lowly cross. The constant friend of man, she has stood by him in his hour of greatest need. She has cheered the prisoner in his cell, and strengthened the martyr at the stake. She has nerved the frail and shrinking heart of woman for high and holy deeds. The worn and weary have rested their fainting heads upon her bosom, and gathered strength from her words and courage from her counsels. She has been the staff of decrepit age, and the joy of manhood in its strength. She has bent over the form of lovely childhood, and suffered it to have a place in the Redeemer's arms. She has stood by the bed of the dying, and unveiled the glories of eternal life; gilding the darkness of the tomb with the glory of the resurrection.

CHAPTER XI: VIRGINIA.

THE Lancaster (Ohio) Gazette, February, 1849, announces the death, at that place, of SAMUEL JENKINS, a colored man, aged 115 years. He was a slave of Capt. Breadwater, in Fairfax county, Virginia, in 1771, and participated in the memorable Campaign of Gen. Braddock.

ISHMAEL TITUS (says the Springfield Republican) died in Williamstown, Mass., January 27th, 1855, at the extraordinary age of 109 or 110 years. He was born a slave in Virginia, and when Gen. Braddock set out on his ill-fated expedition, the master of Ishmael was employed by the Commissary to transport subsistence stores for the army; and, as the wagon was heavily loaded, an additional horse was added to the team, and the boy Ishmael was placed on this third horse as rider; and in that capacity, he followed the army to the scene of its disaster. Like most of the slaves, he had no distinct knowledge of his age; but, judging from his recollection of the event, and his own story, he must have been nine or ten years old at the time. His mental faculties were remarkably active for a person of his years, and after the lapse of nearly a century, he was wont to recount the striking impression made upon his young mind by the red coats of the British soldiers, which he supposed were "colored with blood," — unfortunately too true in this instance.

He ran away from his master, and went into the vicinity of Springfield, Mass., about the close of the Revolution, and was then, apparently, thirty-eight or forty years of age. His story has always been consistent, and no one in that place has ever doubted its correctness. His mind seemed more than a match for his body, and physical infirmities crept upon him, until he seemed to realize all the evils which afflicted "Uncle Ned," and, like him, it is to be hoped that he has received his reward.

Hiram Wilson says that an extremely aged woman lives at the Grand River settlement, Canada, who was a slave girl in Virginia at the time of the French and Indian War of 1755. At the time of the Revolutionary War, she was employed in running bullets for the Americans. Her patriotism was but miserably rewarded, for she was held as a slave till she was about eighty years of age, when she fled to Canada for freedom, where, under monarchical institutions and laws, she is protected in her old age. No one can reasonably rebuke her, for the utterance of an earnest "God save the Queen!"

The Legislature of Virginia, in 1783, emancipated several slaves who had fought in the Revolutionary War, and the example was followed by some individuals, who wished to exhibit a consistency of conduct rare even in those early days of our country's history. The Baltimore papers of September 8th, 1790, make mention of the fact that Hon. General Gates, before taking his departure, will, his lady, for their new and elegant seat on the banks of the East River, summoned his numerous family and slaves about him, and, amidst their tears of affection and gratitude, gave them their freedom; and, what was still better, made provision that their liberty should be a blessing to them.

Sometimes, for other than national services, the colored man's worth is appreciated by men who claim the right to own their brother-men, as is seen in the following clause from the Will of A. P. Upsher, a member of President Tyler's Cabinet: —

"3. I emancipate, and set free, my servant, DAVID RICH, and direct my executors to give him one hundred dollars. I recommend him, in the strongest manner, to the respect, esteem and confidence of any community in which he may happen to live. He has been my slave for twenty-four years, during which time he has been trusted to every extent, and in every respect. My confidence in him has been unbounded; his relation to myself and family has always been such as to afford him daily opportunities to deceive and injure us, and yet he has never been detected in a serious fault, nor even in an intentional breach of the decorums of his station. His intelligence is of a high order, his integrity above all suspicion, and his sense of right and propriety always correct, and even delicate and refined. I feel that he is justly entitled to carry this certificate from me into the new relations which he now must form. It is due to his long and most faithful services, and to the sincere and steady friendship which I bear him. In the uninterrupted and confidential intercourse of twenty-four years, I have never given, nor had occasion to give him, an unpleasant word. I know no man who has fewer faults, or more excellencies, than he."

Throughout this work will be found allusions to several colored persons, bond and free, who were either servants or slaves of General Washington, or through some other relation, were led to cherish grateful and pleasant memories of the treatment they received from him. Some he manumitted, others he specially rewarded for deeds of valor and integrity of conduct;

and, though he did not emancipate the majority of his own slaves until after the decease of Lady Washington, there yet seemed a constant struggle of his better nature to do that which, neglected, has left

— "Posterity's sad eye to run

Along one line, with slaves and Washington."

In a letter written by General Washington to Tobias Lear, in England, in 1794, he assigns the following reasons for empowering Mr. Lear to sell a portion of his landed estate: —

"I have no scruple in disclosing to you, that my motives to these sales are to reduce my income, be it more or less, to specialities, — that the remainder of my days may thereby be more tranquil and free from care, and that I may be enabled, knowing what my dependence is, to do as much good as my resources will admit; for although, in the estimation of the world, I possess a good and clear estate, yet so unproductive is it, that I am oftentimes ashamed to refuse aid which I cannot afford unless I sell part of it to answer this purpose. Besides these, I have another motive, which makes me earnestly wish for these things — it is, indeed, more powerful than all the rest — namely, to liberate a certain species of property which I possess, very repugnantly to my own feelings, but which imperious necessity compels, until I can substitute some other expedient by which expenses not in my power to avoid, however well disposed I may be to do it, can be defrayed."

In Washington's Will, special provision is made for his "mulatto man William, calling himself William Lee," granting him his immediate freedom, an annuity of thirty dollars during his natural life, or support, if he preferred (being incapable of walking or any active employment) to remain with the family. "This I give him," says Washington, "as a testimony of my sense of his attachment to me, and for his faithful services during the Revolutionary War."

The colored soldiers, and others, who were objects of his solicitude, were found North and South, wherever marched the Continental army. From among those in Virginia, the few following cases have been preserved.

The Detroit Tribune, August 10th, 1851, says: — "A short time since, we chronicled the death of a negro who had reached the venerable age of one hundred years. It may not be known to many of our readers, that there is now living, near this city, in the enjoyment of good health and the frugal comforts of life, a negro, who is nearly, or quite, a century old. His name is BENJAMIN MORRIS, and he is residing on the Charles Moran farm, where he has a life lease, and where, by the aid of a few friends, he tills enough ground to earn for himself a plain but comfortable subsistence. His life has been quite eventful. He was born at Snowhill, in Virginia. His master's name was Bob Scofield, as he says, using, probably, the familiar term by which he was known throughout the neighborhood in which he resided. He lived with Scofield until after the Revolutionary War. During the war, he was engaged to drive a baggage wagon; and so well did his behavior please General Washington, who happened to notice him, that his master, at the close of the war, gave him his freedom, at the request of that great and good man. His deed of manumission he has now, — of a truth, the 'palladium of his liberties' in this negro-hunting age and country. From Virginia, Morris went to Cuba, where he stayed but a short time, returning to this country and settling, at Louisville, Ky. Thence he came to Detroit, in time to witness the surrender of Hull, and the closing acts of the war of 1812 upon the frontier. Since then, he has been engaged in labor of various kinds, supporting himself and wife in comfortable circumstances. About three years ago, she died, and he has since lived alone in a little cottage on the Moran farm. He is a member, we believe, of the First Baptist Church of this city, from the members of which he receives such little aids, from time to time, as he needs. He is still quite erect and vigorous, and able to labor a good deal. He walks down to church nearly every Sabbath and returns, a total distance of nearly six miles. We trust the old man is to live many years yet in comfort and peace, to reap the reward of his services to our country, small though they may have been, at a time when the weakest forces told on a country's destinies hanging in equipoise."

A correspondent of the Alexandria (D. C.) Gazette, writing from Fairfax County, Va., November 14, 1835, says: —

Upon a recent visit to the tomb of Washington,. I was much gratified by the alterations and improvements around it. Eleven colored men were industriously employed in levelling the earth and turfing around the sepulchre. There was an earnest expression of feeling about them, that induced me to inquire if they belonged to the respected lady of the mansion. They stated that they were a few of the many slaves freed by George Washington, and they had offered their services upon this last melancholy occasion, as the only return in their power to make to the remains of the man who had been more than a father to them; and they should continue their labors so long as any thing should be pointed out for them to do. I was so interested in this conduct, that I inquired their several names, and the following were given me: — Joseph Smith, Sambo Anderson, William Anderson, his son, Berkley Clark, George Lear, Dick Jasper, Morris Jasper, Levi Richardson, Joe Richardson, Wm. Moss, Wm. Hays, and Nancy Squander, cooking for the men.

That there were exceptions to this community of grateful hearts may be learned from an incident mentioned by James T. Woodbury, Esq., brother of Hon. Levi Woodbury, who, when delivering lectures on the subject of slavery, not unfrequently adverts to the circumstances which first drew his attention to the subject. During his stay in the capital of the United States, he had a wish to visit the tomb of Washington. He was attended by an aged negro, whose business it had been for many years to guide travellers to that consecrated spot. This old man was formerly the slave of General Washington. Mr. Woodbury asked him if he had any children. "I have had a large family," he replied. "And are they living?" inquired the gentleman. The voice of the aged father trembled with emotion, and the tears started to his eyes, as he answered: — "I don't know whether they are alive or dead. They were all sold away from me, and I don't know what became of them. I am alone in the world, without a child to bring me a cup of water in my old age." Mr. Woodbury looked on the infirm and solitary being with feelings of deep compassion. "And this," thought he, "is the fate of slaves, even when owned by so good man as General Washington! Who would not be an Abolitionist?"

In October, 1854, there came to the house of Isaac and Amy Post, in Rochester, as if by instinct to those whose names are synonymous with aid and comfort to all earth's suffering children, an aged colored man, leaning upon his staff, — his clothes poor and ragged, — who represented himself as the son of General Washington's serving man, and that he was fleeing to Canada. Mrs. Angelina J. Knox says, in reference to this case: — "He was born at Mt. Vernon, on the plantation on which the 'father of our country' had lived. His father was a servant of George Washington. Years passed on; his heart pleaded that its pulsations might beat in a land of freedom, and many attempts had he made, but in vain, to be free. Once he was taken in a rice swamp, where he had fled for refuge; the blood hounds scented him, and brought him back to his master. Major Mitchell, of the United States army, had burned into his forehead the letter M., that thus he might be identified as Mitchell's slave. I asked him if his master was a Christian. To which he replied, with a satirical expression, — 'Pious? I guess he was pious! He Free Mason, too, — my last master — O, he biggest Christian!

He 'pears pious. Ha he big man — he 'tempt shoot me, 'cause I won't take off coat, him to whip me. Gun all ready shoot me — I take off coat — he get rope, tie me to hang me — I kitched him, pulled him down, and ran away. Dat is de last of him I ever saw. I pretty tired sleeping in bush. I want to get to Canada — dat's all I want. I want to see my boy dare — dat is what I want. I want to get out dis country. Dey say dat money is de root of all evil; but I hab no money, and go pretty hungry sometimes. Colored folks sometimes 'tray us. Ye aint going to send me back, are ye?' Poor old man — no! no! I will not send you back. But what is the Christianity of this republic doing, but sending you back to bondage? What would the Church do with this old man, with branded brow, who is now looking with a distrustful eye upon every person with whom he meets? O, my country, with extended wings, would that thy protection could overshadow the branded, bleeding fugitive! But, no! True is it, that if this fugitive should stand on the spot where Warren fell — should he clasp the monument on Bunker's Hill — should he flee to the home of John Hancock — even there, the slaveholder may claim him as his chattel slave. Let us, then, shed no more tears at the tomb of Washington at Mt. Vernon — let us no more boast of liberty — let us break every yoke, and let the oppressed go free!"

SIMON LEE, the grandfather of William Wells Brown, on his mother's side, was a slave in Virginia, and served in the War of the Revolution; and, although honorably discharged with the other Virginia troops, at the close of the war, he was sent back to his master, where he spent the remainder of his life toiling on a tobacco plantation. Such is the want of justice toward the colored American, that, after serving in his country's struggles for freedom, he is doomed to fill the grave of a slave!

THE SOUTHAMPTON INSURRECTION.

NATHANIEL TURNER was born Oct. 2d, 1800. In his childhood, from some circumstances, his mother and others said, in his presence, that he would surely be a prophet, as the Lord had shown him things that happened before his birth. This remark made a deep impression upon his mind, and affected all his subsequent conduct. He learned to read with such facility, that he had no recollection whatever of learning the alphabet, and he grew up a prodigy reverenced among his fellows. He was never addicted to stealing, or known to have a dollar in his life, to swear an oath, or drink a drop of spirits. He studiously wrapped himself in mystery, and devoted his hours to fasting and prayer, and communion with the spirit. He had a vision, and saw white spirits and black spirits engaged in battle, and the sun was darkened, the thunder rolled in the heavens, and blood flowed in streams, and he heard a voice, saying "Such is your luck; such you are called to see; and let it come rough or smooth, you must bear it." While laboring in the fields, he discovered drops of blood on the corn, as though it were dew from heaven, and found on the leaves in the woods characters and numbers, with the forms of men, in different attitudes, portrayed in blood.

From his confession, I extract the following: —

"And on the appearance of the sign, [the eclipse of the sun in February, 1831,] I should arise and prepare myself, and slay my enemies with their own weapons.... I communicated the great work I had to do to four in whom I had the greatest confidence, (Henry, Hark, Nelson and Sam). It was intended by us to have begun the work of death on the 4th of July last."

The Richmond Whig of October 31, 1831 in giving an account of Turner's capture, says, — "He is a shrewd, intelligent fellow; he insists strongly upon the revelations which he received, as he understood them, urging him on and pointing to this enterprise. He denied that any except himself and five or six others knew any thing of it. He does not hesitate to say that, even now, he thinks he was right, and if his time were to go over again, he must necessarily act in the same way."

A correspondent of the same paper says, — "Nat had for some time thought closely on this subject, for I have in my possession some papers given up by his wife, under the lash."

"We learn," says the Petersburg Intelligencer, "that the fanatical murderer, Nat Turner, was executed, according to his sentence, at Jerusalem, on Friday last, about one o'clock. He exhibited the utmost composure throughout the whole ceremony, and although assured that he might, if he thought proper, address the immense crowd assembled on the occasion, declined availing himself of the privilege, and told the Sheriff, in a firm voice, that he was ready. Not a limb nor a muscle was observed to move."

Upwards of one hundred slaves were slaughtered in the Southampton tragedy, — many of them in cold blood, while walking in the streets, — and about sixty white persons. Some of the alleged conspirators had their noses and ears cut off, the flesh of their checks cut out, their jaws broken asunder, and, in that condition, they were set up as marks to be shot at. The whites burnt one with red hot irons, cut off his ears and nose, stabbed him, cut his ham-strings, stuck him like a hog, and at last cut off his head, and spiked it to the whipping-post.

The following fact was narrated by the Rev. M. B. Cox, late Missionary to Liberia, soon after the event occurred. Immediately after the insurrection, a slaveholder went into the woods in quest of some of the insurgents, accompanied by a faithful slave, who had been the means of saving his life in the time of massacre. When they had been some time in the woods, the slave handed his musket to his master, informing him, at the same time, that he could not live a slave any longer, and requesting him either to set him free or shoot him on the spot. The master took the gun from the hands of the slave, levelled it at his breast, and shot the faithful negro through the heart.

Dr. Rice, of Virginia, published a sermon, in 1823, predicting very exactly the Southampton insurrection. He says: — "Without pretending to be a prophet, I venture to predict, if ever that horrid event should take place which is anticipated and greatly dreaded by many among us, some crisp-haired prophet, some pretender to inspiration, will be the ringleader as well as the instigator of the act."

MADISON WASHINGTON.

An American slaver, named the Creole, well manned and provided in every respect, and equipped for carrying slaves, sailed from Virginia to New Orleans, on the 30th October, 1841, with a cargo of one hundred and thirty-five slaves. When eight days out, a portion of the slaves, under the direction of one of their number, named MADISON WASHINGTON, succeeded, after a slight struggle, in gaining command of the vessel. The sagacity, bravery and humanity of this man do honor to his name; and, but for his complexion, would excite universal admiration. Of the twelve white men employed on board the well-manned slaver, only one fell a victim to their atrocious business. This man, after discharging his musket at the negroes, rushed forward with a handspike, which, in the darkness of, the evening, they mistook for another musket; he was stabbed with a bowie knife wrested from the captain. Two of the sailor were wounded, and their wounds were dressed by the negroes. The captain was also injured, and he was put into the forehold, and his wounds dressed; and his wife, child and niece were unmolested. It does not appear that the blacks committed a single act of robbery, or treated their captives with the slightest unnecessary harshness; and they declared, at the time, that all they had done was for their freedom. The vessel was carried into Nassau, and the British authorities at that place refused to consign the liberated slaves again to bondage, or even to surrender the "mutineers and murderers" to perish on Southern gibbets.

THE VIRGINIA MAROONS.

The great Dismal Swamp, which lies near the Eastern shore of Virginia, and, commencing near Norfolk, stretches quite into North Carolina, contains a large colony of negroes, who originally obtained their freedom by the grace of God and their own determined energy, instead of consent of their owners, or by the help of the Colonization Society. How long this colony has existed, what is its amount of population, what portion of the colonists are now fugitives, and what the descendants of fugitives, are questions not easily determined; nor can we readily avail ourselves of the better knowledge undoubtedly existing in the vicinity of this colony, by reason of the decided objections of those best enabled to gratify our curiosity — to some extent, at least — to furnishing any information whatever, lest it might be used by Abolitionists for their purposes, — as one of them frankly said when questioned about the matter. Nevertheless, some facts, or, at least, an approximation towards the truth of them, are known respecting this singular community of blacks, who have won their freedom, and established themselves securely in the midst of the largest slaveholding State of the South; for, from this extensive Swamp, they are very seldom, if now at all, reclaimed. The chivalry of Virginia, so far as I know, have never yet ventured on a slave-hunt in the Dismal Swamp nor is it, probably, in the power of that State to capture or expel these fugitives from it. This may appear extravagant; but when it is known how long a much less numerous band of Indians held the everglades of Florida against the forces of the United States, and how much blood and treasure it cost to expel them finally, we may find a sufficient excuse for the forbearance of the "Ancient Dominion" towards this Community of fugitives domiciliated in their midst.

From the character of the population, it is reasonable to infer that the United States Marshal has never charged himself with the duty of taking the census of the Swamp; and we can only estimate the amount of population, by such circumstances as may serve to indicate it. Of these, perhaps the trade existing between the city of Norfolk and the Swamp may furnish the best element of computation. This trade between the Swamp merchants and the fugitives is wholly contraband, and would subject the white participants to fearful penalties, if they could only be enforced; for, throughout the slave States, it is an offence, by law, of the gravest character, to have any dealings whatever with runaway negroes. But, "You no catch 'em, you no hab em," is emphatically true in the Dismal Swamp, where trader and runaway are alike beyond the reach of Virginia law. An intelligent merchant, of near thirty years' business in Norfolk, has estimated the value of slave property lost in the Swamp, at one and a half million dollars. This city of refuge, in the midst of society, has endured from generation to generation, and is likely to continue until slavery is abolished throughout the land. A curious anomaly this community certainly presents; and its history and destiny are alike suggestive of curiosity and interest.

That there are those at the South who desire the abolition of slavery, the following extract from a speech of P. A. Bolling, Esq., in the House of Delegates, in Virginia, 1832 will show: —

"Mr. Speaker, it is in vain for gentlemen to deny the fact, — the feelings of society are fast becoming adverse to slavery. The moral causes which produce that feeling are on the march, and will march on, until the groans of slavery are heard no more in this else happy land. Look over world's wide page! see the rapid progress of liberal feelings! see the shackles falling from nations who have writhed under the galling yoke of slavery! Liberty is going over the whole earth, hand-in-hand with Christianity. The ancient temples of slavery, rendered venerable a by their antiquity, are crumbling into dust; ancient prejudices are fleeing before the light of truth, — are dissipated by its rays, as the idle vapor by the bright sun. The noble sentiment —

"'Then let us pray, that come it may,
As come it will, for a' that,
That man to man, the world o'er,
Shall brothers be, for a' that'

is rapidly spreading. The day-star of human liberty has risen above the dark horizon of slavery, and will continue its bright career until it smiles alike on all men."

The Richmond Enquirer advocates the erection of a monument to the memory of PETER FRANCISCO, a colored man, born a slave in Virginia, but emancipated at the commencement of the Revolution, and enlisted as a soldier. He served all through the war, and was subsequently Sergeant-at-Arms of the Virginia Legislature.

CHAPTER XII: NORTH CAROLINA.

DAVID WALKER was born in Wilmington, North Carolina September 28, 1785. His mother was a free woman but his father was a slave. His innate hatred to slavery was early developed. When yet a boy, he declared that the slaveholding South was not the place for him, and, receiving his mother's blessing, he turned his back upon North Carolina, and, after many trials, reached Boston Mass., where he took up his permanent residence.

He applied himself to study, in order to contribute some thing to the cause of humanity. In 1827, he entered into the clothing business, in Brattle street; married in 1828 and in 1829, published his "APPEAL," which, as Henry H. Garnet truly says, "produced more commotion among slaveholders than any volume of its size that was ever issued from the American press. They saw that it was bold attack upon their idolatry, and that, too, by a black man, who once lived among them. It was merely a smooth stone which this David took up, yet it terrified a host of Goliahs. The Governor of Georgia wrote to the Hon. Harrison Gray Otis, then Mayor of Boston, requesting him to suppress the "Appeal." His Honor replied to Southern censor, that he had no power nor disposition to hinder Mr. Walker from pursuing a lawful course in utterance of his thoughts."

Mr. Walker died in Bridge street, in 1830, aged thirty-four. His son, Edward Garrison Walker, now resides in Charlestown, Mass., with his mother, Mrs. Dewson. Mr. Walker was a faithful member of the Methodist Church in Boston, whose pastor was the venerable Father Snowden.

JONATHAN OVERTON, (says the Edenton Whig,) a colored man, and a soldier of the Revolution, died at this place, at the advanced age of one hundred and years. The deceased served under Washington, and at the battle of Yorktown, besides other less important engagements. He was deservedly held in great respect by our citizens; for, apart from the feeling of veneration which every American must entertain for the scanty remnant of Revolutionary heroes, of which death is fast depriving us the deceased was personally worthy of the esteem and consideration of our community. He has lived among us longer than the ordinary period allotted to human life, and always sustained a character for honesty, industry, and integrity. It is not always that the eulogies or epitaphs of persons, in much more exalted positions than his, contain much truth as does this brief tribute to the humble and patriotic negro. We learn that several gentlemen have made arrangements to have the burial accompanied by every mark of respect.

The Wilmington Journal states that there is an old negro in the county of Sampson, belonging to a Mr. Williamson, he was one hundred and fourteen years old on the last Fourth of July. He has been recently visited by a correspondent of the Journal, who states that he found him cheerful and in fine health, and busily engaged in making himself a pair of pants — without spectacles — he being a tailor by trade. His first master, Archibald Bell, died about ninety-eight years ago, at which time Delph was thirteen years of age. He remembers seeing Lord Cornwallis and his army, as well as other persons and things of note in those early days. He was taken prisoner near the residence of William Fryer. He saw the Tories kill John Thompson — he (Thompson) lingering some three days. The old fellow lives by himself, not another soul being near him. He is a sort of doctor, and travels as much as fifty miles to see sick persons, and many persons visit him for medical aid. He cooks, washes, milks, and makes his own clothes, in a very independent manner. He is four feet high, and weighs one hundred and five pounds. His present owner, Mr. Williamson, is seventy-four, and therefore an old man to the rest of the world, but quite a youth in comparison to Delph. There is little reason for doubting the old negro's age, of which he himself is confident, besides having been known in Sampson from time immemorial almost.

The following is a portion of an "Explanation" which prefaces a volume of poems by GEORGE M. HORTON, a North Carolina slave. The volume was published by Mr. Gales, formerly of North Carolina, but afterwards of the firm of Gales & Seaton, Washington, D. C., who also wrote the "Explanation." Mr. Gales is no Abolitionist and would not be likely, therefore, to exaggerate the talents and character of an African slave: —

"GEORGE, who is the author of the following poetical effusions, is a slave, the property of Mr. James Horton, of Chatham county, North Carolina. He has been in the habit, some years past, of producing poetical pieces, sometimes on suggested subjects, to such persons as would write them while he dictated. Several compositions of his have already appeared in the Raleigh Register. Some have made the way into Boston newspapers, and have evoked expressions of approbation and surprise. Many persons have now become much interested in the promotion of his prospect, some of whom are elevated in office and literary attainments. None will imagine it possible, that pieces produced as these have been, should be free from blemish in composition or taste. The author is now thirty-two years of age, and has always labored in the field on his master's farm, promiscuously with the few others which Mr. Horton owns, in circumstances of the greatest possible simplicity. His master says he knew nothing of his poetry, but as he heard of it from others. George knows how to read, and is now learning to write. All his pieces are written down by others; and his reading, which is done at night, and at the usual intervals allowed to slaves, has been much employed on poetry, such as he could procure, this being the species of composition most interesting to him. It is thought best to print his productions without correction, that the mind of the reader may be in no uncertainty as to the originality and genuineness of every part. We shall conclude this account of George, with an assurance that he has ever been faithful, honest and industrious slave. That his heart has felt deeply and sensitively in this lowest possible condition of human nature, will easily be believed, and is impressive confirmed by one of his stanzas: —

"Come, melting Pity, from afar,
And break this vast enormous bar,
Between a wretch and thee;
Purchase a few short days of time,
And bid a vassal soar sublime,
On wings of Liberty."
RALEIGH, July 2, 1829.

CHAPTER XIII: SOUTH CAROLINA.

THE celebrated Charles Pinckney, of South Carolina, in his speech on the Missouri question, and in defence of slave representation of the South, made the following admissions: —

"At the commencement of our Revolutionary struggle with Great Britain, all the States had this class of people. The New England States had numbers of them; the Northern and Middle States had still more, although less than the Southern. They all entered into the great contest with similar views. Like brethren, they contended for the benefit of the whole, leaving to each the right to pursue its happiness in its own way. They thus nobly toiled and bled together, really like brethren. And it is a remarkable fact that, notwithstanding, in the course of the Revolution, Southern States were continually overrun by the British, and every negro in them had an opportunity of running away, yet few did. They then were, as they still are, as valuable a part of our population to the Union as any other equal number of inhabitants. They were in numerous instances the pioneers, and in all, the laborers of your armies. To their hands were owing the erection of the greatest part of the fortifications raised for the protection of our country. Fort Moultrie gave, at an early period of the inexperience and untried valor of our citizens, immortality to American arms. And in the Northern States, numerous bodies of them were enrolled, and fought, side-by-side with the whites, the battles of the Revolution."

The Charleston Standard and Mercury, of July, 1854 furnishes these facts: —

"CAPTAIN WILLIAMSON, a free man of color, died in this city, on Friday, the 7th instant, at the extraordinary age of one hundred and thirteen years. He was a native of Saint Paul's Parish, and came out of the estate of Mr. William Williamson, a successful merchant of Charleston. Out of this estate, also, came 'Good Old Jacob,' who died a few months since, at the age of one hundred and two years, and whose death was noticed in our papers. When Jacob's obituary notice was read to the Captain, 'Why,' said the old man, 'I used to carry him about in my arms when he was a child.'

"Mr. Williamson, before the Revolution, had removed to his country seat near Wallis Bridge, about fifteen miles from Charleston. There CAPTAIN

WILLIAMSON had charge of his master's large garden of fifty acres, with its fish-pond, shrubbery, and splendid collection of native and exotic plants. The Captain was always a faithful servant, devoted to the service of his master, and afterwards to his mistress who went to England, and there died. She left him free, together with his children. Of these he had fourteen, whom only one survives. For many years, he superintended the farms and gardens of several persons on Charles Neck. He was remarkably intelligent and faithful, and was universally respected by his employers and their neighbors. During the war of the Revolution, he assisted in throwing up the lines for the defence of the city, and was an ardent lover of his country. In further proof of which, we refer Dr. Johnson's reminiscences of the Revolution, where the Captain received honorable notice. There, amongst other instances of his fidelity, it is recorded that, during the troublesome times following the Revolution, he brought mistress a large sum of money due to her for rent, from the Sister's ferry, on the Savannah. For this, he was rewarded by her with a set of silver waistcoat buttons, which he kept and exhibited with 'commendable pride' to visitors of the present generation. By his industry, he accumulated a sufficiency for the comfortable support of himself and his wife, who survives him, and is upwards eighty years of age. For upwards of fifty years, he been a humble and consistent member of the Circular Church. He was charitable and kind to the poor, and willing to assist in every benevolent object. He was highly esteemed by the whites, and respected by his own color, by members of both of whom he was followed to his last resting place, on Saturday evening."

The following interesting account of the trial and execution of a colored man, (said to have been one of the defenders of Fort Moultrie,) which took place at Charleston in the year 1817, must excite the feelings of every benevolent heart against the ruthless prejudices engendered by the foul and leporous stain of slavery. A man belonging to a merchant ship having died, apparently in consequence of poison being mixed with the dinner served up to the ship's company, the cook and cabin boy were suspected; because they were, on account of their occupations, the only persons on board who did not partake of the mess, — the effects of which appeared the moment it was tasted.

As the offence was committed on the high seas, the cook, though a negro, became entitled to a jury, and, with the cabin boy, was put upon his trial. The boy, who was a fine-looking lad, was readily acquitted. The man was then tried. He was of low stature, ill-shapen, and with a strongly-marked and repulsive countenance. The evidence against him was — first, that he was cook, and, therefore, who else could have poisoned the mess? It was, however, overlooked, that two of the crew had absconded since the ship came into port. Secondly, he had been heard to utter expressions of ill-humor before he went on board. That part of the testimony was, indeed, suppressed, which went to explain these expressions. The real proof, no doubt, was written in the color of his skin, and in the harsh and rugged lines of his face. He was found guilty.

Mr. Crafts, Jr., a member of the Charleston bar, and an honor to his profession, who, from motives of humanity, had undertaken his defence, did not think that a man ought to die on account of the color of his skin — although prejudice, with jaundiced eyes, might see nothing but crime and infamy stamped upon it; and moved for a new trial, on the ground of partial and insufficient evidence. But the Judge, who had urged his condemnation with a vindictive countenance, entrenched himself in forms, and found that the law gave him no power on the side of mercy. Mr. C. then forwarded a representation of the case to the President of the United States, through one of the Senators of the State; but the Senator treated with levity the idea of interesting himself in behalf of the life of a negro. He was, therefore, left to his dungeon and the executioner.

Thus situated, he did not, however, forsake himself; and it was now, when prejudice, and a rigor bordering on persecution, had spent their last arrow on him, that he modestly, but firmly, assumed his proper character, — to vindicate not only his own innocence, but the moral equality of his race, and those mental energies, which the white man's pride would deny to the blackness of his skin. Maintaining an undeviating tranquillity, he conversed with ease and cheerfulness, whenever his benevolent counsel, who continued his kind attentions to the last, visited his cell. "I was present (says Lieutenant Hall, from whose travels this account extracted,) on one of these occasions, and observed his tone and manner; he was neither sullen nor desperate, but quiet and resigned, — suggesting whatever occurred to him on the circumstances of his own case, with as much calmness as if he had been uninterested in the event. Yet, as if he deemed it a duty to omit none of the means placed within his reach for vindicating his innocence, he paid the most profound attention to the exhortations of a Methodist preacher, who, for conscience's sake, visited those who were in prison; and, having his spirit strengthened with religion, on the morning of his execution, before he was led out, he requested permission to address a few words of advice to the companions of his captivity. "I have observed much in them," he added, "which requires to be amended, and the advice of a man in my situation may be respected." A circle was accordingly formed in his cell, in which he placed himself, and addressed them at some length, with a sober and collected earnestness of manner, on the profligacy which he had noticed in their behavior while they had been fellow-prisoners — recommending to them the rules of conduct prescribed in that religion in which he now found his support and consolation.

If we regard the quality and condition of the actors only, there is, assuredly, an astonishing difference between this scene, and the parting of Socrates with his friends and disciples. Should we, however, put away from our thoughts such differences as are merely accidental, and seize that point of coincidence which is most interesting and important, namely — the triumph of mental energy over death and unmerited disgrace — the negro will not appear wholly unworthy of a comparison with the sage of Athens. The latter occupied an exalted station in the public eye. Although persecuted, even unto death and ignominy, by a band of triumphant and ruthless despots, he was surround in his last moments by his faithful friends and disciples whose talents and affection he might safely trust the vindication of his fame, and the unsullied purity of his memory. He felt that the hour of his glory must come, and that it would not pass away. The negro had none of these aids; he was a man friendless and despised; the sympathies of society were locked up against him; he was to suffer for an odious crime by an ignominious death; the consciousness of his innocence was confined to his own bosom, there, probably, to sleep for ever; to the rest of mankind he wretched criminal — an object, perhaps, of contempt and detestation, even to the guilty companions of his prison. He had no philosophy with which to reason down the misgivings which may be supposed to precede a violent and ignominious dissolution of life; he could make no appeal to posterity to reverse an unjust judgment. To have borne all this patiently would have been much; he bore it as a hero and a Christian.

Having ended his discourse, he was conducted to the scaffold, where, having calmly viewed the crowd collected to witness his fate, he requested leave to address them. Obtaining permission, he stepped firmly to the edge of the scaffold, and, having commanded silence by his gestures, — "You are come," said he, "to be spectators of my sufferings; you are mistaken;

there is not a person in this crowd but suffers more than I do. I am cheerful and contented; for I am innocent," He then observed, that he truly forgave all those who had taken any part in his condemnation, and believed that they acted conscientiously, from the evidence before them, and disclaimed all idea of imputing guilt to any one. He then turned to his counsel, who, with feelings which honored humanity, had attended him to the scaffold. "To you, Sir," said he, "I am, indeed, most grateful. Had you been my son, you could not have acted by me more kindly;" and observing his tears, he continued, — "This, Sir, distresses me beyond any thing I have felt yet. I entreat that you will feel no distress on my account. I am happy." Then, praying Heaven to reward his benevolence, he took leave of him, and signified his readiness to die; but requested that he might be excused from having his eyes bandaged, wishing, with an excusable pride, to give this last proof of the unshaken firmness with which innocence can meet death. He, however, submitted, on this point, to the representations of the Sheriff, and expired without the quivering of a muscle.

Rev. Theodore Parker gives the following anecdote of a Massachusetts sea-captain. He commanded a small brig, which plied between Carolina and the Gulf States. "One day, at Charleston," said he, "'a man came and brought to me an old negro slave. He was very old, and had fought in the Revolution, and been very distinguished for bravery and other soldierly qualities. If he had not been a negro, he would have become a Captain, at least, perhaps a Colonel. But, in his age, his master found no use for him, and said that he could not afford to keep him. He asked me to take the Revolutionary soldier, carry him South and sell him. I carried him," said the man, "to Mobile, and tried to get as good and kind a master for him as I could, for I didn't like to sell a man that had fought for his country. I sold the old Revolutionary soldier for a hundred dollars to a citizen of Mobile, who raised poultry, and he set him to attend a hen-coop." I suppose the South Carolina master drew the pension till the soldier died. "Why did you do such a thing?" said my friend, who was an Anti-Slavery man. "If I didn't do it," he replied, "I never could get a bale of cotton, nor a box sugar, nor any thing, to carry from or to any Southern port.

JEHU JONES was proprietor of a celebrated hotel in the city of Charleston, situated on Broad street, next to aristocratic St. Michael's church, one of the most public places in the city. He was a fine, portly looking man, active, enterprising, intelligent, honest to the letter, — one whose integrity and responsibility were never doubted. He lived in every way like a white man. His house was unquestionably the best in the city, and had a wide-spread reputation. Few persons of note ever visited Charleston without putting up at Jones's, Where they found not the comforts of a private house, but a table spread every luxury the country afforded. Mr. Jones maintained the popularity of his house many years, rearing a beautiful, intelligent and interesting family, and accumulating forty thousand dollars or more. The most interesting portion of his family were three daughters, the eldest of whom married a gentleman who subsequently removed to New York, where he engaged in a respectable and lucrative business.

Mr. Jones often exerted his influence and contributed his means to redeem persons from slavery. For several years, he carried on an extensive fashionable tailoring establishment, and among his customers were the wealthiest citizens of Charleston. He had a large number of apprentices, among whom was my father, (William G. Nell,) who served seven years and six months.

Jehu, a son of Mr. Jones, visited the North, and was not allowed to return home. The details of this case are similar to hundreds of others, and prove that the right of locomotion is denied in the South to free colored persons from the North, even though they are native-born Southerners. The following extract from South Carolina State Documents is conclusive evidence on this point: —

"Our first and great object is, to prevent the interchange of sentiment between our domestic negroes, whether bond or free, and negroes who reside abroad, or who have left our State. To do this, it becomes imperative to establish a law prohibiting free negroes from coming into the State, and those, in the State from going, under penalty of imprisonment and fine if they return."

This principle strikes down the rights of citizens of other States. Though free-born myself, and unable to trace my genealogy back to slavery, yet I am prohibited from visiting my father's relatives in a Southern city, except at the risk of pains and penalties. Why should not my rights citizen of the Old Bay State be as sacred under the Palmetto Banner as those of any other man, white though he be?

Colored seamen from the free States, and also from British dominions and elsewhere, continue to be removed from vessels and imprisoned, though for many years efforts have been put forth by the several powers to abolish the restriction.

Complexional distinctions, growing out of the institution of slavery, exist, to a great and unhappy extent, even among colored people; and as the Jews and Samaritans of Scripture had no dealings one with another, so in Charleston, as in many other Southern cities, social intercourse and intermarriages occur only as exceptions among the two prominent shades of complexion. In 1810, a Society was in operation in the city of Charleston, of which my father was a member, composed, as set forth in its Constitution, of "free brown men only." Its objects were benevolent; its name, the Humane and Friendly Society; but yet, at the dictation of the spirit of pro-slavery, it was thoroughly proscriptive in its character. This tree of caste, though rooted in the South, shades many cities of the North with its baneful branches; but, through the dissemination of more liberal principles, its influence daily diminishes.

THE BLACK SAXONS.

Mr. Duncan, a rich slaveholder in South Carolina, was one evening indulging in a reverie after reading the History of the Norman Conquest, when a dark mulatto opened the door, and, making a servile reverence, said, in wheedling tones, "Would massa be so good as to giv' a pass to go to Methodist meeting?" Being an indulgent master, he granted the permission to him and several others, only bidding them not to stay out all night. Some time after, when no response was heard to his repeated bell-ringing, it occurred to him that he had given every one of his slaves a pass to go to the Methodist meeting. This was instantly followed by the remembrance, that the same thing had occurred a few days before. Having purchased a complete suit of negro clothes, and a black mask well-fitted to his face, he awaited the next request for a pass to a Methodist meeting, when, assuming the disguise, he hurried after the party. And here, in this lone sanctuary of Nature's primeval majesty, were assembled many hundreds of swart figures, some seated in thoughtful attitudes, others scattered in moving groups, eagerly talking together. He observed that each one, as he entered, prostrated himself till his forehead touched the ground, and, rising, placed his finger on his mouth. Imitating this signal, he passed in with the throng, and seated himself behind the glare of the torches. For some time, he could make out no connected meaning amid the confused buzz of voices, and half-suppressed snatches of songs. But, at last, a tall man mounted the stump of a decayed tree, nearly in the centre, of the area, and requested silence.

"When we had our last meeting," said he, "I suppose most all of you know, that we all concluded it was best for to join the British, if so be we could get a good chance. But we didn't all agree about our masters. Some thought we should never be able to keep our freedom, without we killed our masters in the first place; others didn't like the thoughts of that; so we agreed to have another meeting to talk about it. And now, boys, if the British land here in Caroliny, What shall we do with our masters?"

He stepped down, and a tall, sinewy mulatto stepped into his place, exclaiming, with fierce gestures, "Ravish wives and daughters before their eyes, as they have done to us. Hunt them with hounds, as they have hunted us, Shoot them down with rifles, as they have shot us. Throw their carcasses to the crows, they have fattened on our bones; and then let the Devil take them where they never rake up fire o' nights. Who talks of mercy to our masters?

"I do," said an aged black man, who rose up before the fiery youth, tottering as he leaned both hands on oaken staff. "I do, — because the blessed Jesus always talked of mercy. I know we have been fed like hogs, and shot at like wild beasts. Myself found the body of my likeliest boy under the tree where buckra rifles reached him. But, thanks to the blessed Jesus, I feel it in my poor old heart to forgive them. I have been a member of a Methodist church these thirty years; and I've heard many preachers, white and black; and they all tell me Jesus said, Do good to them that do evil to you, and pray for them that spite you. Now, I say, let us love our enemies; let us pray for them; and when our masters flog us, and sell our pickaninnies, let us break out singing —

"'You may beat upon my body,
But you cannot harm my soul;
I shall join the forty thousand by and by.

"You may sell my children to Georgy,
But you cannot harm their soul;
They will join the forty thousand by and by.

"Come, slave-trader, come in too;
The Lord's got a pardon here for you;
You shall join the forty thousand by and by.'
"That's the way to glorify the Lord."

Scarcely had the cracked voice ceased the tremulous chant in which these words were uttered, when a loud altercation commenced; some crying out vehemently for the blood of the white men, others maintaining that the old man's doctrine was right. The aged black remained leaning on his staff, and mildly replied to every outburst of fury, "But Jesus said, do good for evil." Loud rose the din of excited voices, and the disguised slaveholder shrank deeper into the shadow.

In the midst of the confusion, an athletic, gracefully proportioned young man sprang upon the stump, and, throwing off his coarse cotton garment, slowly turned round and round before the assembled multitude. Immediately, all was hushed; for the light of a dozen torches, eagerly held by fierce, revengeful comrades, showed his back and shoulders deeply gashed by the whip, and still oozing blood. In the midst of that deep silence, he stopped abruptly, and with stern brevity exclaimed, "Boys! shall we not murder our masters?"

"Would you murder all?" inquired a timid voice at his right hand. "They don't all cruellize their slaves."

"There's Mr. Campbell," pleaded another; "he never had one of his boys flogged in his life. You wouldn't murder him, would you?"

"O, No, no, no," shouted many voices; "we wouldn't murder Mr. Campbell. He's always good to colored folks."

"And I wouldn't murder my master," said one of Mr. Duncan's slaves, "and I'd fight any body that set out to murder him. I an't a going to work for him for nothing any longer, if I can help it; but he shan't be murdered, for he's a good master."

"Call him a good master, if ye like!" said the bleeding youth, with a bitter sneer in his look and tone. "I curse the word. The white men tell us God made them our masters; I say, it was the Devil. When they don't cut up the backs that bear their burdens, when they throw us enough of the grain we have raised to keep us strong for another harvest, when they forbear to shoot the limbs that toil to make them rich, they are fools who call them good masters. Why should they sleep on soft beds, under silken curtains, while we, whose labor bought it all, lie on the floor at the threshold, or miserably coiled up in the dirt of our own cabins? Why should I clothe my master in broadcloth and fine linen, when he knows, and I know, that he is my own brother? and I, meanwhile, have only this coarse rag to cover my aching shoulders?" He kicked the garment scornfully, and added, "Down on your knees, if ye like, and thank them that ye are not flogged and shot. Of me they'll learn another lesson!"

Mr. Duncan recognised in the speaker the reputed son of one of his friends, lately deceased; one of that numerous class which Southern vice is thoughtlessly raising up, to be its future scourge and terror.

The high, bold forehead, and flashing eye, indicated an intellect too active and daring for servitude; while his fluent speech and appropriate language betrayed the fact that his highly educated parent, from some remains of instinctive feeling, had kept him near his own person during his life-time, and thus formed his conversation on another model than the rude jargon of slaves.

His poor, ignorant listeners stood spell-bound by the magic of superior mind, and at first it seemed as if he might carry the whole meeting in favor of his views. But the aged man, leaning on his oaken staff, still mildly spoke of the meek and blessed Jesus, and the docility of African temperament responded to his gentle words.

After various scenes of fiery indignation, gentle expostulation, and boisterous mirth, it was finally decided, by a considerable majority, that in case the British landed, they would take their freedom without murdering their masters; not a few, however, went away in a wrathful mood, muttering curses deep.

With thankfulness to Heaven, Mr. Duncan again found himself in the open field, alone with the stars. Their glorious beauty seemed to him, that night, clothed in new and awful power. Groups of shrubbery took to themselves startling forms; and the sound of the wind among the trees was like the unsheathing of swords. Again he recurred to Saxon history, and remembered how he had thought that troubled must be the sleep of those who rule a conquered people.

"And these Robin floods and Wat Tylers were my Saxon ancestors," thought he. "Who shall so balance effects and causes, as to decide what portion of my present freedom sprung from their seemingly defeated efforts? Was the place I saw to-night, in such wild and fearful beauty, like the haunts of the Saxon Robin floods? Was the spirit that gleamed forth there as brave as theirs? And who shall calculate what even such hopeless endeavors do for the future freedom of their race?"

These cogitations did not, so far as I ever heard, lead to the emancipation of his bondmen; but they did prevent his revealing a secret, which would have brought hundreds to an immediate and violent death. After a painful conflict between contending feelings and duties, he contented himself with advising the magistrates to forbid all meetings whatsoever among colored people, until the war was ended.

He visited Boston several years after, and told the story to a gentleman, who often repeated it in the circle of his friends. In brief outline it reached my ears. I have adopted fictitious names, because I have forgotten the real ones.

PROJECTED INSURRECTION IN CHARLESTON.

During the Revolutionary War, Captain Veazie, of Charleston, was engaged in supplying the French in St. Domingo with slaves from St. Thomas. In the year 1781, he purchased DENMARK, a boy of about fourteen years of age, and afterwards brought him to Charleston, where he proved, for twenty years, a faithful slave. In 1800, DENMARK drew a prize of $1500 in the lottery, and purchased his freedom from his master for $600. From that period until the time of his arrest, he worked as a carpenter, and was distinguished for his great strength and activity, and was always looked up to by those of his own color with awe and respect.

In 1822, DENMARK VEAZIE formed a plan for the liberation of his fellow-men from bondage. In the whole history of human efforts to overthrow slavery, a more complicated and tremendous plan was never formed. A part of the plan matured was, that on Sunday night, the 16th of June, a force would cross from James' Island and land on South Bay, and march up and seize the Arsenal and guard-house; another body, at the same time, would seize the Arsenal on the Neck; and a third would rendezvous in the vicinity the mills of Denmark's master. They would then sweep through the town with fire and sword, not permitting a single white soul to escape.

The sum of this intelligence was laid before the Governor, who, convening the officers of the militia, took such measures as were deemed the best adapted to the approaching exigency of Sunday night. On the 16th, at 10 o'clock at night, the military companies, which were placed under the command of Col. R. Y. Hayne, were ordered to rendezvous for guard.

The conspirators, finding the whole town encompassed, at 10 o'clock, by the most vigilant patrols, did not dare show themselves, whatever might have been their plans. In the progress of the subsequent investigation, it was distinctly in proof, that but for these military demonstrations, the effort would unquestionably have been made; that a meeting took place on

Sunday afternoon, the 16th, at 4 o'clock, of several of the ringleaders, at Denmark Veazie's for the purpose of making their preliminary arrangements and that early in the morning of Sunday, Denmark despatched a courier to order down some country negroes from Goose Creek, which courier had endeavored in vain get out of town.

The conspirators, it was ascertained, had held meetings for four years, without being betrayed. The leaders were careful to instruct their followers not to mention their plans to "those waiting men who received presents of old coats, &c., from their masters," as such slaves would be likely to betray them.

DENMARK VEAZIE was betrayed by the treachery of his own people, and died a martyr to freedom. The slave who gave information of the projected insurrection was purchased by the Legislature, who hold out to other slaves the strongest possible motives to do likewise in similar cases, by giving him his freedom.

The number of blacks arrested was one hundred and thirty-one. Of these, thirty-five were executed, forty-one acquitted, and the rest sentenced to be transported. Many a brave hero fell; but History, faithful to her high trust, will engrave the name of DENMARK VEAZIE on the same monument with Moses, Hampden, Tell, Bruce, Wallace, Toussaint, Lafayette, and Washington.

WM. G. NELL was steward on board the ship Gen. Gadsden, when she made good her escape from the British brig Recruit, July 28th, 1812. They put into Boston, where my father took up his abode.

A few days after the escape, the two captains were at the "Indian Queen Tavern," in Bromfield street. The British captain was relating the particulars of the chase, when the Yankee captain (overhearing) acknowledged himself as the one who had given John Bull the slip.

CHAPTER XIV: GEORGIA.

ON the West side of the Apalachicola River, (says the Hon. Joshua R. Giddings, in a narrative from which this account is taken,) some forty miles below the line of Georgia, are yet found the ruins of what was once called "Blount's Fort." Its ramparts are now covered with a dense growth of underbrush and small trees. You may yet trace its bastions, curtains, and magazine. At this time, the country adjacent presents the appearance of an unbroken wilderness, and the whole scene is one of gloomy solitude, associated, as it is, with one of the most cruel massacres which ever disgraced the American arms.

The fort had originally been erected by civilized troops, and, when abandoned by its occupants at the close of the war, in 1815, it was taken possession of by the refugees from Georgia. But little is yet known of that persecuted people; their history can only be found in the national archives at Washington. They had been held as slaves the State referred to; but, during the Revolution, they caught the spirit of liberty, — at that time so prevalent throughout our land, — and fled from their oppressors, and found an asylum among the aborigines living in Florida.

During forty years, they had effectually eluded or resisted all attempts to reënslave them. They were true to themselves, to the instinctive love of liberty which is planted in every human heart. Most of them had been born amidst perils, reared in the forests, and taught from their childhood to hate the oppressors of their race. Most of those who had been personally held in degrading servitude, whose backs had been scarred by the lash of the savage overseer, had passed to that spirit land, where clanking of chains is not heard, where slavery is not known. Some few of that class yet remained. Their grey hairs and feeble limbs, however, indicated that they, too, must soon pass away. Of the three hundred and eleven persons residing in "Blount's Fort," not more than twenty had been actually held in servitude. The others were descended from slave parents, who fled from Georgia, and, according to the laws of the slave States, were liable to suffer the same outrage to which their ancestors had been subjected.

The slaveholders, finding they could not themselves obtain possession of their intended victims, called on the President of the United States for assistance to perpetrate the crime of enslaving their fellow-men.

General Jackson, Commander of the Southern Military District, directed Lieutenant-Colonel Clinch to perform the barbarous task. I was at one time personally acquainted with that officer, and know the impulses of his generous nature and can readily account for the failure of his expedition. He marched to the fort, made the necessary reconnaissance, and returned, making report that "the fortification was not accessible by land."

Orders were then issued to Commodore Patterson, directing him to carry out the orders of the Secretary of War. He, at that time, commanded the American flotilla lying in "Mobile Bay," and instantly issued an order to Lieutenant Loomis to ascend the Apalachicola River with two boats, "to seize the people in Blount's Fort, deliver them to their owners, and destroy the fort."

On the morning of the 17th of September, 1816, a spectator might have seen several individuals standing upon the walls of that fortress, watching with intense interest the approach of two small vessels that were slowly ascending the river under full spread canvass, by the aid of a light southern breeze. They were in sight at early dawn, but it was ten o'clock when they furled their sails and cast anchor opposite the fort, and some four or five hundred yards distant from it.

A boat was lowered, and soon a midshipman and twelve men were observed making for the shore. They were met at the water's edge by some half-dozen of the principal men in the fort, and their errand demanded.

The young officer told them he was sent to make a demand of the fort, and its inmates were to be given up to the "slaveholders, then on board the gun-boat, who claimed them as fugitive slaves!" The demand was instantly rejected, and the midshipman and his men returned to the gun-boats, and informed Lieutenant Loomis of the answer he had received.

As the colored men entered the fort, they related to their companions the demand that had been made. Great was the consternation manifested by the females, and even a portion of the sterner sex began to be distressed at their situation. This was observed by an old patriarch, who had drank the bitter cup of servitude — one who bore on his person the visible marks of the thong, as well as, the brand of his master upon his shoulder. He saw his friends falter, and he spoke cheerfully to them. He assured them that they were safe from the cannon-shot of the enemy — that there were not men enough on board to storm their fort; and, finally, closed with the emphatic declaration, "Give me liberty, or give me death!" This saying was repeated by many agonized fathers and mothers on that bloody day.

A cannonade was soon commenced upon the fort, but without much apparent effect. The shots were harmless; they penetrated the earth of which the walls were composed, and were there buried without further injury. Some two hours were thus spent, without injuring any person in the fort. They then commenced throwing bombs. The bursting of these shells had more effect; there was no shelter from these fatal messengers. Mothers gathered their little ones around them, and pressed their babes more closely to their bosoms, as one explosion after another warned them of their imminent danger. By these explosions, some were occasionally wounded, and a few killed, until, at length, the shrieks of the wounded and the groans of the dying were heard in various parts of the fortress.

Do you ask why those mothers and children were butchered in cold blood? I answer, they were slain for adhering to the doctrine that "all men are endowed by their Creator with the inalienable right to enjoy life and liberty." Holding to this doctrine of Hancock and Jefferson, the power of the nation was arrayed against them, and our army employed to deprive them of life.

The bombardment was continued some hours with but little effect, so far as the assailants could discover. They manifested no disposition to surrender. The day was passing away. Lieutenant Loomis called a council of officers, and put to them the question, "what further shall be done?" An under officer suggested the propriety of firing "hot shot at the magazine." The proposition was agreed to. The furnaces were heated, balls were prepared, and the cannonade was resumed. The occupants of the fort felt relieved by the change. They could hear the deep humming sound of the cannon balls, to which they had become accustomed in the early part of the day, and some made themselves merry at the supposed folly of their assailants. They knew not that the shot were heated, and were, therefore, unconscious of the danger which threatened them.

Suddenly, a startling phenomenon presented itself to their astonished view. The heavy embankment and timbers protecting the magazine appeared to rise from the earth, and the next instant the dreadful explosion overwhelmed them, and the next found two hundred and seventy parents and children in the immediate presence of God, making their appeal for retributive justice upon the government which had murdered them, and the freemen of the North who sustained such unutterable crime.

Many were crushed by the falling earth and timbers; many were entirely buried in the ruins. Some were horribly mangled by the fragments of timber and the explosion of charged shells that were in the magazine. Limbs were torn from the bodies to which they had been attached; mothers and babes lay beside each other, wrapped in that sleep which knows no waking. The sun had set, and the twilight of evening was closing around, when some sixty sailors, under the officer second in command, landed, and, without opposition, entered the fort. The veteran soldiers, accustomed to blood and carnage, were horror-stricken as they viewed the scene before them. They were accompanied, however, by some twenty slaveholders, all anxious for their prey. These paid little attention to the dead and dying, but anxiously seized upon the living, and, fastening the fetters upon their limbs, hurried them from the fort, and instantly commenced their return toward the frontier of Georgia. Some fifteen persons in the fort survived the terrible explosion, and they now sleep in servile graves, or moan and weep in bondage.

The officer in command of the party, with his men, returned to the boats as soon as the slaveholders were fairly in possession of their victims. The sailors appeared gloomy and thoughtful as they returned to their vessels. The anchors were weighed, the sails unfurled, and both vessels hurried from the scene of butchery as rapidly as they were able. After the officers had retired to their cabins, the rough-featured sailors gathered before the mast, and loud and bitter were the curses they uttered against slavery, and against those officers of government who had thus constrained them to murder women and helpless children, merely for their love of liberty.

But the dead remained unburied; and the next day, the vultures were feeding upon the carcasses of young men and young women, whose hearts on the previous morning had beaten high with expectation. Their bones have been bleached in the sun for thirty-seven years, and may yet be seen scattered among the ruins of that ancient fortification.

Twenty-two years have elapsed, and a Representative in Congress, from one of the free States, reported a bill, giving to the perpetrators of these murders a gratuity of five thousand dollars from the public treasury, as a token of the gratitude which the people of the nation felt for the soldierly and gallant manner in which the crime was committed toward them. The bill passed both Houses of Congress, was approved by the President, and now stands upon the records of the third session of the Twenty-Fifth Congress.

These facts are all found scattered among the various public documents which repose in the alcoves of our national library. But no historian has been willing to collect and publish them, in consequence of the deep disgrace which they reflect upon the American arms, and upon those who then controlled the government.

The Savannah Republican of February, 1855, makes the following mention of a venerable colored patriarch:-

"MONSIEUR DE BORDEAUX is a native of St. Domingo. He left that island when about thirty or thirty-five years old, during our Revolutionary War, in company with many French volunteers, and was present at the siege of Savannah, in 1779. He did not play the part of a mere 'looker-on in Venice,' but took part in the struggle, and received a severe and dangerous wound in the hip, which rendered him a cripple for life. He was near Pulaski when he was wounded, and saw the gallant Pole fall. The old man can satisfy the curious, probably, as to where Pulaski died, and what disposition was made of his venerable remains. After the war, Monsieur de Bordeaux returned to St. Domingo. He left the island again, however, during the insurrection, and by a profitable mistake of the captain of the vessel in which he took passage, he was a second time landed at Savannah, where he spent many years with his friend, the late Daniel Leons, of this city. Some fifty or sixty years since he removed to South Carolina, where he has resided ever since.

"Monsieur de Bordeaux is considerable over one hundred years of age; still, he retains a distinct recollection of his vernacular tongue, the French, and possesses all the vivacity of that nation, no one ever having seen him depressed in spirits. He has ever enjoyed the highest character for integrity and truth."

A few years since, a slave, at great hazard, saved the State House at Milledgeville, when in flames. The Legislature purchased him of his master for $1800, and set him free, — thus showing their appreciation of the value of liberty, even to the mind of a slave.

CHAPTER XV: KENTUCKY.

HENRY BOYD was born a slave in Kentucky. Of imposing stature, well-knit muscles, and the countenance of one of Nature's noblemen, at the age of eighteen, he had so far won the confidence of his master, that he not only consented to sell him the right and title to his freedom, but gave him his own time to earn the money. With a general pass from his master, Henry made his way to the Kanawha salt works, celebrated as the place where Senator Ewing, of Ohio, chopped out his education with his axe! And there, too, with his axe, did Henry Boyd chop out his liberty. By performing double labor, he got double wages. In the daytime, he swung his axe upon the wood, and for half the night, he tended the boiling salt kettles, sleeping the other half by their side. After having accumulated a sufficient sum, he returned to his master, and paid it over for his freedom. He next applied himself to learn the trade of a carpenter and joiner. Such was his readiness to acquire the use of tools, that he soon qualified himself to receive the wages of a journeyman. In Kentucky, prejudice does not forbid master mechanics to teach colored men their trades.

He now resolved to quit the dominions of slavery, and try his fortunes in a free State, and accordingly directed his steps to the city of Cincinnati. The journey reduced his purse to the last quarter of a dollar; but, with his tools on his back, and a set of muscles that well knew how to use them, he entered the city with a light heart. Little did he dream of the reception he was to meet. There was work enough to be done in his line, but no master-workman would employ ploy "a nigger." Day after day did Henry Boyd offer his services from shop to shop, but as often was he repelled, generally with insult, and once with a kick. At last, he found the shop of an Englishman, too recently arrived to understand the grand peculiarity of American feeling. This man put a plane into his hand, and asked him to make proof man of his skill. "This is in bad order," said Boyd, and with that he gave the instrument certain nice professional knocks with the hammer till he brought it to suit his practised eye. "Enough," said the Englishman, "I see you can use tools." Boyd, however, proceeded to dress a board in a very able and workmanlike manner, while the journeymen from a long line of benches gathered round, with looks that bespoke a deep personal interest in the matter. "You may go to work," said the master of the shop, right glad to employ so good a workman. The words had no sooner left his mouth, than his American journeymen, unbuttoning their aprons, called, as one man, for the settlement of their wages.

"What, what," said the amazed Englishman, "what does this mean?"

"It means that we will not work with a nigger," replied the journeymen.

"But he is a first-rate workman."

"But we won't stay in the same shop with a nigger. We are not in the habit of working with niggers."

"Then I will build a shanty outside, and he shall work in that."

"No, no; we won't work for a boss who employs niggers. Pay us up, and we'll be off."

The poor master of the shop turned, with a despairing look, to Boyd — "You see how it is, my friend, my workmen will all leave me. I am sorry for it, but I can't hire you."

Even at this repulse, our adventurer did not despair. There might still be mechanics, in the outskirts of the city, who had too few journeymen to be bound by their prejudices. His quarter of a dollar had long since disappeared; but, by carrying a traveller's trunk or turning his hand to any chance job, he contrived to exist till he had made application to every carpenter and joiner in the city and its suburbs. Not one would employ him. By this time, the iron of prejudice, more galling than any thing he had ever known of slavery, had entered his soul. He walked down the river's bank below the city, and, throwing himself upon the ground, gave way to an agony of despair. He had found himself the object of universal contempt; his plans were all frustrated, his hopes dashed, and his dear bought freedom made of no effect! By such trials, weak minds are prostrated in abject and slavish servility, stronger ones are made the enemies and depredators of society, and it is only the highest class of moral heroes that come off like gold from the furnace. Of this class, however, was HENRY BOYD. Recovering from his dejection, he surveyed the brawny muscles that strung his herculean limbs. A new design rushed into his mind, a new resolution filled his heart. He sprang upon his feet, and walked firmly and rapidly towards the city, doubtless with aspirations that might have fitted the words of the poet —

"Thy spirit, Independence, let me share,
Lord of the lion heart and eagle eye!"

The first object which attracted his "eagle eye," on reaching the city, was one of the huge river boats, laden with pig-iron, drawn up to the landing. The captain of this craft was just inquiring of the merchant who owned its contents for a hand to assist in unloading it. "I am the very fellow for you," said Boyd, stripping off his coat, rolling up his sleeves, and laying hold of the work. "Yes, sure enough, that is the very fellow for you," said the merchant. The resolution and alacrity of Boyd interested him exceedingly, and during the four or five days whilst a flotilla of boats were discharging their cargoes of pig-iron with unaccustomed despatch, he became familiar with his history, with the exception of all that pertained to his trade, which Boyd thought proper to keep to himself. In consequence, our adventurer next found himself promoted to the portership of the merchant's store, a post which he filled to great satisfaction. He had a hand and a head for every thing, and an occasion was not long wanting to prove it. A joiner was engaged to erect a counter, but failing by a drunken frolic, the merchant was disappointed and vexed. Rather in passion than in earnest, he turned to his faithful porter — "Here, Henry, you can do almost any thing, why can't you do this job?" "Perhaps I could, Sir, if I had my tools and the stuff," was the reply. "Your tools!" exclaimed the merchant, in surprise, for till now he knew nothing of his trade. Boyd explained that he had learned the trade of a carpenter and joiner, and had no objection to try the job. The merchant handed him the money, and told him to make as good a counter as he could. The work was done with such promptitude, judgment and finish, that his employer broke off a contract for the erection of a large frame warehouse, which he was about closing with the same mechanic who had disappointed him in the matter of the counter, and gave the job to Henry. The money was furnished, and Boyd was left to procure the materials and boss the job at his own discretion. This he found no difficulty in doing; and what is remarkable, among the numerous journeymen whom he employed, were some of the very men who took off their aprons at his appearance in the Englishman's shop! The merchant was so much pleased wit his new warehouse, that he proceeded to set up the intelligent builder in the exercise of his trade in the city. Thus HENRY BOYD found himself raised at once almost beyond the reach of the prejudice which had well-nigh crushed him. He built houses and accumulated property. White journeymen and apprentices were glad to be in his employment, and to sit at his table. He is now a wealthy mechanic, living in his own house in Cincinnati, and his enemies who have tried to supplant him have as good reason as his friends to know that he is a man of sound judgment and a most vigorous intellect.

LEWIS HAYDEN, once a slave in Kentucky, but now a free man in Boston, Mass., in his extensive business and social relations, commands the respect of an increasing circle in the community.

WM. H. CHANNING, in a sketch entitled, "A Day in Kentucky," says:

"I wish to relate what was told me by one of the daughters of Judge K., as we walked over the estate.

"'It all looks bright, and peaceful, and happy, does it not?' said she, as, standing on a little knoll under a group of hickory trees, she pointed over the wide fields to the family mansion and the cluster of slave huts, at whose doors the children, in swarms, were playing, with the noisy glee of the African. 'But,' she continued, after a gloomy pause, 'to us, who know what slavery is, this peace is the green corruption of a stagnant pool, — the peace of death. O! worse, far worse! It is the yawning grave of humanity. Do you see that spreading beech yonder, just on the edge of the hemp field, where the ditch runs? It was there that my brother Frank received the blow on the forehead, of which you observed, perhaps, the scar. I will tell you about it. It was his duty, at that time, to keep the nightly watch; for you know,' she said, turning to me with a smile of bitter irony, 'that we have to be guardians to these poor friends, who love us so as never to leave us.' Well, Frank kept the nightly watch. Armed to the teeth, with a dark lantern, he passed once or twice, or oftener, round the plantation. One stormy night, some two years since, he had reached that spot, when suddenly he heard a crackling sound through the hemp stalks. He cloaked his lantern, drew a pistol, and stepped behind the tree. In a moment, a man, with stealthy tread, approached the ditch, which is the boundary of the farm on that side. Frank flashed the light upon him. It was his own favorite slave, Ned; — of the same age with himself — almost a foster brother, for his mother was Frank's nurse; his fellow rambler in the woods, his play-fellow through early years. Hunting, fishing, swimming, nutting, taming horses, every sport had been shared by them. Frank loved that man, and Ned, I believe in my heart, loved him. He was high spirited and manly, though a negro; strong, bold, and somewhat passionate; and, as we found out afterwards, he had been struck that day by the overseer. It was a dreadful meeting. "Ned," said my brother, "turn back! I cannot in honor let you go. I am my father's watchman. You pass that ditch only over my body. Come! turn back. You know I am your friend; we are all your friends." "Master Frank," answered the noble fellow, — for he was so, though he almost killed my brother, — "Master Frank! God knows I would die for you, but, I forewarn you, I will not be taken. That wretch shall never lay his hand on me again. Let me pass, I beseech you! let me pass." Frank stood firm. Again Ned besought him in vain. He then turned to leap aside. Frank cried, "Beware I shall fire;" and, quick as thought, Ned struck him a stunning blow. He fell, utterly insensible. And what did that man do? Did he leap the ditch and fly? No! he took my bleeding brother on his shoulders, he carried him to the nearest slave-hut, roused the inmates, set him erect by the door, and then, and not till then, made his escape. Time enough elapsed before Frank could come to himself, and be carried to the house, and my father waked, for Ned to get clear off; the darkness, too, and the storm, favored him. He was gone; and I do believe we were all glad. Frank never blamed him. How could he? In the same case, would he not have done the same? Well, two months passed away, when, early one morning, the overseer found Ned asleep under some bushes, and brought him to the house. I will tell you where he had been afterwards; but see the cunning of the creature, a cunning and deceit that we sow in all slaves, and therefore ought to reap. He knelt to my father, and said, "Pardon, master! pardon! I have tried free bread, and it is not good. No friends for the poor slave among the mean white folks over the river, and so I have come back to you, master." My father did not have him punished, but ordered him to be bound with ropes and left in an empty room. The day passed, — two or three days, indeed, — and Ned was still bound. Meanwhile, the overseer threatened him with being sent down the river. You know what that means, don't you? It means, sent to sweat and starve, and die by inches, in the sugar-fields of Louisiana. Ned caught the alarm. By connivance of some one, he got a knife, and, when all was still, cut his ropes, and cautiously made his way out of the house. It was a stormy night, — his tracks were plain, but he could not help it. He ran to the neighboring plantation yonder, where his wife lived, and gave his peculiar whistle under her window. She was awake, and heard him. Poor soul I dare say she had hardly slept, from anxiety, for the two months after he ran away. She raised the window. "Jump down!" whispered Ned; "jump down, just as you are; wait not a second." She jumped, and, catching her in his arms, they escaped together.

"'Next morning, pursuit was made from both plantations; not that my father wished Ned to be taken, but our neighbor was not willing to lose the woman, who was a house servant, and very valuable. The pursuers, however, were deceived by the tracks, which were half buried up, and chilled and blinded by the storm, which was uncommonly severe for this part of the world, and at night gave up the hunt. We heard no more of them till last summer, when, travelling through Canada, whom should we find, as servant at a hotel in Prescott, but this rascal Ned. At first, he was shy and grave, and affected perfect ignorance. But it was always a saying of my father's, "If a nigger has sense enough to run off, and get safely out of the States, he must be a smart fellow, and has sense enough, too, to take care of himself, and he shall be free and welcome;" and Ned soon saw that we were his friends, and told us his adventures. It seems, that when he first escaped, he made his way good to Canada; but no sooner did he feel himself safe, than the thought of his wife in slavery so overcame him, that he instantly resolved to return, at all risks, and free her too. Night and day, he travelled back, till he reached our plantation, when, utterly overcome with fatigue and hunger, he fell asleep and was taken. Then, as I have told you, he "played possum," as the negroes say, till he caught the hint of being sent away, when he again escaped. And now see how a kind Providence aided those poor creatures. Would you believe it? The men who pursued them came to the very barn into which they had crept for concealment when the day broke; they trod, over and over again, upon their bodies, which were covered by the heaps of straw and hay; they cursed and swore, and consulted together, and vowed to take them, at the very ears of their victims; and yet they were kept safe. As soon as it was night, they set off again, through the snow, and hid themselves a second day in a wood, half frozen and famished. The third night they reached the Ohio, by good fortune found a boat, paddled themselves over, and were safe. Friends forwarded them to Canada; and, when we saw them, they were as happy as people could be, with every, prospect of success. And now,' said the beautiful girl, drawing herself up to her full height and folding her arms, 'I know not what you may think, for some of you Northerners seem to me, with all deference, to have the spirit of slaves yourselves; but, Kentuckian as I am, and on this slave soil, I dare to say it, Ned is a hero, — a hero, whom, if he had lived in the good old days of Greece, would have had his deeds immortalized in the strains of some Homer.'

The conversation of this spirited woman gave rise to some thoughts, which I will briefly state, for the benefit of those dull folks, who are too lazy to crack a nut and pick out the kernel.

"1. All slaveholders are riot insensible to the great outrages daily committed by slavery upon justice and affection, nor indifferent to the welfare of those whom they know to be brethren. There are pure-hearted men and women at the South, deserving our respect, our sympathy, counsel, aid, and prayers.

"2. If a Northern man relishes contempt and insult, he can find it, in any quantity and intensity, by professing to be an admirer of their 'peculiar domestic institutions' at the South. Southerners rarely believe such professions, and are apt to think him who makes them a hypocrite, or, if they suppose him sincere, to despise him for a mean-spirited, stupid booby.

"3. If, even under slavery, the African race exhibits such heroic and lovely traits, would they not be noble men, if bound to their white fellow-freemen by the triple bond of gratitude, and mutual confidence, and generous emulation?"

CHAPTER XVI: OHIO.

THE colored citizens of Ohio held a Mass Convention at Cleveland, September 9th, 1852. I cull the following incidents and tributes, as peculiarly appropriate to a military history of Colored Americans.

At sunrise, a salute was fired in the public square, in honor of the day, by the "Cleveland Light Artillery," and another at nine o'clock, as the procession formed, of which the orator of the day subsequently said : — "They are the first thunders of artillery that ever awoke the echoes of these hills in honor of the colored people. But they shall not be the last."

Rev. Dr. J. W. C. Pennington delivered a speech, of which Mr. Howland, a colored phonographic reporter, says, — "The Doctor took the stand and delighted the Convention with a short, brilliant and instructive address on the history of the past, and the part which the colored people have taken in the struggles of this nation for independence, and its various wars since its achievement."

Says the Daily True Democrat, — "The principal feature in the ceremonials of this jubilee was the address of our fellow-citizen, Mr. William H. Day, a performance worthy of its great purpose, and, therefore, most creditable to the author. Not often have we heard an address listened to with so absorbing an attention, nor observed an audience to be more deeply moved, than was Mr. Day's, by some parts of that address. After noticing the day, the 9th of September, which had been selected for their jubilation, and illustrating its preeminent suitableness to the occasion, by happy references to many illustrious events of which it was the anniversary, Mr. Day addressed himself to an able vindication of the claims of his race, in this country, to an equal participation in the exercise and enjoyment of those American rights which large numbers of that race, in common with the men of fairer complexion, had fought, suffered, and died to establish. Behind the orator sat seven or eight veteran colored men. Mr. D.'s apostrophe to those veterans was as touching as admirable, and produced a profound sensation."

Happily, it is in our power to furnish extracts from the speech thus referred to, as follows: —

"'Of the services and sufferings of the colored soldiers of the Revolution,' says one writer, 'no attempt has, to our knowledge, been made to preserve a record.' This is mainly true. Their history is not written. It lies upon the soil watered with their blood: who shall gather it? It rests with their bones in the charnel-house: who shall exhume it? Their bodies, wrapped in sacks, have dropped from the decks where trod a Decatur and a Barry, in a calm and silence, broken only by the voice of the man of God — 'We commit this body to the deep;' and the plunge and the ripples passing, the sea has closed over their memory for ever. Ah! we have waited on shore and have seen the circle of that ripple. We know, at least, where they went down; and so much, to-day, we come to record.

"We have had in Ohio, until very recently, and if they are living, have here now, a few colored men who have thus connected us with the past. I have been told, recently, of one in the Southern portion of the State.

"Another, of whom we all know, has resided, for many years, near Urbana, Champaigne county. He was invited to, and expected at, this meeting. FATHER STANUP (as he is familiarly called) has lived to a good old age. He has been afflicted with recent sickness, and it may have prostrated him permanently. The frosts of a hundred winters will shrivel any oak; the blasts of a century will try any vitality. The aged soldier must soon die. O! that liberty, for which he fought, be bequeathed to his descendants! The realization of that idea would smooth his dying pillow, and make the transit from this to another sphere a pleasant passage. I am credibly informed, that the age of Mr. Stanup is one hundred and nine; that he was with General Washington; and that his position, in this respect, has been recognised by officers of the Government."

"So much for the Revolution. I could add other facts bearing upon this particular, but do not deem it necessary. We have adduced proof sufficient to show any American who breasted the tide of death sweeping over this country in '76. We hold it up, that men who have denied its truth may observe, that the ignorant may be enlightened, and that white Americans may be divested of excuse for basing their exclusive liberty upon the deeds of their fathers. We, to-day, advance with them to the same impartial tribunal, and demand, that if the reason be good in the one case, it be made to apply in the other.

"In May, 1812, the American people again engaged in conflict with Great Britain.

"The naval engagements of that war are, perhaps, unsurpassed by any other; and that on the 11th of September, on Lake Champlain, of that war perhaps the most brilliant of any. Hear what the Common Council of New York city said of that battle to Commodore Macdonough. I read from a newspaper of 1815: —

"'Having approached the chair, his Honor, the Mayor, addressed the Commodore as follow: — "When our northern frontier was invaded by a powerful army, when the heroes who have immortalized themselves on the Niagara were pressed by a superior force, when the capital of the nation was overrun by hostile bands, when the most important city of the South was attacked by the enemy, and when he threatened to lay waste our maritime towns with fire and sword, — at a period so inauspicious and gloomy, when all but those who fully understand and duly appreciate the firmness and resources of the American character began to despair of the Republic, you were the first who changed the fortune of our arms, and who dispelled the dark cloud that hung over our country. With a force greatly inferior, you met the enemy, vaunting of his superior strength, and confident of victory; you crushed his proud expectations, you conquered him; and the embattled hosts which were ready to penetrate into the heart of our country, fled in dismay and confusion.

"'As long as illustrious events shall. be embodied in history, so long will the victory on Lake Champlain, obtained under your auspices, command the respect of mankind. And when you, and all who hear me, shall be numbered among the dead, those who succeed us, to the most extended line of remote antiquity, will cherish with exultation those great achievements which are indissolubly connected with the prosperity and glory of America. — Special Meeting of Common Council, Jan. 7th, 1815.

"To colored men, I remark, as much as to any others, belongs the honor of that battle."

[Mr. Day here exhibited a copy of an old newspaper, the organ of the Government, dated Jan. 12th, 1815, containing the only full account given any where of the names and equipment of the six larger vessels and the ten galleys, and added —]

"I recollect something of one of the men on board the row-galley Viper. That man enlisted under Commodore Macdonough, was apportioned to a row-galley, stood like a man at his post in the thickest of the fight, and where the blood of his fellows literally washed the deck. The honor-marks of that battle he carried to his grave. He sleeps in a secluded graveyard, yet not entirely unhonored by those for whom he perilled all. I hold in my hand 'a List of Acts passed by the Thirteenth Congress at its third session,' the first of which is a series of 'Resolutions, expressive of the sense of Congress of the gallant conduct of Captain Thomas Macdonough, the officers, seamen, marines, and infantry serving as marines, on board the United States squadron on Lake Champlain.'

"This same man was shortly afterward drafted to go to the Mediterranean with Commodore Bainbridge's Relief Squadron.Says Dr. Frost, in his History, — 'Commodore Bainbridge proceeded, according to his instructions, to exhibit his force, now consisting of seventeen sail, before Algiers, Tunis, and Tripoli, and to make arrangements for the security of American commerce in the Mediterranean. Having settled all for the honor and interests of his country, he returned to the United States.' So, according to Dr. Frost, colored men have been of service, where 'the security of American commerce,' and 'the honor and interests of the country' were concerned. The colored marine to whom I have referred received an honorable discharge, March 16th, 1816."

On the platform on this occasion were Mr. JOHN JULIUS, who served under General Jackson at New Orleans; Mr. JOHN BOYER VASHON, who has since deceased, who was in the Jersey prison-ship; and Mr. L. C. FLEWELLEN, who enlisted in Georgia. Mr. Day also alluded to Mr. ROBERT VAN VRANKEN, who marched, in 1815, to Plattsburg; and several others, now residing in the West, whose names escape us, were also mentioned. Mr. Day, in concluding, remarked: —

"I have purposely omitted mention of other matters. I have necessarily been mainly historical. We needed to set forth these facts in form.... I think we have demonstrated this point, that if colored people are among your Pompeys, and Cuffees, and Uncle Toms, they are also among your heroes. They have been on Lakes Erie and Champlain, upon the Mediterranean, in Florida with the Creeks, at Schuylkill, at Hickory Ground, at New Orleans, at Horse Shoe Bend, and at Pensacola. The presence of some of them here to-day is a living rebuke to this land."

Addressing the large crowd of white citizens present, Mr. Day said, — "We can be, as we have always been, faithful subjects, powerful allies, as the documents read here to-day prove: an enemy in your midst, we would be more powerful still. We ask for liberty; liberty here — liberty on the Chalmette Plains — liberty wherever floats the American flag: We demand for the sons of the men who fought for you, equal privileges. We bring to you, to-day, the tears of our fathers, — each tear is a volume, and speaks to you. To you, then, we appeal. We point you to their blood, sprinkled upon your door-posts in your political midnight, that the Destroying Angel might pass over. We take you to their sepulchres, to see the bond of honor between you and them kept, on their part, faithfully, — even until death."

A colored military company has been formed in Cincinnati, — pronounced by competent judges to be well manned, well officered and well drilled. They have chosen the appropriate historic name of "Attucks Guards." July 25th, 1855, Miss Mary A. Darnes, in behalf of an association of ladies, presented the company with a flag. Among the sentiments expressed by her were the following: —

"Should the love of liberty and your country ever demand your services, may you, in imitation of that noble patriot whose name you bear, promptly respond to the call, and fight to the last for the great and noble principles of liberty and justice, to the glory of your fathers and the land of your birth.

"The time is not far distant when the slave must be free; if not by moral and intellectual means, it must be done by the sword. Remember, Gentlemen, should duty call, it will be yours to obey, and strike to the last for freedom or the grave.

"But God forbid that you should be called upon to witness our peaceful homes involved in war. May our eyes never behold this flag in any conflict; let the quiet breeze ever play among its folds, and the fullest peace dwell among you!"

In the State of Ohio, the average property owned by white citizens is $5.90; that of the colored citizens, $6.71. Net property of colored people in Cincinnati, $800,000; in the State of Ohio, $5,000,000. In Cincinnati, among the colored citizens, are to be found three bank tellers, a superior artist in landscape painting — who has visited Rome to perfect his education; besides carpenters, cabinetmakers, stucco-workers, hotel-keepers, shop-keepers, nine daguerreotype artists, — the gallery kept by Mr. Ball (a colored man) being acknowledged the best in the Western country. In Cleveland, a city institution has employed a colored librarian, William H. Day, Esq.

CHAPTER XVII: LOUISIANA.

IN 1814, when New Orleans was in danger, and the proud and criminal distinctions of caste were again demolished by one of those emergencies in which Nature puts to silence, for the moment, the base partialities of art, the free colored people were called into the field in common with the whites; and the importance of their services was thus acknowledged by General Jackson: —

"HEAD QUARTERS, SEVENTH MILITARY DISTRICT, MOBILE, September 21, 1814.

"To the Free Colored Inhabitants of Louisiana:

"Through a mistaken policy, you have heretofore been deprived of a participation in the glorious struggle for national rights, in which our country is engaged. This no longer shall exist.

"As sons of freedom, you are now called upon to defend our most inestimable blessings. As Americans, your country looks with confidence to her adopted children for a valorous support, as a faithful return for the advantages enjoyed under her mild and equitable government. As fathers, husbands, and brothers, you are summoned to rally around the standard of the Eagle, to defend all which is dear in existence.

"Your country, although calling for your exertions, does not wish you to engage in her cause without remunerating you for the services rendered. Your intelligent minds are not to be led away by false representations — your love of honor would cause you to despise the man who should attempt to deceive you. With the sincerity of a soldier, and in the language of truth, I address you.

"To every noble-hearted free man of color, volunteering to serve during the present contest with Great Britain, and no longer, there will be paid the same bounty, in money and lands, now received by the white soldiers of the United States, namely — one hundred and twenty-four dollars in money, and one hundred and sixty acres of land. The non-commissioned officers and privates will also be entitled to the same monthly pay, daily rations, and clothes, furnished to any American soldier.

"On enrolling yourselves in companies, the Major-General commanding will select officers for your government, from your white fellow-citizens.

Your non-commissioned officers will be appointed from among yourselves.

"Due regard will be paid to the feelings of freemen and soldiers. You will not, by being associated with white men, in the same corps, be exposed to improper comparisons, or unjust sarcasm. As a distinct independent battalion or regiment, pursuing the path of glory, you will, undivided, receive the applause and gratitude of your countrymen.

"To assure you of the sincerity of my intentions, and my anxiety to engage your invaluable services to our country, I have communicated my wishes to the Governor of Louisiana, who is fully informed as to the manner of enrollments, and will give you every necessary information on the subject of this address.

ANDREW JACKSON,

Major-General Commanding.

The second proclamation is one of the highest complicated compliments ever paid by a military chief to his soldiers.

December 18, 1814, General Jackson issued, in the French language, the following address to his colored members of his army: —

"SOLDIERS! — When, on the banks of the Mobile, I called you to take up arms, inviting you to partake the perils and glory of your white fellow-citizens, I expected much from you; for I was not ignorant that you possessed qualities most formidable to an invading enemy. I knew with what fortitude you could endure hunger and thirst, and all the fatigues of a campaign. I knew well how you loved your native country, and that you, as well as ourselves, had to defend what man holds most dear — his parents, wife, children, and property. You have done more than I expected. In addition to the previous qualities I before knew you to possess, I found among you a noble enthusiasm, which leads to the performance of great things.

"Soldiers! The President of the United States shall praiseworthy was your conduct in the hour of danger, and the representatives of the American people will give you the praise your exploits entitle you to. Your General anticipates them in applauding your noble ardor.

"The enemy approaches; his vessels cover our lakes; our brave citizens are united, and all contention has ceased among them. Their only dispute is, who shall win the prize of valor, or who the most glory, its noblest reward. By Order,

THOMAS BUTLER, Aid-de-Camp."

The New Orleans Picayune, in an account of the celebration of the Battle of New Orleans in that city, in 1851, says: —

"Not the least interesting, although the most novel feature of the procession yesterday, was the presence of ninety of the colored veterans who bore a conspicuous part in the dangers of the day they were now for the first time called to assist in celebrating, and who, by their good conduct in presence of the enemy, deserved and received the approbation of their illustrious commander-in-chief. During the thirty-six years that have passed away since they assisted to repel the invaders from our shores, these faithful men have never before participated in the annual rejoicings for the victory which their valor contributed to gain. Their good deeds have been consecrated only in their memories, or lived but to claim a passing notice on the page of the historian. Yet, who more than they deserve the thanks of the country, and the gratitude of succeeding generations? Who rallied with more alacrity in response to the summons of danger? Who endured more cheerfully the hardships of the camp, or faced with greater courage the perils of the fight? If, in that hazardous hour, when our homes were menaced with the horrors of war, we did not disdain to call upon the colored population to assist in repelling the invading horde, we should not, when the danger is past, refuse to permit them to unite with us in celebrating the glorious event, which they helped to make so memorable an epoch in our history. We were not too exalted to mingle with them in the affray; they were not too humble to join in our rejoicings.

"Such, we think, is the universal opinion of our citizens. We conversed with many yesterday, and, without exception, they expressed approval of the invitation which had been extended to the colored veterans to take part in the ceremonies of the day, and gratification at seeing them in a conspicuous place in the procession.

The respectability of their appearance, and the modesty of their demeanor, made an impression on every observer, and elicited unqualified approbation. Indeed, though in saying so we do not mean disrespect to any one else, we think that they constituted decidedly the most interesting portion of the pageant, as they certainly attracted the most attention."

The editor, after further remarks upon the procession, adding of its colored members, "We reflected, that beneath their dark bosoms were sheltered faithful hearts, susceptible of the noblest impulses," thus alludes to the free colored population of New Orleans: —

"As a class, they are peaceable, orderly, and respectable people, and many of them own large amounts of property among us. Their interests, their homes, and their affections, are here, and such strong ties are not easily broken by the force of theoretical philanthropy, or imaginative sentimentality. They have been true hitherto, and we will not do them the injustice to doubt a continuance of their fidelity. While they may be certain that insubordination will be promptly punished, deserving actions will always meet with their due reward in the esteem and gratitude of the community."

Yet, if five, even of these veterans, should at any time be seen talking together, they are liable to be arrested for conspiracy, according to the laws of Louisiana!

Hon. Robert C. Winthrop, in his speech in Congress, on the Imprisonment of Colored Seamen, September, 1859, bore this testimony to the gallant conduct of the colored soldiers at New Orleans: — "I have an impression that, not, indeed, in these piping times of peace, but in the time of war, when quite a boy, I have seen black soldiers enlisted, who did faithful and excellent service. But, however it may have been in the Northern States, I can tell the Senator what happened in the Southern States at this period. I believe that I shall be borne out in saying, that no regiments did better service, at New Orleans, than did the black regiments, which were organized under the direction of General Jackson himself, after a most glorious appeal to the patriotism and honor of the people of color of that region; and which, after they came out of the war, received the thanks of General Jackson, in a proclamation, which has been thought worthy of being inscribed on the pages of history."

Chalmette Plains, the scene of the famous Battle of New Orleans, are five miles below that city, on the left bank of the Mississippi. There is an elaborate engraving of this battle, eighteen by twenty inches, executed by M. Hyacinth Laclotte, the correctness of which was certified to by eleven of the superior officers residing in New Orleans, July 15, 1815, when the drawing was completed.

The report "No. 8," from the American Army, corroborates the following interesting statements, which have been kindly furnished me by Wm. H. DAY, Esq., of Cleveland: —

"From an authenticated chart, belonging to a soldier friend, (writes Mr. Day,) I find that, in the Battle of New Orleans, Major-General Andrew Jackson, Commander-in-Chief, and his staff, were just at the right of the advancing left column of the British, and that very near him were stationed the colored soldiers. He is numbered 6, and the position of the colored soldiers, 8. The chart explanation of No. 8 reads thus: — '8. Captains Dominique and Bluche, two 24 pounders; Major Lacoste's battalion, formed of the men of color of New Orleans, and Major Daquin's battalion, formed of the men of color of St. Domingo, under Major Savary, second in command.'

"They occupied no mean place, and did no mean service.

"From other documents in my possession, I am able to state the number of the 'battalion of St. Domingo men of color' to have been one hundred and fifty; and of 'Major Lacoste's battalion of Louisiana men of color,' two hundred and eighty.

"Thus there were over four hundred 'men of color' in that battle. When it is remembered that the whole number of soldiers claimed by Americans to have been in that battle reached only 3,600, it will be seen that the 'men of color' were present in much larger proportion than their numbers in the country warranted.

"Neither was there colorphobia then. Major Planche's battalion of uniformed volunteer companies, and Major Lacoste's 'men of color,' wrought together; so, also, did Major Daquin's 'men of color,' and the 44th, under Captain Baker.

"Great Britain had her colored soldiers in that battle: the United States had hers. Great Britain's became freemen and citizens: those of the United States continued only half-free and slaves."

It has long been well known, that to the colored soldiers belonged the honor of first erecting the cotton-bale defences which so signally contributed to General Jackson's victory. We have no means now of confirming the statement, but the following letter contains some very significant historical reminiscences: —

WAYLAND, Feb. 19, 1855.

MR. WILLIAM C. NELL:

My DEAR SIR, — The fact to which I alluded in our brief conversation respecting the interesting memorials you have collected of the services of colored citizens in the Revolutionary War, and other wars, was, that some thirty years ago, I was informed by a colored man from Louisiana, that the idea of erecting a bulwark of cotton-bags at the battle of New Orleans, was suggested by a colored man, a native of Africa. Whether that statement is true, I am unable to say, and in all probability it would be very difficult to ascertain. The Commander on that occasion, a man of the fiercest prejudices, and all persons around him, would have an obvious interest and pride in concealing any agency which a poor and despised negro may have had in causing the adoption of that happy expedient. It was celebrated as a stroke of genius in Gen. Jackson. It strikes me as strange that no account of the first flash of the thought, whosoever it was, has been given. There cannot be a doubt that it saved the city of New Orleans and some thousands of lives, and raised the spirit of the whole country from the depression consequent upon a war of doubtful necessity and more than doubtful success; a war waged upon more plausible pretexts than the Mexican, but, in reality, for objects no less sectional and criminal.

I think the story derives some countenance from a passage in an Old Portuguese writer, of which the following is a literal translation: —

"On the following day, which was great Thursday of the year 1546, when morning came, it was found that a breastwork composed of earth, with its embrasures and heavy ordnance, had been raised near to our fortress, having its walls topped by a great quantity of cotton-bags, sheathed with rawhides to resist our fire. Our people were astonished at the silence and suddenness with which it had been erected. It was evidently no contrivance of a barbarous and disorderly multitude, for during the whole conflict, our enemies showed equal valor and discipline. Immediately they opened upon our fortress with decided effect, silencing four of our guns, which were doing them most harm.

"The good success of this day guided their conduct for succeeding ones, and during five nights, they built five forts, at proportionate distances, so as to be prepared for a general assault by several breaches."

The army of the Sultan of Cambay, employed against the Portuguese in this, the siege of Diu, was composed of various races inhabiting the cotton-growing zone of Asia and Africa. Two Abysinnians of high rank and distinguished valor are specially mentioned. It is probable that this mode of fortification was familiar to the natives of those countries, and has remained so to the present day. In the interior of Africa, it would be peculiarly convenient and important, subject, as the dwellers are, to sudden incursions for the capture of their wives and children, to supply the Christian and Arab markets of human flesh.

The work to which I have referred is, "The Life of Don John de Castro, Fourth Vice-Roy of India, by Jacinto Freire de Andrade," first published at

Lisbon, 1651. It has passed through several editions, and been translated into different languages.

I was also informed by the same person, a fugitive from Louisiana, that the slaves who took the field in compliance with Jackson's invitation, and fought for the country, were promised, before the battle, that they should have their freedom; that after it was over, they sent a committee to the General to claim the fulfilment of this promise, and that he made no reply, except to bid them "go home and mind their masters."

It is well known that a large number of slaves did fight bravely in that battle, and that they neither received their freedom nor any other mark of the gratitude of this false and degenerate republic. Two thousand years ago, when the opinion was universal, that nine-tenths of the men, and all the women, were made for slaves, and the small remnant of males for masters, the Athenians, and even the Spartans, set at liberty the slaves who had helped them win their victories and shared their glorious daring and dangers. They seem to have thought thus much due to their honor and self-respect as gentlemen, the doctrines of equal rights and reciprocal duties being yet undeveloped in the dark void of ages. But we, a nation calling ourselves Christian as well as republican, have actually fallen below the low standard of humanity and magnanimity preached by Aristotle and practised by the cruel and treacherous Spartans two thousand years ago. In the name of Heaven, how is it that we are cursed with a callousness as impenetrable as the Thugs of India or the father-eaters of Sumatra?

Wishing you success and satisfaction in your useful labors, I remain,

Yours, very truly,

D. LEE CHILD.

Among the colored veterans was JORDAN B. NOBLE, who was a drummer in the seventh regiment of infantry, which led on the attack of the British army on the night of December 23d, 1814. The two armies lay within gunshot of each other from that night until the 12th of January, 1815. It is Mr. Noble's custom to issue, every New Year's day, the following card: —

JORDAN B. NOBLE, THE VETERAN DRUMMER,

Who had the pride and satisfaction of beating to arms the American Army, on the 23d of December, 1814, and on the 8th of January, 1815, and the members of his Band, ADOLPH BROOKS and WILLIAM SAVAGE, who served with him in Mexico, in the First Regiment of Louisiana

Volunteers, Col. J. B. WALTON, Commander, under Gen. TAYLOR, in 1846, beg to present their congratulations of the season and best wishes to the officers of the regular and militia service, under whom they had the honor to serve; wishing them long lives, increased honors, and that the National Flag of our great country may ever be sustained by their faithful arms and gallant hearts.

And beg to remain ever,

Their obedient servants.

JORDAN D. NOBLE, DRUMMER

In proof of the estimation in which this colored veteran is held by his fellow-citizens, the New Orleans Daily Delta mentions the following "happy incident" as having occurred at the celebration of the "Eighth," at the St. Charles Theatre: —

"The bill announced that old Jordan, the matchless drummer, would appear and beat the drum as he beat it on the morning of the battle to reveille the Americans to action, and as he beat it again at night to soothe them to repose, after the arduous duties of the victorious day were past. Full one-third of the audience visited the St. Charles for no other purpose than to pay a tribute of respect to old Jordan; and as the old veteran appeared, a loud and long cheer welled up from the audience, and was borne far beyond the precincts of the building; again and again was he called out, and it seemed as if the audience would never tire of his music. The old veteran bowed his acknowledgments, and apparently felt more proud of the enthusiastic applause bestowed upon him than he would to have been seated on the imperial throne of Hayti. When the tattoo was beat, we were forcibly struck with the remarkable coincidence, that at the same hour, on the same day and date, thirty-nine years ago, he beat the same tune upon the battle-field of Chalmette."

A benefit was also tendered him, at the same theatre, on the evening of April 24th, 1854; and at the Fourth of July celebration following, JORDAN B. NOBLE was complimented and, according to the Delta, "no speech or toast produced a finer effect than his."

JOHN JULIUS was a member of the gallant colored regiment. He is a tall, good-looking, brown-skinned Creole of Louisiana, now about sixty-five years of age. He still bears the terrible gashes of the bayonet conspicuously on his neck. He was one of those who encountered the British hand-to-hand on the top of the breastworks. JULIUS BENNOIT (for that is his name, though commonly called John Julius) is a man of strict integrity of character, having all the delicate sensibility of a Frenchman; and he laments more at the injustice done him in the neglect of the authorities to grant him his claim of money and lands, according to the promises set forth in the proclamation, than any reverse of fortune he has ever met.

He is enthusiastic on the subject of the battle scenes of Chalmette Plains, and anxious that all who converse with him should know of his position in the conflict with Sir Edward Packenham. He exhibits the complete draught of the battle, and explains with lively satisfaction all its points of interest.

At a private dinner-party in New Orleans, some years after the battle, a relative of Gen. Packenham happened to be present, when the colored servant in waiting improved a chance moment to say, — "I saved General Packenham's life on the battle-ground." He was overheard by his master, who reprimanded him, admitting, however, that he was at the battle-ground, and did good service.

Many of the slaves who engaged in the battle were induced to do so from promises of freedom; but the sequel proved that a false hope had been held out to them, numbers being ordered to the cotton-fields to resume their unrequited toil, for the benefit of those for whom their own lives had been jeoparded on the bloody field of battle. The British took advantage of these violated pledges, and induced many colored Americans, panting for the freedom which, theirs as a birthright, had been confirmed by deeds of valor and patriotism, to accept free homes under the banner of England.

ANTHONY GILL was one of the soldiers remanded to work again for his master, when he was accosted by General Packenham, who, learning that he was a slave, told him to put down his hoe, follow him, and become a free man. He did so; and is now undisputed owner of fifty-two acres of free soil, in St. Johns, N. B. His son resides in Boston, Mass.

This is but one of numerous instances, of which there are abundant testimonies.

"When the British evacuated Charleston, in 1782, (says Ramsay, in his History of South Carolina,) Governor Matthews demanded the restoration of some thousands of negroes who were within their lines. These, however, were but a small part of the whole taken away at the evacuation, but that number is very inconsiderable when compared with the thousands that were lost from the first to the last of the war. It has been computed by good judges, that, between the years 1775 and 1783, the State of South Carolina lost TWENTY-FIVE THOUSAND NEGROES." [At least a fifth part of all the slaves in the State at the beginning of the war.]

"The forces under the command of General Provost marched through the richest settlements of the State, where are the fewest white inhabitants in proportion to the number of slaves. The hapless Africans, allured with the hope of freedom, forsook their owners, and repaired in great numbers to the Royal Army. They endeavored to recommend themselves to their new masters by discovering where their owners had concealed their property, and were assisting in carrying it off."

And the same candid historian, describing the invasion of next year says: — "The slaves a second time flocked to the British Army."

Dr. Ramsay, being a native and resident of Charleston, enjoyed every facility for ascertaining the facts in the case; but his testimony does not stand alone; Col. Lee, of Virginia, in his "Memoirs of the War in the Southern Department," confirms the statement.

"Lord Dunmore, Governor of Virginia, (says Burke, in his History of Virginia,) after escaping from Williamsburg, in 1775, to a vessel in James River, offered liberty to those slaves who would join him. It appears, from the history, that one hundred of them were soon after enumerated among his forces. How many more joined him does not appear."

Mr. Jefferson, then Secretary of State, in a letter to Hammond, Minister of Great Britain, dated Philadelphia, December 15, 1791, says: — "On withdrawing the troops from New York, a large embarkation of negroes, the property of the inhabitants of the United States, took place. A very great number was carried off in private vessels, without admitting the inspection of the American Commissioners."

In the Secret Journal of the Continental Congress, under date of March 29, 1799, we find the following: — "The Committee, appointed to take into consideration the circumstances of the Southern States, and the ways and means for their safety and defence, report that the State of South Carolina (as represented by the Delegates of the said State, and by Mr. Huger, who has come here at the request of the Governor of the said State, on purpose to explain the circumstances thereof) is UNABLE to make any effectual efforts with militia, by reason of the great proportion of citizens necessary to remain at home, to prevent insurrection among the negroes, and to prevent the desertion of them to the enemy; — that the state of the country, and the great number of these people among them, expose the inhabitants to great danger, from the endeavors of the enemy to excite them to revolt or desert."

Hon. John Quincy Adams, in a letter to Lord Castlereagh dated February 17, 1816, says: — "In his letter of the fifth of September, the undersigned had the honor of enclosing a list of seven hundred and two slaves carried away, after the ratification of the treaty of peace, from Cumberland Island, and the waters adjacent ....A number perhaps still greater was carried away from Tangier Island, in the State of Virginia, and from other places."

The same important admission was made in debate, on the floor of Congress, 30th March, 1790, some time after the war, by Mr. Burke, a Representative from South Carolina. "There is not a gentleman," said he, "on this floor, who is a stranger to the feeble situation of our State, when we entered into the war to oppose the British power. We were not only without money, without an army or military stores, but were few in number, and likely to be entangled with our domestics, in case the enemy invaded us."

Similar testimony to the weakness engendered by slavery was also borne by Mr. Madison, in debate in Congress. "Every addition," said that distinguished gentleman, "they (Georgia and South Carolina) receive to their number of slaves, tends to weaken them, and render them less capable of self-defence."

And at a still later day, Mr. Justice Johnson, of the Supreme Court of the United States, and a citizen of South Carolina, in his elaborate life of General Green, speaking of negro slaves, makes the same admission. He says: — "But the number dispersed through these (Southern) States was very great; so great as to render it impossible for the citizens to muster freemen enough to withstand the pressure of the British arms."

Hon. Wm. Jay says: — "We find at the South no one element of military strength. Slavery, as we have seen, checks the progress of population, of the arts, of enterprise, and of industry. But, above all, the laboring class, which in other countries affords the materials of which armies are composed, is regarded at the South as the most deadly foe and the sight of a thousand negroes with arms in their hands would send a thrill of terror through the stoutest hearts, and excite a panic which no number of the veteran troops of Europe could produce. Even now, laws are in force to keep arms out of the hands of a population which ought to be a reliance in danger, but which is dreaded by day and night, in peace and war."

The burning of Washington City was a signal instance of the military weakness of the South, as detailed in Ball's Compilation. "The city was burnt in the last war with Britain, for which the Americans may thank their pet 'institution' as much as the invading army. When the British in the Chesapeake evinced their intention to make a descent an Washington or Baltimore, the President ordered all the regular troops to the defence of the latter, and called on the States of Pennsylvania, Maryland and Virginia for volunteers for the protection of the capital. All know the result. The city was taken and burnt, while the Americans, lacking numbers to compete with their enemies, were obliged to return, although, had the Virginia troops, which were but a few miles distant, come up, they would have been able to make a stand."

The cause of their delay is thus explained: — "When the requisition on Virginia reached her Governor, General Madison, who was brother of the President, and at that time commandant of that division of the militia whose services were required, he promptly issued his orders, collected his quota, and commenced his march for the scene of action. Scarcely, however, had his force passed from Orange, Culpepper, Madison, and the adjoining counties, from which it had been principally raised, before the slaves in all that section were seen in commotion. A rumor, the source of which nobody knew, had spread among them, that some powerful foreign prince, — from Africa, we believe they had it, — with a sufficient force to accomplish his purpose, had arrived on the coast, to give freedom to the slaves of Virginia. This rumor soon became confirmed news with them. They simultaneously quitted work, and, without manifesting the least disposition to injure the whites, began, in their joyful excitement, to run from plantation to plantation, collect in bodies, and prepare to go off to meet their expected deliverers. The white inhabitants, in the mean time, who, as has ever been the case with the whole South, were sensitively alive to the fear of a slave insurrection, and were now thoroughly alarmed by this movement of the blacks, harmless as was the shape it had taken, sent off express after express to General Madison, whose force had made a temporary halt in the vicinity of the Potomac, from which it was on the point of moving on to Washington, and begged him to return with his troops and quell the apprehended insurrection of the slaves. This at once completely paralyzed the movements of Madison. He immediately marched back with the principal part of his force, leaving the rest, we believe, to remain on the spot, to await the event, and be in readiness to return if wanted. Finding, after a few days, that the force with which he had returned was sufficient to overawe the slaves, though he did not dare to withdraw them from the infected district, he finally sent orders for the remnant he had left on the Potomac to march on to Washington, as they then did, but reached the place too late to be of any service."

A letter from New Orleans, addressed to Le Republican, has some interesting matter respecting the population of mixed blood in that city. It alludes to the brilliant feat of arms of Dec. 20, 1814, "when the colored population rivalled in bravery and patriotism the other improvised soldiers," and to the battle of Jan. 8, of the same year, where they figured, and contributed to finish the foreign invasion of our soil, and goes on to say, that it is an error to confound the colored population of Louisiana with that elsewhere. They constitute, the writer affirms, an elite set, having nothing in common with those of the surrounding States. "The French and Spanish blood from which they are sprung has not degenerated among us: it has preserved the primitive warmth and generosity which distinguish those two chivalric nations." Notwithstanding they are not allowed to participate in the public schools, although forced to pay school taxes, they have received an elementary education, and a good number of them shine in science, arts and letters. There is, we are told, now in Paris, a Creole of Louisiana, who is walking in the steps of Alexander Dumas, and whose dramatic pieces are represented at the Theatre Francais. There is another in Louisiana, who has effected a complete revolution in sugar making, by a refining invention; and yet, this man has not been able to obtain a patent in his own name for the invention which enriches his country. "Medicine, music, finance, wholesale commerce and farming, have their representatives in this class of society; and there are in Louisiana fortunes honorably acquired by their proprietors, belonging to this class, which would secure for their owners a distinguished rank in Parisian society, were they to settle in that capital. I will not speak here," says the letter writer, "of the native citizens reputed to be bons blancs. They are very few, if we may believe an old Creole of the highest respectability, who said upon'Change, that he knew more than five hundred persons of this sort sprung from maroon negresses, and now enjoying the rights of citizenship."

CHAPTER XVIII: FLORIDA.

TONEY PROCTOR, a free man of color, died in Tallahassee, at the residence of H. L. Rutgers, Esq., on the 15th of June, 1855, in the 112th year of his age. The Tallahassee Sentinel thus notices the death of this remarkable man: —

"'UNCLE TONEY,' as he was familiarly called, must have been, at the time of his death, at least one hundred and twelve years old, and the probabilities are that he was several years older. It is known, as a historical fact, that he was at the battle of Quebec, on the 13th of September, 1759, some ninety-six years ago. His recollection of that event was clear and distinct. He was there in the capacity of a body servant to an English officer, and was sixteen years of age or more at the time of sailing, in company with the English sailors, from the Island of Jamaica, to return no more to the place of his nativity. He was subsequently engaged in the same capacity, though under a different officer, during the early period of the Revolutionary War between this and the mother country. He was in the vicinity of Boston at the time the tea was thrown overboard, and afterwards at the battle of Lexington. He came to Florida long before the change of flags, and settled in St. Augustine, where he purchased his freedom, married, and reared a large family. During his long residence in the 'Ancient City,' where he experienced many reverses — living through a period much longer than is allotted to an ordinary life-time — his conduct was such as to command the esteem and respect of its inhabitants, as well under the administration of the United States as the dominion of Spain.

"At the change of flags, he considered himself an American citizen, and remained in St. Augustine, true to his allegiance, during the campaigns and military regime of General Jackson; and subsequently rendered himself very useful to General Harney and others, as an Indian interpreter in the late Seminole war.

"Coming out of that protracted and disastrous war reduced in circumstances, with nothing to rely upon for support except a claim upon the Government for service rendered, but little of which was ever recognised and paid, he came, some ten years or more ago, to Tallahassee, to live with his son George.

"In 1849, George went a gold-hunting, with the intention, if successful, of returning in a few years, at the furthest, and relieving himself of his embarrassments. In the mean time, his family, as well as 'Uncle Toney,' were left in charge of Mr. Rutgers.

"The circumstances attending his death were very remarkable. He died of no disease. His health continued good and his spirits cheerful down to within a day or so of his death. The first evidence of decay was that of sight; time, in other respects, working but little change in his appearance. Death seemed to come over him like falling into a gentle sleep. The vital spark, like the socket of a candle, literally burned out.

UNCLE TONEY was much beloved by his own people. He was a zealous member of the Baptist Church. His funeral was one of the largest processions we remember to have seen."

CONDITION AND PROSPECTS OF COLORED AMERICANS.

CHAPTER I: CITIZENSHIP.

IN 1790, (says Judge Jay,) Congress passed an act prescribing the mode in which "any alien, being a white person," might be naturalized, and admitted to the rights of an American citizen. Two years after, an act was passed for organizing the militia, which was to consist of each and every free able-bodied white male citizen, &c. No other government on earth prohibits any portion of its citizens from participating in the national defence. But, not with this insult to colored citizens, another, and perhaps a still more wanton and malignant one, was offered by the government in the act of 1810, organizing the Post-Office Department. The fourth section enacts that "no other than a free white person shall be employed in carrying the mail of the United States, either as post-rider or driver of a carriage carrying the mail," under a penalty of fifty dollars.

Any vagabond from Europe, any fugitive from our own prisons, may take charge of the United States mail; but a native-born American citizen, of unimpeachable morals, and with property acquired by honest industry, may not, if his skin be dark, guide the horses which draw the carriage in which a bag of newspapers is deposited!

The following letter of instructions from the Postmaster General to one of his deputies, written in 1828, is a curious commentary on this law: —

SIR, — The mail may not, in any case whatever, be in the custody of a colored person. If a colored person is employed to lift the mail from the stage into the post-office, it does not pass into his custody, but the labor is performed in the presence and under the immediate direction of the white person who has it in custody; but if a colored person takes it from a tavern and carries it himself to the post-office, it comes into his custody during the time of carrying it, which is contrary to law.

"I am, &c.,

JOHN McLEAN."

In the United States Senate, July 29, 1842, the bill regulating enlistments in the Navy was discussed. Mr. Calhoun moved an amendment, that white men only should be enlisted, except for cooks, servants, and stewards, for which offices negroes or mulattoes might be employed.

Mr. Woodbury, of New Hampshire, supported the amendment.

Mr. Phelps, of Vermont, and Mr. Clayton, of Delaware, objected; and each cited instances of the colored man's valor, and enforced his claim to being enrolled as other Americans.

The amendment was, however, adopted, by a vote of twenty- four to sixteen ; as was, also, that of Mr. Preston, (of South Carolina,) prohibiting the enlistment of negroes in the Army. And this, notwithstanding the fact, that the victory upon Champlain has been well-known to have been achieved, in part, by the valor of colored men. That upon Erie, so far as aided by colored men's valor, has been in doubt, and in some quarters has been denied. Says Mr. Day, "I desire to refer you to the proof of the position, that colored men were with Commodore Perry on Lake Erie, and that they were as good hands as others. Writing to Commodore Chauncey, the senior officer, Captain Perry, said — 'The men that came by Mr. Champlin are a motley set, blacks, soldiers, and boys. I am, however, pleased to see any thing in the shape of a man.' So much as to the fact that there were 'blacks' to help man the squadron.

"To show that many of the colored men upon Lakes Erie and Champlain were among the best, I quote the following from a letter of Commodore Chauncey to Captain Perry: —

ON BOARD THE "PIKE," OFF BURLINGTON BAY, July 13th.

SIR, — I have been duly honored with your letters of the 23d and 26th ultimo, and notice your anxiety for men and officers. I am equally anxious to furnish you, and no time shall be lost in sending officers and men to you, as soon as the public service will allow me to send them from this lake. I regret that you are not pleased with the men sent you by Messrs. Champlin and Forrest; for, to my knowledge, a part of them are not surpassed by any seamen we have in the fleets; and I have yet to learn, that the color of the skin, or the cut and trimmings of the coat, can affect a man's qualifications or usefulness. I have nearly fifty blacks on board of this ship, and many of them are among my best men; and those people you call soldiers have been to sea from two to seventeen years, and I presume that you will find them as good and useful as any men on board of your vessel, — at least, if I can judge by comparison, for those which we have on board this ship are attentive and obedient and, as far as I can judge, many of them excellent seamen; at any rate, the men sent to Lake Erie have been selected with a view of sending a fair proportion of petty officers and seamen, and I presume upon examination, it will be found they are equal to those upon this lake.

"So far as to the capacity of colored men with Commodore Perry."

The managers of the Park Theatre, in New York city, in testimony of the bravery of the lamented Captain Lawrence and his crew, manifested in the brilliant action with the British sloop-of-war "Peacock," invited him and them to a play in honor of the victory achieved on that occasion. The crew marched, together into the pit, and nearly one half of them were negroes.

In March, 1855, Hon. T. D. Eliot, of Massachusetts, succeeded in obtaining the compensation Of PETER AMEY, a colored man of New Bedford, who fought on board the "Essex," in 1812. His motion was opposed by Mr. Chastain, of Georgia; but as Mr. Eliot intimated that he should then probably oppose other private claims, Mr. Seward, of Georgia, remarked that Georgia would lose her claims, and Mr. Chastain withdrew his opposition, and the bill passed to a third reading.

The Homestead Bill was adopted by Congress in March, 1854, with an amendment to limit its grant of land to white persons only. Thomas Davis, of Rhode Island, Joshua R. Giddings, of Ohio, and Gerrit Smith, of New York, with others, ably and strenuously advocated the rights of colored Americans, but were voted down, seventy-one to sixty-three.

Public bodies and the press have, during the past few years, discussed several questions bearing on the right of colored men to the privileges of citizenship. The following facts showing the theory and practice of this government, capricious as the latter has been, yet furnish precedents favorable to the colored man.

Distinctions of color are not recognised in the letter of the United States Constitution; yet that instrument leaves it in the power of Congress and individual States to trample on or acknowledge, as tyranny may dictate, the rights of colored citizens.

Congress can as well naturalize Asiatics, South Americans and Africans, as Europeans; and yet, for reasons best known to the Slave Power which rules this nation, the instances are few and far between where colored aliens have received naturalization papers. One case, however, occurred, as early as 1804, where a colored man received a certificate of naturalization, of which the following is a copy:

CITY OF NEW YORK, ss.

Be it remembered, that GEORGE DEGRASSE, of the city of New York, servant, who hath resided within the limits and jurisdiction of the United States for the term of five years, and within this State of New York for the term of one year at least, appeared in the Court of Common Pleas, called the Mayor's Court, and which is a common law court of record held in and for the city and county of New York in the State of New York, on Thursday, the fifth day of July, in the year one thousand eight hundred and four, and having made proof to the satisfaction of said Court that he is a person of good moral character, attached to the principles of the Constitution of the United States, and well disposed to the good order and happiness of the same, and having in the said Court taken the oath prescribed by law to support the Constitution of the United States, and did in open Court absolutely and entirely renounce and abjure all allegiance and fidelity to every foreign prince, potentate, state or sovereignty, and particularly to the King of the United Kingdom of Great Britain and Ireland, of whom he was then a subject, the said GEORGE DEGRASSE was thereupon, Pursuant to the laws of the United States in such case made and provided, admitted by the said Court to be, and he is accordingly to be, considered a citizen of the United States.

Given under the seal of the said Court, the day and year above written. Per curiam,

T. WOODMAN, Clerk.

Mr. DEGRASSE has since resided in New York city, where, for more than fifty years, he has regularly voted for United States and State officers.

The following account of Dr. JOHN V. DEGRASSE, a son of the above-named, by a correspondent of the New YorkIndependent, will be found of interest in this connection: —

"August 24th, 1854, Mr. DEGRASSE was admitted in due form a member of the 'Massachusetts Medical Society.' It is the first instance of such honor being conferred upon a colored man in this State, at least, and probably in the country; and therefore it deserves particular notice, both because the means by which he has reached this distinction are creditable to his own intelligence and perseverance, and because others of his class may be stimulated to seek an elevation which has hitherto been supposed unattainable by men of color. The Doctor is a native of New York city, where he was born June, 1825, and where he spent his time in private and public schools till 1840. He then entered the Oneida Institute, Beriah Green, President, and spent one year; but as Latin was not taught there, he left and entered the Clinton Seminary, where he remained two years, intending to enter college in the fall of 1843. He was turned from this purpose, however, by the persuasions of a friend in France, and after spending two years in a college in that country, he returned to New York in

November 1845, and commenced the study of medicine with Dr. Samuel R. Childs, of that city. There he spent two years in patient and diligent study, and then two more in attending the medical lectures of Bowdoin College, Me. Leaving that institution with honor in May, 1849, he went again to Europe in the autumn, of that year, and spent considerable time in the hospitals of Paris, travelling, at intervals, through parts of France, England, Italy, and Switzerland. Returning home in the ship 'Samuel Fox,' in the capacity of surgeon, be was married in August, 1852, and since that time, he has practised medicine in Boston. Earning a good reputation here by his diligence and skill, he was admitted a member of the Medical Society, as above stated. Many of our most respectable physicians visit and advise with him whenever counsel is required. The Boston medical profession, it must be acknowledged, has done itself honor in thus discarding the law of caste, and generously acknowledging real merit, without regard to the hue of the skin."

In the Doctor's study hangs his diploma, and a beautiful painting, ("The Ship Outward Bound,") executed by a young colored artist, Mr. EDWARD BANNISTER, which is enclosed in an elaborate gilt frame, the work of a young mechanic, Mr. JACOB ANDREWS, — the whole being a joint presentation to their professional friend. Such tributes of genius and skill harmonize well with every worthy effort for the elevation of those in this land with whom the donors are identified, by complexion and condition.

In 1811, JOHN REMOND was successful in his application for naturalization, in form as follows: —

ESSEX, SS.

At the Supreme Judicial Court of the Commonwealth of Massachusetts, begun and holden at Ipswich, within and for the county of Essex, oil the fourth Tuesday of April, Anno Domini 1811, JOHN REMOND, late of the Island of Curacoa and town of Curacoa, formerly subject to the government of the States General, but now to George the Third, King of the United Kingdom of Britain and Ireland, now resident at Salem, in said county of Essex, Hair-Dresser, took and subscribed the oath and declaration required by law. And thereupon he, the said JOHN REMOND, was admitted to become a citizen of the United States, according to the laws in such case made and provided.

In testimony whereof, I have hereunto set my hand, and affixed the seal of said Court, on this second day of May, Anno Domini 1811.

ICHABOD TUCKER,

Clerk of the Court aforesaid.

Several distinguished colored Americans have succeeded in obtaining passports. The following circumstance is related in a letter from the Rev. A. A. Phelps, dated May 24, 1834, to William Goodell: — "On Tuesday evening, I took tea at Mr. Forten's, (a well-known manufacturer and merchant of Philadelphia — a man of color,) in company with Brothers Leavitt, Pomeroy, and Dr. Lansing. It was a very pleasant interview, and not the least pleasing thing about it is the following: — We were scarcely seated, before in came Robert Vaux, Esq., with a passport for Robert Purvis and wife, under the seal of the Secretary of State, certifying that the said Purvis and wife were citizens of the United States. Mr. Purvis is son-in-law to Mr. Forten. He was about to visit Europe for his health, and in some of the countries on the Continent, as in France, a passport is necessary, certifying who the person is, where from, &c. The application was made through Robert Vaux, Esq., and on the representation of the case by him, it was at once granted."

Mr. Robert Purvis, in a letter to Mr. Garrison, dated London, July 13, 1834, says: — "I had, at the House of Commons, an introduction to the Hon. Daniel O. Connell. On my being presented to the Irish patriot as an American gentleman, he declined taking my hand; but when he understood that I was not only identified with the Abolitionists, but with the proscribed and oppressed colored men of the United States, he grasped my hand, and, warmly shaking it, remarked, — "Sir, I will never take the hand of an American, nor should any honest man in this country do so, without first knowing his principles in reference to America slavery, and its ally, the American Colonization Society."

Rev. PETER WILLIAMS also received a passport from John Forsyth, Secretary of State, the 17th of March, 1836, requesting "all whom it may concern to permit safely and freely to pass, Rev. Peter Williams, a citizen of the United States, and in case of need, to give him all lawful aid and protection."

Rev. PETER WILLIAMS, JR., was born in Brunswick, N. J., December, 1786. His father was proprietor of the largest tobacco manufactory then in the city of New York, and was the first to introduce steam power to drive its machinery. Mr. WILLIAMS was for twenty years (until his death, in 1840) pastor of St. Phillips' Episcopal Church. Aside from his pulpit efforts, he contributed many able, eloquent and practical effusions, through pamphlets and newspapers, in aid of the colored American's elevation. We learn, from a memoir by Dr. James Mc'Cune Smith, that "he had mastered Logic and Algebra, read Latin with some facility, was extravagantly fond of Metaphysics, and, what is remarkable with the slender advantages he enjoyed, he had formed a style in composition so clear, concise and elegant, that few men of twice his years and with every advantage, have excelled it. His oration on the Abolition of the Slave Trade, delivered January, 1808, when he was just twenty-one years of age, was discredited as having emanated from his pen, — and it was deemed necessary that his certificate to that effect should be published, confirmed by Rt. Rev. Benjamin Moore, Bishop of the Protestant Episcopal Church, and others.

During the reign of terror to which Anti-Slavery men and women were subjected, in the years 1833, '4 and '5, Mr. Williams was induced by his Bishop, for church reasons, to abstain from taking part in the anti-slavery agitation. His letter was published, and created much sensation at the time, especially among many of his former associates. It is due, however, to his memory, to state, (which we do upon the most reliable authority,) that the Bishop suppressed those passages which Mr. Williams had confidently relied upon to modify the objections of his friends. His natural diffidence of character deterred him from making an explanation. From that letter the following reminiscences are extracted: —

"In the Revolutionary War, my father was a decided advocate of American Independence, and his life was repeatedly jeopardized in its cause. Permit me to relate an instance, which shows that neither the British sword nor British gold could make him a traitor to his country. He was living in the State of Jersey, and parson Chapman, a champion of American liberty of great influence throughout that part of the country, was sought after by the British troops. My father immediately mounted a horse and rode round among his parishioners to notify them of his danger, and to call on them to help in removing him and his goods to a place of safety. He then carried him to a private place, and as he was returning, a British officer rode up to him, and demanded, in a most peremptory manner, —

"'Where is parson Chapman?'

"'I cannot tell,' was the reply.

"On that, the officer drew his sword, and, raising it over his head, said, — 'Tell me where he is, or I will instantly cut you down.'

"Again he replied, — 'I cannot tell.'

"Finding threats useless, the officer put up his sword, and drew out a purse of, gold, saying, — 'If you will tell me where he is, I will give you this.'

"The reply still was, 'I cannot tell.'

"The officer cursed him, and rode off.

"This attachment to the country of his birth was strengthened and confirmed by the circumstance, that the very day on which the British evacuated New York was the same on which he obtained his freedom by purchase, through the help of some republican friends of the Methodist Church; and to the last year of his life, he always spoke of that day as one which gave double joy to his heart, by freeing him from domestic bondage, and his native city from foreign enemies.

"Reared with these feelings, though fond of retirement, I felt a burning desire to be useful to my brethren and my country, and when the last war between this country and Great Britain broke out, I felt happy to render the humble services of my pen; my tongue, and my hands, towards rearing fortifications to defend our shores against invasion. I entreated my brethren to help in the defence of the country, and went with them to the work; and no sacrifice has been considered too great by me for the benefit of it or them."

WILLIAM WELLS BROWN, on leaving the United States for Europe, obtained, through the intercession of a friend, a passport signed by Wm. B. Calhoun, Secretary of State for Massachusetts. The following letter from Mr. Brown, covering the passport obtained in London, countersigned by a son of Ex-Governor John Davis, is instructive and interesting: —

LONDON, Nov. 22, 1849.

WENDELL PHILLIPS, Esq:

DEAR FRIEND — I observe in the American papers an elaborate discussion upon the subject of passports for colored men. What must the inhabitants of other countries think of the people of the United States, when they read, as they do, the editorials of some of the Southern papers against recognizing colored Americans as citizens? In looking over some of these articles, I have felt ashamed that I had the misfortune to be born in such a country. We may search history in vain to find a people who have sunk themselves as low, and made themselves appear as infamous by their treatment of their fellow-men, as have the people of the United States. If colored men make their appearance in the slave States as seamen, they are imprisoned until the departure of the vessel. If they make their appearance at the capital of the country, unless provided with free papers, they are sold for the benefit of the Government. In most of the States we are disfranchised, our children are shut out from the public schools, and embarrassments are thrown in the way of every attempt to elevate ourselves. And after they have degraded us, sold us, mobbed us, and done every thing in their power to oppress us, then, if we wish to leave the country, they refuse us passports, upon the ground that we are not citizens. This is emphatically an age of discoveries; but I will venture the assertion, that none but an American slaveholder could have discovered that a man born in a country was not a citizen of it. Their chosen motto, that "all men are created equal," when compared with their treatment of the colored people of the country, sinks them lower and lower in the estimation of the good and wise of all lands. In your letter of the 15th ult., you ask if I succeeded in getting a passport from the American Minister in London, previous to going to Paris to attend the Peace Congress. Through the magnanimity of the French Government, all delegates to the Congress were permitted to pass freely without passports. I did not, therefore, apply for one. But as I intend soon to visit the Continent, and shall then need one, I called a few days since on the American Minister, and was furnished with a passport, of which the following is a copy. If t will be of any service in the discussion upon that subject, you are at perfect liberty to use it: —

"LEGATION OF THE UNITED STATES OF AMERICA IN ENGLAND.
PASSPORT NO. 33.
The undersigned, Envoy Extraordinary and Minister Plenipotentiary of the United States of America at the Court of the United Kingdom of Great Britain and Ireland, begs all whom it may concern to allow safely and freely to pass, and in case of need, to give aid and protection to
MR. WILLIAM W. BROWN,
a citizen of the United States, going on the Continent.
Given under my signature, and the imprint of the seal of the legation in London, Oct. 31, 1849, the 74th year of the independence of the United States.
For the Minister,
JOHN C. B. DAVIS,
Secretary of Legation."

So you see, my friend, that though we are denied citizenship in America, and refused passports at home when wishing to visit foreign countries, they dare not refuse us a passport when we apply for it in old England. There is a public sentiment here, that, hard-hearted as the Americans are, they fear. When will the Americans learn, that if they would encourage liberty in other countries, they must practice it at home? If they would inspire the hearts of the struggling millions in Europe, they should not allow one human being to wear chains upon their own soil. If they would welcome the martyrs for freedom from the banks of the Danube, the Tiber and the Seine, let them liberate their own slaves on the banks of the Mississippi and the Potomac. If they would welcome the Hungarian flying from the bloody talons of the Austrian eagle, they must wrest the three millions of slaves from the talons of their own. They cannot welcome the wanderer from the battle-fields of freedom in the old world, as long as the new world is the battle-field of slavery. Should the Kossuths and the Wimmers visit America, the would be reminded of their friends they left in chains in Austria, by the clanking chains of the American slave.

I was asked a few clays since, at a meeting, if I was not afraid that the abolitionists would become tired, and give up the cause as hopeless. My answer was, that the slave's cause was in the hands of men and women who intended to agitate and agitate, until the iron hand of slavery should melt away, drop by drop, before a fiery public sentiment.

WM. W. BROWN.

At a reception meeting tendered Mr. Brown in Boston, October 13th, 1854, WENDELL PHILLIPS, Esq., in the course of an eloquent speech, said: —

"I still more rejoice that Mr. Brown has returned. Returned to what? Not to what he can call his 'country.' The white man comes 'home.' When Milton heard, in Italy, the sound of arms from England, he hastened back — young, enthusiastic, and bathed in beautiful art as he was in Florence. 'I would not be away,' he said, 'when a blow was struck for liberty.' He came to a country where his manhood was recognised, to fight on equal footing. The black man comes home to no liberty but the liberty of suffering — struggle in fetters for the welfare of his race. It is a magnanimous sympathy with his blood that brings such a man back. I honor it. We meet to do it honor. Franklin's motto was, Ubi libertas ibi patria — Where liberty is, there is my country. Had our friend adopted that for his rule, he would have stayed in Europe. Liberty for him is there. The colored man who returns, like our friend, to labor, crushed and despised, for his race, sails under a higher flag: his Motto is — 'WHERE MY COUNTRY IS, THERE WILL I BRING LIBERTY"

As recently as the first of January, 1854, JOHN REMOND, of Salem, Mass., obtained a passport from the then Secretary of State, William L. Marcy.

Although, on some occasions, the officials of the United States government have refused to acknowledge colored Americans as citizens, — denying them passports and the like, — yet, with a strange inconsistency, they are sometimes made recipients of honors and emoluments not to be obtained by others than citizens of the United States.

At a meeting of the Bar of the County of Suffolk, Mass., held at the office of the Clerk of the Circuit Court of the United States, on Thursday, June 27, 1850, Ellis Gray Loring, Esq., was chosen Chairman, and Charles Theodore Russell, Esq., Secretary.

On motion of Charles Sumner, Esq., it was

Resolved, That ROBERT MORRIS, Esq., be recommended for admittance to practice as a Counsellor and Attorney of the Circuit and District courts of the United States.

(Signed,)

ELLIS GRAY LORING, Chairman.

CHAS. THEO. RUSSELL, Sec'y.

In accordance with this resolve, Mr. MORRIS presented himself before Justice Sprague, of the United States District Court, — who, it is presumed, had ample evidence of his color, — and, was duly admitted to practice in the Courts of the United States.

MACON B. ALLEN, another colored lawyer, was admitted in Maine, to the Cumberland Bar, on examination, and subsequently in Massachusetts, to the Suffolk Bar, on certificate. Among those who congratulated him on his appointment were Hon. John G. Palfrey, and Professor Greenleaf, of Harvard University.

GEORGE B. VASHON was also admitted, on examination, before the New York Bar, in 1848. A correspondent of the Philadelphia Inquirer alludes to his admission as Attorney, Solicitor and Counsellor of the Supreme Court of the State, and adds, that he evinced a perfect knowledge of the rudiments of law, and a familiar acquaintance with Coke, Littleton, Blackstone, and Kent.

When it is remembered that most lawyers are admitted by certificate, great credit will be awarded Messrs. ALLEN and VASHON, who passed the ordeal of open court examination with signal credit.

Messrs. MORRIS and ALLEN are now Justices of the Peace for Massachusetts.

The Constitution of the United States declares "that the citizens of each State shall be entitled to all the privileges and immunities of citizens in the several States."

The Act of February 21, 1799, granting patents for useful improvements, authorizes the issuing of a patent only to a "citizen." Cannot a man of color obtain one? Such has been done, and he would be a bold officer who should refuse one on the ground of color. The Act of 1831, on the subject of copyright, is one of the same character.

So the Act of December 31, 1792, concerning the registering and recording of ships or vessels. It is enacted, that no vessel shall be considered or treated as an American vessel, unless she is owned and commanded by an "American citizen;" — men of color have owned vessels, and they have always been considered American vessels.

So by the Act of February 18, 1793, for enrolling and licensing vessels for the coasting trade and the fisheries, a like oath must be taken by the owner before she can be permitted to engage in the same — a "citizen" only can do it; but cannot and have not men of color?

So the militia law uses the words white male citizens; implying that there are other citizens besides white ones; for else the word citizens would not have been used. It is true, colored men are exempt from military duty, but so are all persons under eighteen, or over forty-five, years of age, and all females; but yet, Congress can call all these into the army or navy, or militia; and none will contend that exemption from military service proves political inferiority.

So the Act of May 15, 1820, makes it criminal for a "citizen" to engage in the slave trade. Can people of color do it? And yet penal laws are construed strictly.

So the Act of May 28, 1796, for the relief and protection of American seamen, declares that any "citizen" sailor can obtain from the custom-house officer a certificate of his citizenship; men of color have often done this, and can again.

So the Act of July 20, 1790, for the regulation of seamen in the merchant's service, provides, that every ship or vessel belonging to a "citizen or citizens" of the United States, of a certain burthen, on a foreign voyage, shall, under a severe penalty, be provided with a medicine chest. Are not men of color bound to comply with this law?

Impressed colored sailors have been claimed by the National Government as "citizens of the United States."

If a man of color in New York or Pennsylvania should sue a white citizen of Connecticut in the Federal Court, would it be a good plea in abatement that one of the parties is a man of color?

The question of colored citizenship came up as a national question, and was settled, during the pendency of the Missouri question, in 1820.

It will be remembered, that that State presented herself for admission into the Union, with a clause in her Constitution prohibiting the settlement of colored citizens within her borders. Resistance was made to her admission into the Union upon that very ground; and it was not until that State receded from her unconstitutional position, that President Monroe declared the admission of Missouri into the Union to be complete.

According to Niles's Register, August 18th, vol. 20, pages 338 and 339, the refusal to admit Missouri into the Union was not withdrawn until the General Assembly of that State, in conformity to a fundamental condition imposed by Congress, had, by an act passed for that purpose, solemnly enacted and declared, "That this State (Missouri) has assented, and does assent, that the fourth clause of the twenty-sixth section of the third article of their Constitution should never be construed to authorize the passage of any law, and that no law shall be passed in conformity thereto, by which any citizen of either of the United States shall be excluded from the enjoyment of any of the privileges and immunities to which such citizens are entitled, under the Constitution of the United States."

A free colored citizen of the county of West Chester, in the State of New York, named GILBERT HORTON, was employed as a sailor on board a coasting vessel, which touched at a port in the District of Columbia. Horton went on shore, and while peaceably walking in one of the streets of the city of Washington, was seized and thrown into jail as a fugitive slave.

After he had been in jail a month, the following notice appeared in the National Intelligencer, August 1st, 1826: —

"Was committed to the jail of Washington county, District of Columbia, on the 2d of July last, as a runaway, a negro man by the name of Gilbert Horton. He is five feet four inches high, stout made, has large full eyes, and a scar on his left arm near the elbow. Had on, when committed, a tarpaulin hat, linen shirt, blue cloth jacket and trousers. Says that he was born free in the State of New York, near Peekskill. The owner or owners of the above described negro, if any, are requested to come and prove him and take him away, or he will be sold for his jail fees and other expenses, as the law directs.

"RICHARD BURR,

"FOR TENCH RINGOLD, Marshal."

This advertisement happened to meet the eye of the Hon, Wm. Jay, a son of the celebrated Governor John Jay, who took immediate measures to procure a meeting of the citizens of West Chester county. That meeting adopted a series of resolutions, requesting his Excellency De Witt Clinton to demand from the proper authorities the instant liberation of Horton, as a free citizen of the State of New York. In reply to the Governor's letter, he was informed that the Marshal, having become satisfied that Horton was a free man, had liberated him. The truth probably was, that the Marshal had notice of the proceedings of the State of New York, and knowing (what was generally well known) that De Witt Clinton was not a man to be trifled with, and that he would, at any hazard, maintain and defend the rights of his own State, and every citizen of it, with a firmness and a perseverance not to be evaded or eluded, preferred the immediate liberation of Horton, by what might seem to be a voluntary act, to a compulsory discharge, in pursuance of a requisition from the Governor of a free State.

The following is a copy of the letter of De Witt Clinton to John Q. Adams, President of the United States, in the case alluded to: —

ALBANY, 4th September, 1826.

SIR, — I have the honor to inclose copies of the proceedings of a respectable meeting of inhabitants of West Chester county, in this State, and of an affidavit of John Owen, by which it appears that one GILBERT HORTON a free man of color, and a CITIZEN of this State, is unlawfully imprisoned in the jail of the city of Washington, and is advertised to be sold by the Marshal of the District of Columbia. From whatever authority a law authorizing such proceedings may have emanated, whether from the municipality of Washington, the Legislature of Maryland, or the Congress of the United States, it is, at least, void and unconstitutional in its application to a CITIZEN, and could never have intended to extend further than to fugitive slaves. As the District of Columbia is under the exclusive control of the national government, I conceive it my duty to apply to you for the liberation of Gilbert Horton, as a freeman and a citizen, and feel persuaded that this request will be followed by immediate relief. I have the honor to be, &c.,

"DE WITT CLINTON."

SOLOMON NORTHUP, a citizen of Washington county, State of New York, was kidnapped in 1841, and conveyed to Louisiana, and there held as a slave for twelve years; but, through an almost miraculous chain of circumstances, he was enabled to impart the fact to his friends at Saratoga, His Excellency, Washington Hunt, demanded from the authorities of Louisiana the safe delivery of Solomon Northup, a free citizen of the State of New York. The demand was complied with, and he was restored to his family and friends.

HOSEA EASTON thus forcibly alludes to the claims of colored Americans to the rights and privileges of citizenship: —

"In this country, we behold the remnant of a once noble, but now heathenish people. I would have my readers lose sight of the African character. For at this time, circumstances have established as much difference between them and their ancestry, as exists between them and any other race or nation. In the first place, the colored people who are born in this country, are Americans in every sense of the word, — Americans by birth, genius, habits, language, &c. They are dependent on American climate, American aliment, American government, and American manners, to sustain their American bodies and minds; a withholding of the enjoyment of any American privilege from an American man, either governmental, ecclesiastical, civil, social or alimental, is in effect taking away his means of subsistence; and consequently, taking away his life. Every ecclesiastical body which denies an American the privilege of participating in its benefits, becomes his murderer. Every State which denies an American a citizenship, with all its benefits, denies him his life. The claims the colored people set up, therefore, are the claims of Americans. Their claims are founded in an original agreement of the contracting parties, and there is nothing to show that color was a consideration in the agreement. It is well known, that when the country belonged to Great Britain, the colored people were slaves. But when America revolted from Britain, they were held no longer by any legal power. There was no efficient law in the land except martial law, and that regarded no one as a slave. The inhabitants were governed by no other law, except by resolutions adopted from time to time by meetings convoked in the different colonies. Upon the face of the warrants by which these district and town meetings were called, there is not a word said about the color of the attendants. In convoking the Continental Congress of the 4th of September, 1774, there was not a word said about color. At a subsequent period, Congress met again, to get in readiness twelve thousand men to act in any emergency; at the same time, a request was forwarded to Connecticut, New Hampshire, and Rhode Island, to increase this army to twenty thousand men. Now, it is well known that hundreds of the men of which this army was composed were colored men, and recognised by Congress as Americans. * * *

"Excuses have been made in vain to cover up the hypocrisy of this nation. The most corrupt policy which ever disgraced its barbarous ancestry has been adopted by both Church and State, for the avowed purpose of withholding the inalienable rights of one part of the subjects of the government. Pretexts of the lowest order, which are neither witty nor decent, and which rank among that order of subterfuges under which the lowest of ruffians attempt to hide when exposed to detection, are made available. * * * I have no language to express what I see, and hear, and feel, on this subject. Were I capable of dipping my pen in the deepest dye of crime, and of understanding the science of the bottomless pit, I should then fail in presenting to the intelligence of mortals on earth, the true nature of American deception. There can be no appeals made in the name of the laws of the country, or philanthropy, or humanity, or religion, that are capable of drawing forth any thing but the retort, — you are a negro! If we call to our aid the thunder tones of the cannon and the arguments of fire-arms, (vigorously managed by black and white men, side by side,) as displayed upon Dorchester Heights, and at Lexington, and at White Plains, and at Kingston, and at Long Island, and elsewhere, the retort is, you are a negro! If we present to the nation a Bunker's Hill, our nation's altar, (upon which she offered her choicest sacrifice,) with our fathers, and brothers, and sons, prostrate thereon, wrapped in fire and smoke — the incense of blood borne upward upon the wings of sulphurous vapor, to the throne of national honor, with a halo of national glory echoing back, and spreading over and astonishing the civilized world; — and if we present the thousands of widows and orphans, whose only earthly protectors were thus sacrificed, weeping over the fate of the departed; and anon, tears of blood are extorted, on learning that the government for which their lovers and sires had died refuses to be their protector; — if we tell that angels weep in pity, and that God, the eternal Judge, 'will hear the desire of the humble, judge the fatherless and the oppressed, that the man of the earth may no more oppress,' the retort is, YOU ARE A NEGRO! If there is a spark of honesty, patriotism, or religion, in the heart or the source from whence such refuting arguments emanate, the devil incarnate is the brightest seraph in paradise.

Hon. Norton S. Townshend, in submitting to the Senate a bill in accordance with the wish of petitioners for equal suffrage, remarked, "That the reasons were so ably set forth in the following memorial of J. Mercer Langston, that nothing further seemed to be required; and as Mr. Langston had been appointed by a State Convention of colored people, and therefore spoke by authority, the committee adopt the language of the memorial, making it a part of their report."

From the memorial thus highly complimented, I make the following extracts. It was presented to the General Assembly of the State of Ohio, April 19, 1854: —

"What, then, are the grounds upon which we claim the elective franchise?

"In answering this question, we have to say, in the first place, that we are men. Nor is it necessary to enter upon an argument in support of so self-evident a proposition. We possess the physical, the intellectual and the moral attributes common to humanity. We have the same feelings, desires, and aspirations that other men have; and we are capable of the same high intellectual and moral culture. As men, then, we have rights, inherent rights, which civil society is bound to respect, nay, more, which civil society is bound to protect and defend. Prominent among those rights, and one which we deeply love and cherish, is the elective franchise, is the privilege of saying who shall be our rulers, and what shall be the character of the laws under which we live. By none is this right held in higher estimation than by the colored men. And those greatly mistake who think that we, are contented without it. We are not. We know that it is one of our dearest rights. We feel that we ought to have it. We feel that civil society is under obligation to secure it to Us, and protect us in its enjoyment. The first consideration that we offer, therefore, in favor of granting our claim, is the fact that it is a dictate of justice and fair dealing, between civil society and men living within its jurisdiction.

* * * * * * * *

"We could, with propriety, however, claim so much at your hands, if we were foreigners. But when it is remembered that we are native-born inhabitants, and by our birth citizens, the consideration which has just been offered appears doubly significant, and therefore doubly forcible. It is needless for us, in grounding our claim to the elective franchise upon our nativity, to remind you, that it is a principle fully recognised by the Constitution of the country, that natural birth gives citizenship, otherwise, our naturalization laws are absurd and nonsensical. Says Chancellor Kent, in confirmation of our view, 'Citizens, under our Constitution and laws, mean free inhabitants born within the United States, or naturalized under the laws of Congress. If a slave, born in the United States, be manumitted, or otherwise lawfully discharged from bondage, or if a black man be born within the United States, and born free, he becomes thenceforward a citizen.' If Chancellor Kent's principle be correct, we may ask, with some degree of force, where is the right to disfranchise us where is the right to strip us of our citizenship? Said the Hon. Mr. Baldwin, in the United States Senate, 'When the Constitution of the United States was framed, colored men voted in a majority of these States; they voted in the State of New York, in Pennsylvania, in Massachusetts, in Connecticut, Rhode Island, New Jersey, Delaware and North Carolina; and long after the adoption of the Constitution, they continued to vote in North Carolina and Tennessee also. The Constitution of the United States makes no distinction of color. There is no word 'white' to be found in that instrument. All free people then stood upon the same platform in regard to their political rights, and were so recognised in most of the States of the Union.

* * * * The free colored citizens of these States are as much entitled to the rights of citizenship, as are men of any other color or complexion whatever. * * * * To this day, in the State of Virginia, free colored persons, born in that State, are citizens.

"We claim our enfranchisement also upon the ground that we are patriotic. It is a fact that we love this country. We love her Constitution, and we love those free institutions that might and ought to be built up all over this land under its benign influence. Indeed, at no time have we manifested for this country any other spirit than that of deep, abiding affection. And that, too, when we have been outraged and abused most barbarously. * * * *

"'Their right,' (colored Americans) in the truthful language of John G. Whittier, 'like that of their white fellow-citizens, dates back to the dread arbitrament of war. Their bones whiten every stricken field of the Revolution; their feet tracked with blood the snows of Jersey; their toil built up every fortification south of the Potomac; they shared ,the famine and nakedness of Valley Forge, and the pestilential horrors of the old Jersey prison ship.' Have we, then, no claim to an equal participation in the blessings which have 'grown out of the national independence,' which we fought to establish? Is it right, is it just, is it generous, is it magnanimous, to withhold from us these blessings and 'starve our patriotism'? What foreigner, what Irish or German emigrant, has ever given such evidences of deep devotion to your government? And yet, you have taken pains to make a special arrangement by which, in due time, they are to enter upon the full enjoyment of citizenship. To this arrangement we would not object. We simply ask that we, who have given such strong and significant proofs of our love of this country and its laws, be clothed in the livery of free and independent citizenship.

"As touching this point, we would also submit the views of Hon. William H. Seward, as presented in the following letter: —

WASHINGTON, May 16, 1850.

"'DEAR SIR: — Your letter of the 6th inst. has been received. I reply to it cheerfully and with pleasure.

'It is my deliberate opinion, founded upon careful observation, that the right of suffrage is exercised by no citizen of New York more conscientiously, or more sincerely, or with more beneficial results to society, than it is by the electors of African descent. I sincerely hope that the franchise will before long be extended, as it justly ought, to this race, who of all others need it most.

'I am, very respectfully, your obedient servant,

WILLIAM H. SEWARD.'

"Thus it will be seen that, in the estimation of such men — men who have bestowed some thought upon our condition and our conduct — that we are not all so ignorant and degraded that we are incapable of exercising the elective franchise in an intelligent and manly manner.

"Permit us to say, in conclusion, then, in view of these considerations, we hold that it is unjust, anti-democratic, impolitic, and ungenerous, to withhold from us the right of suffrage."

Mr. Langston has since had satisfactory proof that colored men are regarded as citizens by a good portion of the Buckeyes. Here is his announcement: —

"They put upon their ticket the name of a colored man, who was elected clerk of Brownhelm township, by a very handsome majority, indeed. Since

I am the only colored man who lives in this township, you can easily guess the name of the man who was so fortunate as to secure this election. To my knowledge, the like has not been known in Ohio before. It proves the steady march of the anti-slavery sentiment, and augurs the inevitable destruction and annihilation of American prejudice against colored men. What we so much need, just at this juncture and all along the future, is political influence; the bridle by which we can check and guide to our advantage the selfishness of American demagogues. How important, then, it is, that we labor night and day to enfranchise ourselves."

WILLIAM J. WATKINS SUMS Up the argument in behalf of the citizenship of colored men as follows: —

"It is said that the minister refused the negro a passport, On the ground that a black man was not considered a citizen of the United States. We gravely ask the question, If we are not citizens, then what are we? What constitutes citizenship in this country? Is color a constitutional disqualification? If so, there are a great many so-called white men who are not citizens, for we know not a few who would be taken for colored men, if the complexion were the standard. Neither does the texture of the hair exclude any one from the privileges of American citizens, that is, in compliance with the edict of the Constitution. It is just as constitutional to ostracise all the bald heads, or 'heads with sandy hair,' as to thrust a man, in the country, with woolly hair, outside the pale of American citizenship.

"We believe the Government recognizes the existence of but two classes of population, natives, or citizens, and aliens.

"Colored men, born on the soil, cannot be aliens; of course not. They cannot, therefore, be naturalized. Who ever heard of a colored American being naturalized in the United States? This government naturalizes foreigners only. We must, then, be CITIZENS. Our white fellow-citizens may withhold our right, but they cannot annihilate it.

"And now, with the broad, blazing sunlight of the Revolution flashing across our path, and revealing to the gaze of all men the prowess and patriotism of colored Americans, in the hour that tried men's souls, we are told we are not citizens. Shame upon this ingrate Government! But we will continue to regard ourselves as citizens, and as such demand our rights. We ask no favors, at the hands of the United States."

CHAPTER II: ELEVATION.

COEVAL with the establishment of The Liberator in Boston, in the year 1831, the dormant energies of the oppressed colored Americans became actively aroused, and the ways and means of elevation were prolific themes in their social gatherings. Among the causes contributing to this hopeful state of things may be mentioned the pamphlet of DAVID WALKER, published during the eventful period of Mr. Garrison's imprisonment in a Baltimore jail, for being an Anti-Slavery man, which was signally effective in rousing the eloquence of Walker. This appeal waked up some feeling at the South, and a corresponding degree of vitality among the colored people. But the most potent instrumentality that inspired the hearts of the colored Americans with faith, hope, and perseverance "for the good time coming," was the publication of that fearless, uncompromising sheet, The Liberator, which, when commenced, had arrayed against it the 30,000 churches, and clergy of the country — its wealth, its commerce, its press. At that time, there was the most entire ignorance and apathy on the slave question. In that dark hour, The Liberator was unfurled to the breeze, in the eyes of the nation, within sight of Bunker Hill, and in the birth-place of American liberty, consecrated to the cause till every chain be broken, and every bondman set — free its Editor pledging himself to the work in these immortal words: — "I am in earnest! I will not equivocate — I will not excuse — I will not retreat a single inch — and I WILL BE HEARD!" For twenty-five years has that clarion voice sounded in the ears of this guilty nation, and twenty-three millions of people complain, to-day, that they hear of nothing but slavery! It has unmasked the hydra-headed monster, Colonization, and secured an audience for the colored man, who before could hardly utter his thoughts.

Before The Liberator was issued, Mr. Garrison delivered Anti-Slavery lectures in Boston, at Julien Hall, and the old Athenaeum Hall, Pearl street. Among the colored friends present, on one very interesting occasion, at the latter place, were Rev. Thomas Paul and Rev. Samuel Snowden. The hearty amen of Father Snowden was responded to by the eloquent eye and earnest hand-shaking of the other favorite colored pastor, both of whom then vowed their devotion to the cause and its enthusiastic young advocate, to which pledge their life was remarkably consistent.

I remember, when a boy, in January, 1832, looking in at the vestry window of Belknap Street Church, while the Editor of The Liberator and a faithful few organized the first Anti-Slavery Society.

The immediate result of the labors of the Anti-Slavery press and the public lecturers, was the formation of exclusive organizations among the colored people. They, and the great body of the Abolitionists, did not then see eye to eye in the matter of combined action, for many of the latter supposed their Anti-Slavery mission was ended when they had publicly protested against slavery, without being careful to exemplify their principles in every-day practice. Many of the colored people, too, seemed to think that enough of heaven was opened unto them, when white people would talk Anti-Slavery; the idea of social political equality seemingly never being dreamed of by them.

In accordance with this view, a society was formed, called the "Massachusetts General Colored Association," of which Hosea and Joshua Easton, John E. Scarlett, Thomas Cole, James G. Barbadoes, William G. Nell, and others, now numbered with the dead, were members, — together with Thomas Dalton, John T. Hilton, Frederick Brimley, Coffin Pitts, Walker Lewis, and others of the "Old Guard," who yet remain with us. The object of this Association was the promulgation of Anti-Slavery truth. In January, 1833, it made application to be received as an auxiliary to the Massachusetts (then New England) Anti-Slavery Society, through the following letter: —

BOSTON, January 15, 1833.

To the Board of Managers of the New England Anti-Slavery Society:

The Massachusetts General Colored Association, cordially approving the objects and principles of the New England Anti-Slavery Society, would respectfully communicate their desire to become auxiliary thereto. They have accordingly chosen one of their members to attend the annual meeting of the Society as their delegate, (Mr. JOSHUA EASTON, of North Bridgewater,) and solicit his acceptance in that capacity.

THOMAS DALTON, President.

WILLIAM G. NELL, Vice President.

JAMES G. BARBADOES, Secretary.

Of course, this request was cordially granted; but they and their white friends soon learned that complexional Anti-Slavery societies, as such, were absurdities, to say the least, and hence, such distinctions soon melted into thin air; and if the spirit of Susan Paul takes cognizance of events familiar to her when in the flesh, she is now rejoicing in her association with the Anti-Slavery societies of that time, their "Martyr Acre," and her share in the perils consequent upon the burning of Pennsylvania Hall.

From the time of the mobbing of William Lloyd Garrison and George Thompson, and the women's meeting at Francis Jackson's, in Hollis street, where Harriet Martineau consecrated herself to the cause, and historically identified herself with the colored people, colored and white have met together on one Anti-Slavery platform, where, "like kindred drops, they mingle into one."

John Remond and Prince Farmer, of Salem, and Susan Paul, of Boston, became life-members of the Massachusetts Anti-Slavery Society in 1835. Subsequently, other names were enrolled from New Bedford and elsewhere, and colored persons also connected themselves with the American Anti-Slavery Society. And if there are any colored friends who do not now participate freely with their white brethren and sisters, in their efforts for the slave's redemption and their own elevation, it is only because they choose to absent themselves, and not because of objections on the part of others.

The presence of ROBERT PURVIS on the platform of the American A. S. Society as presiding officer, or of CHARLES LENOX REMOND, President, for several years, of the Essex County Anti-Slavery Society, with the distinguished position occupied by themselves and WILLIAM WELLS BROWN as orators, fully justifies what MARIA WESTON CHAPMAN claims for the American Anti-Slavery Society, when she says it is "church and university, high school and common school, to all who need real instruction and true religion. Of it what a throng of authors, editors, lawyers, orators, and accomplished gentlemen of color have taken their degree! It has equally implanted hopes and aspirations, noble thoughts and sublime purposes, in the hearts of both races. It has prepared the white man for the freedom of the black man, and it has made the black man scorn the thought of enslavement, as does a white man, as far as its influence has extended. Strengthen that noble influence! Before its organization, the country only saw here and there in slavery some 'faithful Cudjoe or Dinah,' whose strong natures blossomed even in bondage, like a fine plant beneath a heavy stone. Now, under the elevating and cherishing influence of the American Anti-Slavery Society, the colored race, like the white, furnishes Corinthian capitals for the noblest temples. Aroused by the American Anti-Slavery Society, the very white men who had forgotten and denied the claim of the black man to the rights of humanity, now thunder that claim at every gate, from cottage to capitol, from schoolhouse to university, from the railroad carriage to the house of God. He has a place at their firesides, a place in their hearts — the man whom they once cruelly hated for his color. So feeling, they cannot send him to Coventry with a horn-book in his hand, and call it instruction! They inspire him to climb to their side by a visible, acted gospel of freedom. Thus, instead of bowing to prejudice, they conquer it."

In 1831, the plan of Arnold Buffum for a colored college at New Haven was thought favorably of by the friends, white and colored, and Mr. Garrison, during his first mission to England, was expected to secure funds for the same; but a variety of causes prevented his receiving any donations, and the persecution of Prudence Crandall at Canterbury, Conn, and the attack upon the school-house at Canaan, N. H., bad the effect to open the doors of colleges and seminaries to youth, irrespective of complexion, and the necessity (or what seemed to be such) for a colored college was superseded.

Since that time, colored students have been admitted at Wilbraham, Leicester, Andover, Dartmouth, and at the majority of the institutions of learning in the New England, Central, and Western States.

In June, 1831, six months after the advent of The Liberator, the first Annual Convention of the People of Color was held in Philadelphia. New York, Pennsylvania, Maryland, Delaware and Virginia were the only States represented. This Convention appointed Provisional Committees, and named for Boston, Hosea Easton, Robert Roberts, James G. Barbadoes, and the late lamented Rev. Sam. Samuel Snowden. Since then, there have been several Conventions held by colored Americans in different parts of the country, and no one can deny that some good has resulted therefrom.

The Hamiltons, the Sipkinses, and a constellation of others from the Empire State, with those named elsewhere from the various sections, acted according to the light and promise of the times. Let us fulfil, during our mission, the prophecy of our fathers, who, in passing away, have left us the legacy of their prayers and fondest aspirations for success. While they have wept in remembrance of the past, when denied even a tithe of our present opportunities, their hearts were made glad in the anticipation of better associations for their sons, — the gaining of access to various avenues of improvement in morals, science, and the mechanic arts, and through such mediums, effecting an opening for their brethren to the position of free and independent citizenship.

In the Declaration of Sentiments adopted by the American Anti-Slavery Society in Philadelphia, in 1833, they pledged themselves to secure to the colored population of the United States all the rights and privileges which belong to them as men and as Americans, "come what may to our persons, our interests, or our reputation." The colored persons who signed this declaration were, Robert Purvis, of Pennsylvania, and James G. Barbadoes, of Massachusetts. The Anti-Slavery women of the United States assembled in Convention at New York, May, 1837, and published a circular, from which the following is extracted: —

"Those Societies that reject colored members, or seek to avoid them, have never been active or efficient. The blessing of God does not rest upon them, because they 'keep back a part of the price of the land,' — they do not lay all at the apostle's feet.

"The abandonment of prejudice is required of us as a proof of our sincerity and consistency. How can we ask our Southern brethren to make sacrifices, if we are not even willing to encounter inconveniences? First cast the beam from thine own eye, then wilt thou see clearly to cast it from his eye."

This circular was signed by Mary S. Parker, President, and Angelina E. Grimke, Secretary. Miss Sarah Douglass was among the colored members, and one of the Central Committee, and their published appeal contained these dedicatory lines by Sarah Forten, a colored lady: —

"We are thy sisters. God has truly said,
That of one blood the nations he has made.
O, Christian woman! in a Christian land,
Canst thou unblushing read this great command?
Suffer the wrongs which wring our inmost heart,
To draw one throb of pity on thy part!
Our skins may differ, but from thee we claim
A sister's privilege and a sister's name."

At the annual meeting of the New England Anti-Slavery Society, in January, 1836, Rev. Professor Follen offered the following resolution, which was unanimously adopted:

"Resolved, That we consider the Anti-Slavery cause the cause of philanthropy, with regard to which all human beings, white men and colored men, citizens and foreigners, men and women, have the same duties and the same rights."

In support of this resolution, Mr. Follen said, — "We have been advised, if we really wished to benefit the slave and the colored race generally, not unnecessarily to shock the feelings, though they were but prejudices, of the white people, by admitting colored persons to our Anti-Slavery meetings and societies. We have been told that many who would otherwise act in unison with us were kept away by our disregard of the feelings of the community in this respect....But what, I would ask, is the great, the single object of all our meetings and societies? Have we any other object than to impress upon the community this one principle, that the colored man is a man? and, on the other hand, is not the prejudice which would have us exclude colored people from our meetings and societies the same which, in our Southern States, dooms them to perpetual bondage?"

Rev. Theodore S. Wright, at the Anti-Slavery Convention in Boston, May, 1836, alluding to the Oneida Institute, testified as follows: — "God is there teaching abolition by training white and colored young men together. The most efficient coöperation I ever received was from those with whom I have associated in the seats of learning, — my respected classmates. They have always been ready to aid and counsel me. My heart has always gladdened to see them. It is important to make the two races feel kindness and respect for each other, even if but few do, so it will have an effect on others. Get two men to love each other, though of two nations, and it will make them love the whole class."

James M'Cune Smith, J. V. DeGrasse, and their brethren in the medical profession, as also the trio of college Professors, Wm. G. Allen, Charles L. Reason and George B. Vashon, Rev. H. H. Garnet, S. R. Ward, Amos G. Beman, and others, are manifestly more competent in their various callings for having graduated at institutions where they contended for mental superiority with the more favored class of white students.

This principle is beautifully illustrated at Oberlin College. Among the classmates at this institution, at one time, were Lucy Stone, John M. Langston, Sallie Holley, Wm. H. Day, and others of both complexions and sexes.

But, shout some, "Instruction! Instruction! Found schools and churches for the blacks, and thus prepare for the abolition of slavery!" This, in the language of another, "is shallow and short-sighted. The demand is the preparation; nothing can supply the place of that. And exclusive instruction, — teaching for blacks, — a school founded on color, — a church in which men are herded ignominiously, apart from the refining influence of association with the more refining highly educated and accomplished, — what are they? A direct way of fitting white men for tyrants, and black men for slaves."

When Dr. James M'Cune Smith returned from Edinburgh, in 1837, at whose University he had drank deep of the Pierian stream of classic literature, the colored citizens of his native New York tendered him a public welcome. Ransom F. Wake, in their behalf, congratulated him on having passed five years in a land where "a man's a man," without regard to his complexion, — where the gentleman, the scholar, the Christian and the patriot did not restrict their benevolence to geographical limits, nor to the mean, degrading, illiberal, detestable and unholy distinction of color which prevails in our otherwise happy land.

Dr. Smith happily responded. Among other appropriate remarks, he said: — "I have striven to obtain education, at every sacrifice and every hazard, and to apply such education to the good of our common country. I have blessed the chance which threw me upon the sympathies of, and opened up to me an association with, the Wardlaws and the Heughs, the Andersons and the Murrays, — men whose names are the property, neither of the city nor the time in which they dwell, but will be held in grateful remembrance so long as civil and religious liberty shall be remembered; and I was further permitted, to the extent of my humble energies, (he says,) to battle side-by-side with them in the cause of the immediate and universal emancipation of slaves."

Dr. Smith was then obliged to leave his home to obtain the education his heart longed for. Now, no colored man need quit the United States for that purpose.

In 1843, Dr. Smith delivered a lecture before the New York Philomaethan and Hamilton Lyceum, on the Destiny of the People of Color, in which he advances the idea, "that we (the colored Americans) are to remain amid the institutions which enthral us, in order to bring liberty to the one by purifying the other." And in 1849, in a letter on the Equal School Rights Question in Boston, he said: — "It has ever been my solemn conviction, that separate organizations of all kinds, based upon the color of the skin, keep alive prejudice against color, and that no organizations do this more effectually than colored schools. All arguments in favor of the especial appropriateness of colored teachers for colored children must cease when colored children are freely and equally admitted into white schools. In this latter case, all the signs of degradation are removed; free and manly instincts — the grand instinct of equality — grow out of the facts of equality; colored teachers are no longer needed for the especial purpose of teaching colored children that they are free and equal; these children feel and know that they are free and equal, and it is only in proportion to their merits and acquirements, only in free and open competition, that colored teachers should then take their equal chances with others in obtaining teacherships in common schools."

In the year 1838, William Whipper, and other talented and distinguished colored Americans, conducted a periodical called "The National Reformer," the organ of an Association in which such men as James Forten, John P. Burr, Rev. Charles W. Gardiner, Robert Purvis, and Rev. Daniel A. Payne, were members. At one of its meetings, the following resolution was adopted: —

"Resolved, That the erecting what are termed white and colored churches fosters the spirit of prejudice and insults the spirit of true reform, by refusing to be associated in Christian fellowship with their brethren of a different complexion, while they both acknowledge the same God as their ruler, and expect to inherit the same destiny in a future world."

The "National Reformer" of September, 1838, endorsed the American Anti-Slavery platform in the following language: — "With them (the Society) we make common cause; satisfied to await the same issue with them, we are willing to labor for its achievement, and terminate our lives as martyrs in support of its principles; under this banner we will rally our countrymen, without distinction of caste or complexion. Show forth to the world that the white man and the colored, the rich and the poor, the bond and the free, can all, on the platform of our common nature, live as brethren, in harmony, peace, and unity, and you will have levelled to the ground the most powerful barrier against universal emancipation."

Rev. J. W. C. PENNINGTON, in his lectures before the Glasgow Young Men's Christian Association, and the St. George's Biblical Literary and Scientific Institute of London, laid down the following as the basis of his argument: — "The colored population of the United States have no destiny separate from that of the nation of which they form an integral part. Our destiny is bound up with that of America. Her ship is ours; her pilot is ours; her storms are ours; her calms are ours. If she breaks upon any rock, we break with her. If we, born in America, cannot live upon the same soil upon terms of equality with the descendants of Scotchmen, Englishmen, Irishmen, Frenchmen, Germans, Hungarians, Greeks, and Poles, then the fundamental theory of the American Republic fails and falls to the ground."

"We oppose," says the National Anti-Slavery Standard of June 18, 1840, "all exclusive action on the part of the colored people, except where the clearest necessity demands it. Is it not the grand object of our enterprise to show the world that our struggle is for great rights? Are we not purposed to overthrow any and every arrangement of society that hinders us from the attainment of this end? Then why should our friends seek to put themselves in a position, to say the least, that looks like an admission of the rightfulness of such lines of demarcation? Where, then, is the goodness or depth of that philosophy that leads you to separate yourselves, for an hour, from those who are your coadjutors in this great work?

"The fetter galls and cuts deeply, but we cannot unlock it instantly; in your desire to become free men, be careful that you do not tear down what you build up.

"Teach the Abolitionists to make common cause with you; teach them to forget, and forget yourselves, as fast as possible, that you are colored men and women. A man is a man, and the rights of man are what we are seeking to procure.

"As long as exclusive colored conventions are held, the white slavite will let them hold them in peace, and strength and shape is given daily to that system of ostracism from social, political and religious influence, which, of all things else, crushes the colored man at the North, and makes him twin brother to the bond-slave of the South."

The great movement now going on in the United States, on the part of foreigners and their descendants, is to coalesce with those to the "manner born." From a paper devoted to the interests of the Irish in this country, I take the following pertinent suggestion: —

"The more an Irishman abstracts himself from those associations exclusively Irish, the greater is his chance of, amalgamation with Americans, among whom his destiny is cast, and in whose fraternity he is, after all, to look for the meed of his industrious career. It may be safely observed, that those Irishmen who have thriven best in the United States are those who have taken an independent stand, and, separating themselves from all clannish connections, have worked their way alone."

The New York Tribune has recently said, that "nine out of every ten Catholic parents prefer their children instructed in good common schools, rather than in the specially Catholic schools in the several States;" and it is equally true, that even the social organizations and clubs, so peculiar to many old countrymen, are fast being regarded by the intelligent as inconsistent, in America, while they are contending for the position of American citizens. Shall we, colored citizens, Native-Americans born, prove less republican than those who are Americans only by adoption? Eagles fly alone; they are but sheep that always herd together.

In the year 1847, a call was issued for a Convention to be held in Troy, N. Y. Massachusetts, and some other States, regarding this as exclusive, it was, by general consent, modified to a call for a National Convention of Colored Americans and their friends. Had this arrangement been acceded to sooner, several Anti-Slavery societies would have sent delegates, white and colored. One colored delegate was furnished with credentials by the Northampton Anti-Slavery Society. The feeling, at that time, among prominent white and colored Anti-Slavery friends was, that exclusive colored conventions belonged to the past, and their resurrection was not desirable. The great question was that of abandoning, as soon as possible, all separate action, and becoming part and parcel of the general community.

The following is an extract from. some remarks made by the author at the Troy Convention, October, 1847: — The fear of colored children sinking under the weight of prejudice in a white institution is not a conclusive argument against their exercising the right of entrance. The colored youth should be stimulated to establish such a character in these seats of learning, by his energy in study and gentlemanly deportment towards teachers and pupils, as to disarm opposition, show himself an equal, and, in despite of cold looks and repulsive treatment, hew a path to eminence and respect; and, like the gem, which shines brighter by attrition, become himself, among good scholars, the very best.

"Perseverance will accomplish wonders. History is replete with examples where young persons have thus, by a harmonious association, converted enemies into good friends, Colored men are daily learning of new avenues opening for their improvement in all the varied business and social relations of life, and do not wish to be behind the age. The intelligent among them will jump on board the car of freedom, and if there are those who will cling to the flesh-pots of Egypt, why, they should not complain if the advancing train jostle them from the track.

"Any person, of ordinary capacity, must know that, to become elevated, he must cultivate and practice the same traits which are elevating others around him; and if it is (as, indeed, we all feel it to be) harder for the colored man than any other, why, then, let him work the harder, and, eventually, the summit will be attained. We shall not be transported, en masse, as the fabled palace of Aladdin was, by the hands of a magician, and set down upon some Elysian plain; but each for himself must aim for the height, and an excelsior march will soon place his feet, like the patriarch's of old, upon Pisgah's top, where the promised land of equality will be presented, in full view, to his longing eyes."

From the report of the Cambridge (Mass.) School Committee, submitted in 1851, we make the following extract: —

"In the Broadway Primary School, a singular fact was noticed — viz., the mixture of four different races among the pupils — the Anglo-Saxon, Teutonic, Celtic, and African; but, by the influence Of the teacher and of habit, there exists perfect good feeling among them, and there is no apparent consciousness of a difference of race or condition."

A gentleman who attended the examination of this last mentioned school, in April, 1854, said of it in one of the public prints: — "Colored boys and girls were classified with those not colored like themselves, and all without the least apparent sign that such a spectacle was otherwise by ordinary. The various exercises were participated in by them with commendable tact, zeal and deportment; and, in the Committee's summing up, the marks of distinction for studies, punctual attendance, and exemplary deportment, during the term, were very flattering. In map-drawing, a colored pupil excelled all others."

From FREDERICK DOUGLASS'S speech in Ford Street church, Rochester, N. Y., March 13, 1848, I make the following extract: —

"I am well aware of the anti-Christian prejudices which have excluded many colored persons from white churches, and the consequent necessity for erecting their own-places of worship. This evil I would charge upon its originators, and not the colored people. But such a necessity does not now exist to the extent of former years. There are societies where color is not regarded as a test of membership, and such places I deem more appropriate for colored persons than exclusive or isolated organizations.

"I look upon all complexional distinctions, such as negro pews, negro berths on steamboats, negro cars, Sabbath or week-day schools or churches, &c., as direct obstacles to the progress of reform, and as the means of continuing the slave in his chains."

At the anniversary celebration of Franklin's birthday by the printers of Rochester, N. Y., in January, 1848, Mr. Douglass and myself accepted an invitation to be present. The landlord of the Irving House protested against our participation in the celebration, called us intruders, and told us that it was a "violation of the rules of society for colored people to associate with whites," &c. But, through the interposition of Alexander Mann, Esq., editor of the Rochester American, seconded by James Vick, Esq., the question was put to the company, and decided in our favor by almost an unanimous vote.

The following were among the sentiments offered on the above occasion: —

By FREDERICK DOUGLASS. Gentlemen of the Rochester Press — Promoters of knowledge, lovers of liberty, foes of ignorance, despisers of prejudice, — may you continue to give the world noble examples by a free and intelligent union of black with white.

By WM. C. NELL. Free Speech and a Free Press — The hand-maids of liberty, "the wide world o'er." May the printers of Rochester, in glorious emulation of their honored prototype, Franklin, ever prove the uncompromising defenders of both.

It has been my lot to listen, from early childhood to colored clergymen of various sects and denominations, and with sorrow do I record the fact, that in but few cases have they exhibited the capability at all worthy of their calling as teachers. The recollection of the many deficiencies, apparent, at times, even to the school children among the congregation, is sufficient to excite a tear of deep regret in view of the unprofitable connection between pastor and people. A few years since, the colored citizens of Boston, regretting that those among them who aspired to lead in religious matters did not evince the proper degree of zeal for intellectual improvement, adopted the following resolutions: —

"Resolved, That the apathy manifested by our colored ministers of the gospel, in reference to the promulgation of the arts and sciences among us as a people, tends more to retard our intellectual emancipation than the influence of any class of persons, except the slaveholders.

"Resolved, That it is the duty of our people to give their support to such ministers of the gospel as show proof of the best intellectual and spiritual cultivation."

When this is done will the beautiful language of the Psalmist be realised, — "Our sons will be as plants grown up in their youth, and our daughters as corner-stones, polished after the similitude of a palace."

The names of some honorable exceptions now occur to me of clergymen stationed in cities and towns, who have done their duty, by precept and example, in the general elevation of their brethren; but in my native city, Boston, two prominent clergymen deserve special mention.

Many years ago, the Rev. THOMAS PAUL presided over a large congregation. He was possessed of fine talents, enriched by active intercourse with, and the friendship of, celebrated individuals in civil and literary relations, both at home and in England. I can remember, among his merits, the efforts originated and promoted by him for the education and welfare of those with whom his fortunes were allied. Saying this, is but rendering justice to a good man, now in his grave.

At a later day, JOHN T. RAYMOND occupied the same pulpit, and proudly do I testify to one fact conspicuous in his ministry. Education, Anti-Slavery and Temperance always received from him deserved attention. Lecturers on the various reforms were cordially solicited to address his church, in which exercises he participated with credit to himself and satisfaction to others. He believed and taught, that "man, educated, will ever be better than when ignorant."

Colored men and. women, especially the younger portion, are looking forward, aiming to expand their minds, and they will not be satisfied with any thing short of what tends to "improve, elevate, and refine." While colored churches do exist, let the pulpit be filled by those to whom the aspiring mind can look up with confidence. Even this is an advanced step, and will better prepare all for the advent of a brighter day.

"Did we at the North (says Win. J. Watkins) occupy a position analogous to that of our Southern brethren, were we compelled, on account of our complexion, to occupy the highest seat in the synagogue, or hide ourselves in some remote corner, and catch the crumbs as they fall from the white man's table, then would there be extenuating circumstances sufficient to justify us in worshipping God exclusively under our own vine and fig tree. But no such Mitigating circumstances present themselves. Churches in which we can unite and worship God as men and brethren are thrown wide open for our reception, but how few of us wend our way thither! In Boston, there is a colored population of not quite two thousand, and yet we have five colored churches."

In the year 1848, an attempt was made in Boston to form a colored Anti-Slavery Society. At a crowded meeting in Belknap Street Church, January 24th, a resolution opposing such a scheme was advocated by Wm. Wells Brown, Robert Morris, Esq., Edward B. Lawton, John T. Hilton, and others, and adopted as the sense of the meeting.

A combination of influences, in 1853, resulted in a call for a National Convention of Colored People, to be held at Rochester, N. Y., July 6th. At a meeting held in Boston, June 20th, the following resolution was adopted: —

"Resolved, That we, in common with our fellow-citizens of the several States, respond to the call for a National Convention of Colored Americans, though it would have been more in unison with the advanced state of sentiment among Reformers, had the call embraced colored Americans and their friends."

One argument in favor of Colored Conventions has been, that, in some States, the colored people are so oppressed by local customs, as to be apparently forbidden to have intercourse with the whites, and hence, that while some parts of the country may not need such an auxiliary, to others it may be important. It must be admitted, that there is some plausibility in this statement, and yet, it is only a superficial and not an enlarged view of the question. Instead of their desiring the more advanced to come down to them, they should labor to come up themselves, that Illinois and Indiana, with their Black Laws repealed, and Pennsylvania, with her colored suffrage restored, may stand side by side with the more liberal and liberty-practising States in other parts of the Union. When rights are to be discussed and contended for, it is of vital importance that we invoke a union of all true hearts, as they have wisely contemplated in Toronto, Canada, where the Constitution of their Provincial Union embodies measures to further promote literature, general intelligence, active benevolence, and the principles of universal freedom, not based on complexional considerations.

Associations, like individuals, to a certain extent, are controlled by the surrounding atmosphere; as, for instance, when the Massachusetts State (colored) Council met in New Bedford, the fact that Protective Unions already existed open to colored and white stockholders equally, — that colored children shared equal school privileges with the whites, — that a colored man, the President of the Council, was an officer in pay of the city, and that they anticipated that the time, would soon come when colored and white jurymen would sit on the same panel, — these facts, and their legitimate consequences, visible in the body politic, had the effect to prevent the Council from adopting any exclusive measures, and even from endorsing the Colored Industrial School.

The position of those colored Americans who complain of their brethren for not taking steps backward to accommodate their lower level, is analogous to the slaves asking freemen to put on chains, barbarians requiring a people to abandon civilization, the Pope of Rome abolishing railroads, or those ancients who burned the Alexandrian Library, because they had no literature of their own.

There is a glaring inconsistency in exclusive colored action on the part of those who claim to be Anti-Slavery reformers. The idea, carried out to its legitimate conclusion, would frustrate all such hopes as were cherished by many of seeing FREDERICK DOUGLASS elevated to the United States Congress; for, on their theory, a colored Congress must be organized, as the only one where consistency would allow of his credentials being presented.

That colored Americans should not be isolated, but participate with other Americans in the duties of legislation, as every where else, is an essential element in the Anti-Slavery philosophy, but one, of course, equally derided by Colonizationists and slaveholders. In the Colonizationist for September, 1833, Cyril Pearl alluded to Mr. Garrison as the man who encourages the colored population to expect the time when "our State and National assemblies will contain a fair proportion of colored representatives."

How indignant does the colored man feel, when some Colonizationist denies his equal rights in churches, public places and conveyances, by saying, "Why don't you go among your own people, where you belong?" And yet, in many instances, the very individuals whose sensibilities are thus wounded, are themselves active in upholding colored institutions. By such a course, they blunt the Sword of their denunciations against colorphobia.

Others protest against the blending of colored with white, for fear of the loss of identity on the part of colored people; and further, for the reason that it will have a tendency to turn aside patronage from colored professional men, traders and mechanics. All this is either an ignorant or wilful perversion of the matter. "Competition is the life of trade." If colored genius will but imitate the successful examples among the whites, the public will surely reward the persevering effort.

Hon. Rufus Choate, in opposing the colored military petition in the Massachusetts Constitutional Convention, remarked, that "though the colored man should win Bunker Hills, the color will cleave to him still," — a sentiment based on Henry Clay's Colonization speech in the Senate, Feb. 7th, 1839, when he asked, "Do they (the Abolitionists) not perceive, that in thus confounding all the distinctions which God himself has made, they arraign the wisdom and goodness of Providence itself? It has been his divine pleasure to make the black man black and the white man white, and to distinguish them by other repulsive constitutional differences." So far as the conduct of some colored people is concerned, they are constantly strengthening that statement. It is possible so to deport ourselves, that the idea of color shall be forgotten. Do not let it be our fault, that the white people are for ever being reminded of the fact. We need not always give color to the idea. Rather let us give them the impression that we are men and women, which is far preferable. Let our enemies, and not ourselves, rear the barriers of separation and exclusiveness.

Why do we content ourselves with reposing at the base of the hill, when, by an ascent to its summit, we can obtain ingress to its marble halls, where none may molest or make afraid! Why do we yet hanker after the flesh-pots of Egypt, when the "delectable mountains" of the long-promised land of Equality greet our vision, and humane hearts and helping hands conjure and beckon us to come and occupy!

Mr. Garrison has, at times, been supposed to be a colored man, because of his long, patient and persevering devotion to our cause. He himself (although there is no need of his words to that effect) often expresses himself as wholly identified with us — "colored all over"; and yet, there are those, for whom he and others have made themselves martyrs, who can propose societies and action for elevation, from which William Lloyd Garrison, Wendell Phillips, Gerritt Smith, and their fellow-philanthropists, would be excluded. When my head or heart accepts this theory, I shall be in a fit condition to believe in the Colonization dogma, that our Almighty Father has interposed an insurmountable barrier between the white and colored portion of His children and that we are, indeed, a peculiar, isolated, distinct race, and always to be so; a state of things in the contemplation of which angels weep, and fiends clap their hands for joy.

"But," ask some, "do Colored Conventions result in no good?" To this it is but necessary to reply, that, when a body of intelligent and aspiring colored men assemble to interchange opinions, the relation, of course, is often an instructive one, and the white communities wherein they meet are sometimes favorably affected by their presence; but this, and, indeed, all that the most sanguine adherents can legitimately anticipate therefrom, is not an equivalent for the infraction of Anti-Slavery principle, to say nothing of the great sacrifice of time and effort, always the penalty of Colored Conventions.

Let us be in perpetual session of the whole on the subject of human rights, reporting progress from time to time; form business relations, (when possible,) like the firm of Williams & Plumb, in New York, colored and white in Partnership; organize Protective Unions, and Industrial Colleges, of all who think and act alike, irrespective of complexion; and secure places in every workshop, book-store, or seminary, where, by dint of perseverance, opposition may be melted away, — and the work of elevation is accomplished.

But, though Colored Conventions may not solve the problem of a people's elevation, "all is not lost" thereby. As was once said in the old Republic, "Sparta does not depend upon one man;" so should we not attach all our faith to one man, or body of men, or set of measures, but avail ourselves of them all, and then only as means to a noble end, — the elevation of humanity. Let each man, woman, and child, aim to excel in those branches now monopolized by the favored classes. Can Colored Conventions teach a better lesson? Let us encourage the genius that may be exhibited by young colored men and women, — not to inflate their vanity, but to develop into healthy growth the qualities that might otherwise lie dormant. Lot us be charitable to those whom vice and intemperance may have turned from the paths in which we ourselves love to walk; and, as was said by Mrs. Child, "those whom we now term Tom, Dick, and Harry, will, under our kind ministrations, become Mr. Thomas, Mr. Richard, and Mr. Henry." Let us, as advised by Rev. Daniel A. Payne, "hold licentious men in the same repute as licentious women." Let us banish from the social circle that spirit of detraction and backbiting, which is always the bane of society.

It was my happy privilege, not long since, to meet a company of colored men in my native city, among whom was a young man upon whom had been conferred the degree of Master of Arts, he having passed through a course of theology, and being now engaged in reading law, with a prospect of an early admission to the Bar in one of the Western States. In conversation with him were two young physicians, one just graduated at Dartmouth College, the other a student at Bowdoin, having perfected his medical education by three years' attendance at the hospitals in Paris.

In various cities and towns may now be found those home circles, where mental and moral worth, genius and refinement, lend their charms in giving to the world assurance that, despite accidental differences of complexion, here you behold a colored man, there a colored woman, competent to fill any station in civilized society. Let us organize and sustain intelligent and happy homes, for in them, as has been truly said, may be found the substitute for both Church and State.

The following testimony in regard to the character of the colored people of this country is taken from a speech of CHARLES LENOX REMOND, at the New England Anti-Slavery Convention, May 30, 1854: —

"Since my friend Prince, of Essex, called attention to the character of the colored people, allow me to ask you to look in that direction for a moment; for, while men live in Boston, go upon 'Change, walk up and down the public streets, all the while coming in contact with colored people, they do not understand their character; they do not know that, notwithstanding the constant pressure, from the commencement of our nation's history, which has been exerted upon their manhood, their morality, upon all that is noble, magnanimous and generous in their characters, they have exhibited as many instances of noble manhood, in proportion to their number, as have been displayed by their more favored brethren of a white complexion. It was said here by Mr. Prince, that the colored race is at once morally and physically brave. Do not consider me, Mr. Chairman, in alluding to this subject, as feeling vain in regard to it; I only ask that the whole truth respecting my people may be known, and there I will leave the success of their cause. But I ask the people not to act blindly with regard to it; not to make up their opinions with this great weight of prejudice on their minds. I ask them to look upon this question impartially, generously, magnanimously, patriotically, and I believe they will be converted to our movement.

"Sir, I have taken note, for the last eighteen years, of the course pursued by colored people in Anti-Slavery meetings, for there was a time when the number of colored people present was greater than at the present time; and yesterday, I had evidence that there was some courage left with them yet. I refer to this incident only as an illustration of the character of this people generally in our country. There was a meeting of Anti-Slavery friends in the basement of Tremont Temple, and a call was made for persons to come forward and give in their names, that they might be called upon, at any moment, to discharge not only a responsible, but dangerous duty, [rescuing Anthony Burns,] and my heart has not been so much encouraged for many a long day, as when I witnessed a large number of the colored men present walk up to that stand, with an unfaltering step, and enrol their names.

"Why is it that the Anti-Slavery cause should recommend itself to every well-wisher of his country? Because there are men, white men, who have never been deprived of their citizenship, nor subjected to persecution, outrage and insult, who are honored for the patriotism they have exhibited; and if the demonstration of that feeling, or principle, or Sentiment, or whatever you may please to call it, is worthy of honor in the white man, then it is also worthy of honor in the colored man; and the last evening that I had the privilege of speaking in this I house, I endeavored, briefly, to make it clear that, on every occasion where manhood and courage have been required in this country, the number of colored people volunteering their services has been equal to that of white people, in proportion to their number, from the earliest moment of our nation's existence.

"I think I may safely say, Sir, that the courage and patriotism of the colored man are of a higher character than those of the white man. There is not a man of fair complexion before me, who has not something in this country to protect which the colored man does not possess; and, Sir, when I see them, in the moment of danger, willing to discharge their duty to the country, I have a proof that they are the friends, and not the enemies, of the country."

From the Address issued by the Colored Convention held at Rochester, N. Y., in 1853, and signed by Frederick Douglass, J. M. Whitfield, H. O. Wagoner, Rev. A. N. Freeman, and George B. Vashon, I make this extract: —

"Fellow-citizens, we have had, and still have, great wrongs of which to complain. A heavy and cruel hand has been laid upon us.

"As a people, we feel ourselves to be not only deeply injured, but grossly misunderstood. Our white fellow-countrymen do not know us. They are strangers to our character, ignorant of our capacity, oblivious of our history and progress, and are misinformed as to the principles and ideas that control and guide us, as a people. The great mass of American citizens estimate us, as being a characterless and purposeless people; and hence we hold up our heads, if at against the withering influence of a nation's scorn and contempt.

"It will not be surprising that we are so misunderstood and misused when the motives for misrepresenting us and for degrading us are duly considered. Indeed, it will seem strange, upon such consideration, (and in view of the ten thousand channels through which malign feelings find utterance and influence,) that we have not fallen even lower in public estimation than we have done. For, with the exception of the Jews, under the whole heavens, there is not to be found a people pursued with a more relentless prejudice and persecution, than are the free colored people of the United States.

"Without pretending to have exerted ourselves as we ought, in view of an intelligent understanding of our interest, to avert from us the unfavorable opinions and unfriendly action of the American people, we feel that the imputations cast upon us, for our want of intelligence, morality, and exalted character, may be mainly accounted for by the injustice received at your hands. What stone has been left unturned to degrade us? What hand has refused to fan the flame of popular prejudice against us? What American artist has not caricatured us? What wit has not laughed at us in our wretchedness? What songster has not made merry over our depressed spirits? What press has not ridiculed and contemned us? What pulpit has withheld from our devoted heads its angry lightning, or its sanctimonious hate? Few, few, very few; and that we have borne up with it all — that we have tried to be wise, though denounced by all to be fools — that we have tried to be upright, when all around us have esteemed us as knaves — we have striven to be gentlemen, although all around us have been teaching us its impossibility — that we have remained here, when all our neighbors have advised us to leave — proves that we possess qualities of head and heart, such as cannot but be commended by impartial men. It is believed that no other nation on the globe could have made more progress in the midst of such an universal and stringent disparagement. It would humble the proudest, crush the energies of the strongest, and retard the progress of the swiftest. In view of our circumstances, we can, without boasting, thank God, and take courage, having placed ourselves where we may fairly challenge comparison with more highly favored men."

The following encouraging items have been recently gleaned from the field of improvement of colored people.

A diploma has been awarded to a colored girl in Portsmouth, N. H., and also to a young colored lad at one of the Boston public schools, to which he (the only colored boy in the school) had secured access but a few months previous.

At the semi-annual examination of the State Normal School, in Salem, Mass., a hymn was sung, the production of Miss C. L. Forten, a young colored pupil.

This year's graduating class at Dartmouth College contained one colored young man, (Edward Garrison Draper.) The class procured lithographic portraits of each other, to exchange fraternally, and, to give color to their consistency, Draper's was among them as a brother beloved.

A colored aspirant for classical knowledge has just obtained admittance to an institution in Connecticut, after several years' refusal by the faculty.

A town in Worcester county, Mass., has chosen a colored man on the School Committee.

A colored citizen of Boston has received an appointment as Auctioneer.

Mrs. F. J. Webb, the dramatic reader, is winning golden opinions from poets, authors, and the public.

CHAPTER III: CONCLUSION.

FROM the foregoing pages, it will be seen that the various conflicts by sea and land, which have challenged the energies of the United States, have been signalized by the devotion and bravery of colored Americans, despite the persecutions heaped, Olympus high, upon them, by their fellow countrymen. They have ever proved loyal, and ready to worship or die, if need be, at Freedom's shrine. The amor patriæ has always burned vividly on the altar of their hearts. They love their native land:

"For, O! there's a magical tie to the land of our home,
Which the heart cannot break, though the footsteps may roam;
Be that land where it may, at the line or the pole,
It still holds the magnet that draws back the soul;
'T is loved by the free man — 't is loved by the slave,
'T is dear to the coward — more dear to the brave;
Ask of any the spot they like best on the earth,
And they they'll answer, with pride, 't is the land of our birth."

Let it not be inferred, however, that because many colored soldiers were, from the force of circumstances, assigned a subordinate position by themselves during the war, that their more immediate descendants are to remain satisfied with a half-way excellence. But, like Crispus Attucks, leading on Boston citizens to resist tyranny, 1770, — Major Jeffrey, Latham and Freeman, each gallant and brave, — Jordan B. Noble, the drummer of Chalmette Plains, — and the many others, in more or less responsible departments, during their country's trial hour, so, henceforward, in our battle for equality, each should aim to be incorporated with the mass of Americans, — unite, when possible, as affinities may lead, with the various political literary, benevolent, ecclesiastical, business and social, organizations of the land, and so prove valiant and consistent soldiers in Freedom's army, without arranging ourselves in a colored section.

There is, however, a historical propriety in setting forth the service's of those colored Americans, who, in the "day of small things," have labored earnestly for the welfare of humanity. If others fail to appreciate the merit of the colored man, let us cherish the deserted shrine. The names which others neglect should only be the more sacredly our care. Let us keep them for the hoped-for day of full emancipation, when, in the possession of all our rights, and redeemed from the long night of ignorance that has rested over us, we may recall them to memory, recollecting, with gratitude, that the stars which shone in our horizon have ushered in a glorious dawn.

The light which radiated from the prison-cell Of WILLIAM LLOYD GARRISON, in Baltimore, is yet diffusing itself over the land. The past, present and future agitation of the slavery question in these United States owes itself to that man, and the hour when he nobly dedicated his life to the emancipation of the slave, and the elevation of the nominally free colored Americans.

"I CAN WAIT," were the memorable words of John Q. ADAMS, when his mouth was gagged on the floor of Congress. The world will bear witness, that we have waited; and, O! how patiently! We have learned

"How sublime a thing it is

To suffer and be strong;"

but, though familiar with, we shall never grow reconciled to, the treatment: —

"Our hearts, though ofttimes made to bleed,

Will gush afresh at every wound."

The Revolution of 1776, and the subsequent struggles in our nation's history, aided, in honorable proportion, by colored Americans, have (sad, but true, confession) yet left the necessity for a second revolution, no less sublime than that of regenerating public sentiment in favor of Universal Brotherhood. To this glorious consummation, all, of every complexion, sect, sex and condition, can add their mite, and so nourish the tree of liberty, that all may be enabled to pluck fruit from its bending branches; and, in that degree to which colored Americans may labor to hasten the day, they will prove valid their claim to the title, "Patriots of the Second Revolution."

The Anti-Slavery war waged for the last twenty-five years has indeed been prolific in noble words and deeds, and is remarkable for the succession of victories, always the reward of the faithful and persevering. To compare the present with the past — those dark hours when the bugle blast was first sounded among the hills and valleys of New England, — we can hardly believe the evidence daily presented of the onward progress of those mighty principles then proclaimed to the American nation. The treatment of the colored man in this country is a legitimate illustration of "hating those whom we have injured," and brings to my recollection that chapter in Waverly where Fergus Mac Ivar replies to his friend, when being led to execution — "You see the compliment they pay to our Highland strength and courage. Here we have lain until our limbs are cramped into palsy, and now they send six soldiers with loaded muskets to prevent our taking the castle by storm." The analogy is found in the omnipotent and omnipresent influence of American pro-slavery in crushing every noble and praiseworthy aspiration of the persecuted colored man. As in nature, the smiles of summer are made sweeter by the frowns of winter, the calm of ocean is made more placid by the tempest that has preceded it, so in this moral battle, these incidental skirmishes will contribute to render the hour of victory indeed a blissful realization.

So sure as night precedes day, war ends in peace, and winter wakes spring, just so sure will the persevering efforts of Freedom's army be crowned with victory's perennial laurels!

APPENDIX: MILITARY CONVENTION AT WASHINGTON.

JANUARY 8th, 1855, the soldiers of the war of 1812 celebrated the anniversary of the battle of New Orleans by a Convention at Washington, having for its object the furtherance of the bill before Congress giving one hundred and sixty acres of land to all the soldiers of the last war with Great Britain. Among those present was a colored man, named GEORGE R. ROBERTS, a well-known resident of Baltimore, and now over seventy years of age. He attended in quest of a pension for services in behalf of his country. He was a privateer, was captured and carried to Jamaica, and, with half a dozen others, barely escaped the honors of yard-arm promotion. The National Era informs us that he was requested, by vote, to make a statement of his experience. He was introduced by Col. Baldwin, and (says the Washington Sentinel) "made his statement in an earnest and impressive manner, relating the incidents of his captivity and condemnation to death by the British, of his exchange and return home, and of his subsequent services under the celebrated privateer commander, Captain Thomas Boyle, of Baltimore. His recital was received with applause."

The Washington Convention was characterized by the presence, not only of white and black, but also of red Americans, all participating in its proceedings, — a striking and significant fact.

Gen. Coombs addressed the old soldiers in behalf of the red men who once owned this beautiful country, but who now had scarcely enough of it for a graveyard. He said some of them had fought by his side during the last war with Great Britain with perfect self devotion, and had shared with him captivity and suffering. He would scorn to be the beneficiary of a Government that would take every thing away and give nothing in return.

THE CLAIMS OF THE RED MAN.

The reader has already learned, from the foregoing pages, some facts in regard to the history of New England red men, and their devotion to liberty. The following is a copy of a petition sent, some years. ago, by an Indian of the Catawba tribe, to the Assembly of South Carolina: —

"I am one of the lingering emblems of an almost extinguished race. Our graves will soon be our habitations. I am one of the few stalks that still remain in the field, when the tempest of the revolution is past. I fought against the British for your sake. The British have disappeared, and you are free. Yet from me the British took nothing, — nor have I gained any thing by their defeat. I pursue the deer for my subsistence; the deer are disappearing, and I must starve. God ordained me for the forest, and my habitation is the shade; but the strength of my arm decays, and my feet fail in the chase. The hand which fought for your liberty is now open for your relief. In my youth, I bled in battle that you might be independent; let not my heart in my old age bleed for the want of your commiseration.

PETER HARRIS."

"The Indians are now but few in number," (Says WENDELL PHILLIPS, Esq., in an eloquent appeal in behalf of the red man, published in the Massachusetts Quarterly Review,) "separated from the dominant races, isolated at school and church, and found, after the lapse of a century, and the trial of three generations, in such a plight, that humanity weeps, and the best statecraft is dumb and confounded. While the humanity of the State gathers up the blind, the dumb, the idiotic, and the insane, — while strong friends compel attention to the slave, — let us see, for once, the mercy of the majority toward those whose only plea is their feebleness, their friendliness, and their wrongs. The first word from Indian lips that our annals have preserved is 'Welcome!' Let us so govern, that the last farewell of the going-out of the race may be — 'Thanks!'"

A cluster of brilliant gems adorn this tribute of the gifted author, whose heart, tongue and pen are a free-will offering to the oppressed of every clime or kin; and to himself may be most truthfully applied a quotation familiar to his own lips, when awarding honor to some of Nature's noblemen, — "The ocean: of his philanthropy knows no shore."

PAYMENT FOR SLAVES LOST OR KILLED IN THE PUBLIC SERVICE.

In 1816, a bill was pending in the House of Representatives, to pay "for property lost or destroyed in the public service." A motion was made so to amend the bill as to grant compensation for "slaves lost or killed in the public service, in the same manner as other property." This motion was rejected, only thirty-two members voting in its favor. [Vide House Docs.,

No. 401, 1st Session, 21st Congress, where the Committee state the fact, and refer to the National Intelligencer of Dec. 28, 1816.]

The next case was that of D. Auterive. He had claims against the United States for wood and other necessaries furnished the Army, and for the loss of time and expense of nursing a slave who was wounded in the service of government at New Orleans. The case of D. Auterive was reported by the Committee on Claims, — the Chairman who made the report, and two other members of the Committee, being slaveholders. It states that "slaves, not beingregarded as property, could not be paid for as such." This case was fully considered in the House, and the views of the Committee sustained.

The bill to pay the people of West Florida for slaves, lost in 1814, was again brought up in 1843, and was rejected, by a vote of 116 to 36.

The case of "Pacheco" was reported upon first by the Committee on Claims, in 1842, — just eight days after Mr. Giddings resigned, on account of the censure passed on him by the House. He was Chairman of that Committee then, and they would not allow such a report. It was subsequently reported upon by other committees, and the last time in 1848, when the Northern members of the Committee made a minority report, drawn up by Mr. Giddings, at the request of Hon. John Dickey.

From the correspondence and speeches of Hon. J. R. Giddings, I am permitted to present the following facts: —

Referring to the Pacheco case, he says, — "The claimant, in 1835, residing in Florida, professed to own a negro man named Lewis. This man is said to have been very intelligent, speaking four languages, which he read and wrote with facility. The master hired him to an officer of the United States, to act as a guide to the troops under the command of Major Dade, for which he was to receive twenty-five dollars per month. The duties were dangerous and the price was proportioned to the danger. At the time these troops were massacred, this slave, Lewis, deserted to the enemy, or was captured by them. He remained with the Indians, — acting with them in their depredations against the white people, — until 1837, when, General Jessup says, he was captured by a detachment of troops under his command. An Indian chief, named Jumper, surrendered with Lewis, claimed him as a slave, having, as he said, captured him at the time of Dade's defeat. General Jessup declares that he regarded him as a dangerous man; that he was supposed to have kept up a correspondence with the enemy from the time he joined Major Dade until the defeat of that officer.

To insure the public safety, he ordered him sent with the Indians, believing that, if left in the country, he would be employed against our troops. He was sent West, and the claimant now asks that we shall pay him one thousand dollars as the value of this man's body."

With his (the slave's) extraordinary intelligence, with a knowledge of the wrongs he and his people had suffered at the hands of those who claimed them as property, he must have thirsted for vengeance. He could have felt no attachment or respect for a people at whose hands he had received nothing but abuse and degradation.

Judge McLean, in a case brought before the United States Supreme Court, admitted that, though some local laws had given the character of property to slaves, the Constitution acts upon them as persons, and not as property.

Mr. Giddings, in the United States House of Representatives December 28, 1848, challenged proof that the House, the United States Supreme Court, or any respectable Court of any free State, has decided slaves to be property, under the Federal Constitution; and yet, July 26, 1852, Mr. Charlton, of Georgia, aided by Mr. Rusk, of Texas, and Mr. Cass, of Michigan, though opposed by Mr. Sumner, (in behalf of Mr. Chase, who had prepared for the debate, but was at this time absent, not expecting the business to be then presented,) succeeded in obtaining compensation for James C. Watson, of Georgia, for his slaves, taken by the Creeks in the Seminole War.

This was the sequel to many years' able and unsuccessful efforts of the friends of freedom in Congress against the acknowledgment by that body, that man can hold property in man.

TRIBUTES OF LAFAYETTE AND KOSCIUSKO.

Among the Europeans; who left their homes and rallied in defence of American Independence, history records no more illustrious names than LAFAYETTE and KOSCIUSKO. Not being tainted with American colorphobia, they each expressed regret that their services had been made a partial, instead of a general, boon. Read this extract from Lafayette's letter to Clarkson: — "I would never have drawn my sword in the cause of America, if I could have conceived that thereby I was founding a land of slavery."

During his visit to the United States, in 1825, he made inquiries for several colored soldiers whom he remembered as participating with him in various skirmishes. Lafayette was consistent. Having bravely and disinterestedly aided in vindicating our rights, he did not incur the reproach of hypocrisy, by turning and trampling on the rights of others. For the purpose of applying his principles to men of color, he purchased a plantation in French Guiana. His first step was to collect all the whips and other instruments of torture and punishment, and make a bonfire of them in presence of the assembled slaves. He then instituted a plan of giving a portion of his time to each slave every week, with a promise, that as soon as any one had earned money enough to purchase an additional day of the week, he should be entitled to it, and when, with his increased time to work for himself, he could purchase another day, he should have that, and so on, until he was master of his whole time. In the then state of Anti-Slavery science, this gradual and sifting process was deemed necessary to form the character of slaves, and to secure the safety of the masters. Abolitionists would not elect this mode now. They would turn slaves at once into free laborers or leaseholders on the same estate, if possible, where they have been as slaves. Before Lafayette's views were fully executed, the French Revolution occurred, which interrupted his operations and made the slaves free at once. But mark the conduct of the ungrateful and blood-thirsty blacks. While other slaves in the Colony availed themselves of the first moment of freedom to quit the plantations of their masters, Lafayette's remained, desiring to work for their humane and generous friend.

KOSCIUSKO, the gallant Pole, was young when the news reached his ear that America was endeavoring to release her neck from Britain's yoke. He promptly devoted himself to the service, and displayed a heroism which won universal respect. Washington loved and honored him, and the soldiers idolized his bravery; but his manly heart was saddened to learn that the colored man was not to be a recipient of those rights which many a sable soldier had fought to obtain. Kosciusko, however, with the feeling that all Americans should have been proud to exhibit, (but, sad to tell, few did so,) endeavored to render some signal compensation to those with whose wrongs his own had taught him to sympathise; and, as a grateful tribute to the neglected and forgotten colored man, he appropriated $20,000 of his hard earnings to purchase and educate colored children. But, by the laws of Virginia, where the bequest appropriated was to be carried into effect, this generous object was defeated.

On the last visit to the United States of this illustrious donor, the will was put into the hands of Thomas Jefferson, who was appointed Executor, to purchase slaves and educate them, so as, in his own words, "to make them better sons and better daughters." Jefferson transferred the trust to Benjamin L. Lear. In 1830, the bequest, amounting then to $25,000, was claimed by the legal heirs of Kosciusko. Interested parties subsequently recommended that the fund, if recovered, should be employed by the trustees in buying and educating slave children, with the view of sending them to Liberia, — an object far enough at variance from the donor's intention.

This matter has been in litigation a long while, and I have been unable to learn the conclusion. The circumstance reminds me of the following question, once put to a Florida planter of twenty-five years standing: — "Has any property, left by will to any colored person, ever been honestly and fairly administered by any white person?" Mark his answer: "Such instances might possibly have happened, but never to my knowledge."

HEROIC COLORED MEN.

A correspondent of the New York Observer, writing from the West, says — "Before leaving our boat, we must not omit to notice one of the waiters in the cabin. He is a man of history. That tall, straight, active, copper-colored man, with a sparkling eye and intelligent countenance, was Col. CLAY'S servant at Buena Vista. Fearless of danger, and faithful to his master, he attended the Colonel into the midst of the fatal charge, saw him fall from his horse, and, surrounded by the murderous Mexicans, at last carried the mangled dead body from the field. The Hon. HENRY, in gratitude for such fidelity to his gallant son, has allowed this man to hire himself out for five years, and to retain half the proceeds; and at the end of that time, gives him his freedom."

"That is," says the Boston Christian Register, "a human being perils his life to save the life or bear off the body of another human being, and for this act, he is to receive one-half of his own earnings, for five years, and at the end of that time, to be made a present of — to himself!"

In a letter published in The Voice of the Fugitive, Jan. 1, 1853, HIRAM WILSON says: — "I had an interview on yesterday morning with a colored man. I will not at present give his name, but he was a servant to General Taylor through the Mexican war — was with him at Palo Alto, Monterey and Buena Vista. He held a beautiful testimonial in regard to his gentlemanly conduct and martial character from the hand of Col. Grayson. He had large scars upon his person from wounds he received in the bloody battles. What was rather remarkable, he told me he saved the life of Gen. Taylor at Monterey. A Mexican was aiming at the General a deadly blow, when he sprang in between the assailant and the assailed, and slew the Mexican, but received a deep wound from a lance. So it would seem that a colored man gave to the United States a President, by saving his life in a terrific battle! I examined the sear left from the wound he received at the time, which was as long as my finger. He was emancipated by President Taylor about one month before his death, but represents that his brother-in-law was not acting an honorable part towards him as the reason for his coming to Canada. 'Republics are ungrateful,' so it is said, even to their most gallant heroes. How honorable, how creditable to the United States, that such a man must fly to Canada for freedom!!!"

COLONIZATION

The history of the American Colonization Society, since its formation by slaveholders, in 1817, is sufficiently familiar, perhaps, to most of the friends of humanity. Ever since that period, colored people all over the land have protested against it as an apologist for slavery and justifier of slaveholders, as the enemy of immediate emancipation, aiming to expel from the land of their birth the colored population, not for "any color of crime, but for the crime of color," and preventing, as far as possible, their elevation in the United States.

Among the resolutions expressive of the sense of the colored people on the colonization question, the following, submitted by Philip A. Bell, at a mass meeting in New York city, January 8, 1839, is selected: —

Resolved, That our sympathies for the slave, the love we bear our native land, our respect and veneration for the institutions and government of our country, are so many cords which bind us to our home, the soil of our birth, which has been wet by the tears and fertilized by the blood of our ancestors, and from which, while life lasts, in spite of the oppressor's wrongs, we will never be seduced or driven, but abide by principle, and, placing our trust in the Lord of Hosts, we will tell the white Americans, that their country shall be our country, we will be governed by the same laws and worship at the same altar, where here they live we will live, where they die there will we be buried, and our graves shall remain as monuments of our suffering and triumph, or of our failure and their disgrace.

THE FUGITIVE SLAVE LAW.

The reign of terror which burst upon the land in 1850, by the passage of the atrocious Fugitive Slave Law, sounded the alarm for meetings of consultation and vigilance in every community where its immediate victims were located, and their action has been published broadcast to the world. The seizure of Hamlet, Long and Boulding, in New York, Garnet and others, in Philadelphia, Thomas Sims and Anthony Burns, in Boston, with each attendant chain of associations, has created a healthy agitation, ominous, we hope, at no distant day, of its final repeal.

The following resolutions, submitted at a public meeting in Boston, October 5th, 1850, by Wm. C. Nell, (and unanimously adopted,) may be accepted as embodying the general feeling: —

Resolved, That in view of the imminent danger, present and looked for, we caution every colored man, woman and child, to be careful in their walks through the highways and byways of the city by day, and doubly so if out at night, as to WHERE they go — HOW they go — and WHO they go with; to be guarded on nigh side, off side and all sides; as watchful as Argus with his hundred eyes, and as executive as was Briareus, with as many hands; if seized by any one, to make the air resound with the signal-word, and, as they would rid themselves of any wild beast, be prompt in their hour of peril.

Resolved, That any Commissioner who would deliver up a fugitive slave to a Southern highwayman, under this infamous and unconstitutional law, would have delivered up Jesus Christ to his persecutors for one-third of the price that Judas Iscariot did.

Resolved, That in the event of any Commissioner of Massachusetts being applied to for remanding a fugitive, we trust he will emulate the example of Judge Harrington, of Vermont, and "be satisfied with nothing short of a bill of sale from the Almighty."

Resolved, That though we gratefully acknowledge that the mane of the British Lion affords a nestling-place for our brethren in danger from the claws of the American Eagle, we would, nevertheless, counsel against their leaving the soil of their birth, consecrated by their tears, toils and perils, but yet to be rendered truly, the "land of the free and the home of the brave." The ties of consanguinity bid ALL remain who would lend a helping hand to the millions now in bonds. But at all events, if the soil of Bunker Hill, Concord and Lexington is the last bulwark of liberty, we can no where fill more honorable graves.

STRIKE OF THE AMISTAD CAPTIVES FOR LIBERTY.

On the 28th of June, 1839, the Spanish schooner Amistad, Ramen Ferrer, master, sailed from Havana for Porto Principe, a place in the island of Cuba, about 100 leagues distant, having on board as passengers, Don Pedro Montes and Jose Ruiz, with 54 fresh African negroes, just brought from Lemboko, as slaves. Among the slaves was one called in Spanish, Joseph Cinquez. He was the son of an African Prince. On the fifth night after leaving port, Cinquez, with a few chosen men among the fifty-four slaves, revolted, striking down the captain and cook, and took possession of the vessel. The two sailors took the boat and went on shore, and Montes was required, on pain of death, to navigate the vessel to Africa. He steered eastwardly in the day time, but put about at night, and thus kept near the American coast, until the 26th of August, when they were taken by Lieut. Gedney, United States Navy, and carried into New London. Judge Judson, of the United States Court, was sent for, and after a short examination of the two Spaniards, and a Creole cabin boy, without a word of communication with the negroes, the latter were bound over for trial as pirates, although their utter ignorance of any European language, and the admission of Ruiz himself, showed that they were fresh Africans, and of course could not be slaves by the laws of Spain. At this time, it was the united voice of the public press and of public men, that, as a matter of course, they would either be tried and executed here, or delivered up to the Spaniards; and they would have been returned to their claimants had not the eminent talents Of JOHN QUINCY ADAMS frustrated the designs of the Administration.

They were released in 1841, by the United States Court, and "they now sing of liberty on the sunny hills of Africa, beneath their native palms, where they hear the lion roar, and feel themselves as free as that king of the forest." They are living within a few miles of the Missionary Station at Sherbron Island. Cinquez has built a town, of which he is chief.

FUGITIVE SLAVES AT CHRISTIANA, PENN.

In the month of September, 1850, a colored man, known in the neighborhood around Christiana to be free, was seized and carried away by men known to be professional kidnappers, and has never been seen by his family since. In March, 1851, in the same neighborhood, under the roof of his employer, during the night, another colored man was tied, gagged, and carried away, marking the road along which he was dragged with his own blood. No authority for this outrage was ever shown, and he has never been heard from. These, and many other acts of a similar kind, had so alarmed the neighborhood, that the very name of kidnapper was sufficient to create a panic.

In September, 1851, (as narrated by a correspondent of the New York Tribune,) "a slaveholder, with his son and nephew, from Maryland, accompanied by United States officers of this city and Baltimore, went to Christiana after two fugitive slaves. The blacks, having received notice of their coming gathered, a considerable number of them, in the house which the slave-catching party were expected to visit. The door was fastened, and the blacks retired to the upper part of the house. When the slaveholder and his company approached, they were warned off. A parley was held, the slaveholder declaring, as it is said and believed, 'I will go to h — l, or have my slaves.' The door was broken in, a horn was sounded out of one of the upper windows, and, after an interval, a company of blacks, armed, gathered on the spot, and the negroes in the house made a rush down and crowded the whites out.

"Here, the parley was resumed, the spokesman of the blacks telling the white men to go away; they were determined, he said, to die rather than go into slavery, or allow any one of their number to be taken. He declared, moreover, that the blacks would not fire, but if the whites fired, they were dead men. Shortly, first the nephew, then the slave-owner and his son, fired revolvers, wounding a number of the blacks, but not seriously. One man had his ear perforated by a ball; the clothes of others were pierced and torn; but, as the blacks, said afterwards, 'the Lord shook the balls out of their clothes.' The fire of the whites was returned. The slave-owner fell dead, and his son very dangerously wounded. The whites then retired. One of the United States officers summoned the posse, but in vain. Some of the neighbors, Quakers and Anti-Slavery persons, went and took up the wounded man and carried him to one of their homes, where, while they told him, in Quaker phrase, that 'they had no unity with him in his acts,' and abhorred the wicked business in which he had been engaged, every attention was paid him, and medical aid instantly sent for. The effect of this treatment upon the young man, as our informant told us, may be easily imagined. He wept, and vowed, if he lived, to correct the impression people had at his home about Abolitionists. The doctor pronounced his wounds mortal.

"People soon gathered in large numbers at this scene of blood. The excitement was intense. Opinions and feelings conflicted, of course, but there was a strong feeling in behalf of the blacks. While the crowd were talking, and during the ferment, two blacks (brick-makers) passed. One of the crowd exclaimed, 'There go two fellows who should be shot!' The black men paused and faced the crowd, and said calmly something to this effect, — 'Here we are; shoot us, if you choose; we are a suffering people, any how. God made us black; we can't help that; shoot us, if you will.' The revulsion was instantaneous and strong, and any man who had muttered a word against the blacks would have been knocked down on the spot."

Several men, white and colored, were arrested for participation in the killing of Gorsuch, the kidnapper; but, though the United States Government expended about fifty thousand dollars in the prosecution, they failed to convict any of the party.